JOURNAL FOR THE STUDY OF THE NEW TESTAMENT
SUPPLEMENT SERIES
75

Executive Editor
Stanley E. Porter

Editorial Board
Richard Bauckham, David Catchpole, R. Alan Culpepper,
Joanna Dewey, James D.G. Dunn, Robert Fowler, Robert Jewett,
Elizabeth Struthers Malbon, Dan O. Via

JSOT Press
Sheffield

Patronage and Power

A Study of Social Networks in Corinth

John K. Chow

Journal for the Study of the New Testament
Supplement Series 75

Copyright © 1992 Sheffield Academic Press

Published by JSOT Press
JSOT Press is an imprint of
Sheffield Academic Press Ltd
343 Fulwood Road
Sheffield S10 3BP
England

Typeset by Sheffield Academic Press
and
Printed on acid-free paper in Great Britain
by Billing & Sons Ltd
Worcester

British Library Cataloguing in Publication Data

A catalogue record for this book is available
from the British Library

ISSN 0143-5108
ISBN 1-85075-370-9

Contents

Preface	7
Abbreviations	9
INTRODUCTION	11
Social-Historical Studies on Corinth	12
Purpose	28
Method of Study	28
Plan of Study	36
Chapter 1	
PATRONAGE IN ROMAN CORINTH	38
Patronage and Society	41
Patronage and Institutions	64
Conclusion	80
Chapter 2	
THE CHURCH IN ROMAN CORINTH	83
The Corinthian Network	83
Personal Relations in the Church	87
Patronal Relations in the Church	101
Conclusion	112
Chapter 3	
THE POWER OF THE PATRONS	113
Opponents in 1 Corinthians	114
The Corinthians and the Pagans	120
The Powerful Patron	123
The Rich Patron	130
The Political Patron	141
The Priestly Patron	157
Conclusion	166

Chapter 4
THE RESPONSE OF PAUL   167
    Paul's Exhortations   169
    Paul's Defence   172
    Paul's Directives   175
    Conclusion   187

CONCLUSION   188

Bibliography   191
Index of References   221
Index of Authors   227

Preface

I had a dream. I dreamed that one day I would go on a world-seeing trip. Thank God, my dream has come true! Now I feel that it is *kairos* to go home. But before I go, I find it necessary to do some reckoning and to express my deepest gratitude to all those who, in one way or another, have played a part in my dream.

First, I would like to thank those who have helped to shape my dream, especially Dr George Wilson, Jr (fellow-dreamer and precious friend, servant and master), Dr Jerry Moye (fellow-dreamer, precious friend, and teacher), Professor Eduard Schweizer (spiritual counsellor), Dr Bill Hendricks, and Dr and Mrs S. Southard.

Secondly, I wish to thank some friends and organizations for helping to make my dream possible, especially Dr and Mrs L. Wong, Mr and Mrs C.N. Tsang, Mr and Mrs T.K. Chow, brothers and sisters of the North Point Baptist Church (Hong Kong), the trustees of the Hong Kong Baptist Theological Seminary, the Ming-Yee Foundation (Hong Kong), and the ORS Awards scheme.

Thirdly, I sincerely thank those who have helped to open up new dimensions or clarify unclear visions in my dream, especially Professor James Dunn (patron and mentor), Professor James Beckford (most helpful guide), Professor Abraham Malherbe (pastor), Professor W. Wuellner (sobering critic), Dr Andrew Lincoln and Dr A.J.M. Wedderburn (helpful examiners), Professor Howard Kee, Dr Richard Roberts, Dr Andrew Chester, Dr David Hunt, Dr Bill Williamson, Dr Robert Banks, Dr John Hurd, Dr Victor Furnish, Professor C.E.B. Cranfield, Dr David Gill, respondents to my paper at the 1989 Tyndale New Testament Study Group, other scholars and mind-openers whom I met through reading their books.

Fourthly, I would like to thank those who have made my sometimes melancholic dream more pleasant and comfortable—Suk-Har (most loving wife) and Mo-Yat (most beloved boy), our families in Hong Kong, Rev and Mrs L.K. Lo, Dr and Mrs W.O. Lee, Mr and Mrs Y.P. Kok, Dr and Mrs Y.K. Yu, Mrs Williamson, Dr Nicholas Taylor (good companion), Dr Bruce Longenecker, Mr and Mrs R. Reynolds, and other friends at Durham.

Lastly, I would like to thank those who have helped to make the publication of this book possible, especially Dr David Hill (gracious editor), the editorial staff at the Sheffield Academic Press, Mrs Ruth Moye and Mr Morning Chu. I would also like to dedicate this work to those, romantic perhaps, brave Chinese, past and present, who made great sacrifices for a more worthy dream—the dream of a better China free from the sickness of human patronage. May we continue to dream until it comes true. May our dream soon come true!

J.K.M.C.
May, 1992
Homantin Hill, Hong Kong

ABBREVIATIONS

ABR	*Australian Biblical Review*
AES	*Archives Européennes de Sociologie*
AHR	*American Historical Review*
AJA	*American Journal of Archaeology*
AJP	*American Journal of Philology*
AJS	*American Journal of Sociology*
ANRW	*Aufstieg und Niedergang der römischen Welt*
AQ	*Anthropology Quarterly*
ASR	*American Sociological Review*
BA	*Biblical Archaeologist*
BAGD	W. Bauer, W.F. Arndt, F.W. Gingrich and F.W. Danker, *A Greek–English Lexicon of the New Testament*
BARev	*Biblical Archaeology Review*
BCH	*Bulletin de correspondance hellénique*
Bib	*Biblica*
BJRL	*Bulletin of the John Rylands University Library of Manchester*
BJS	*British Journal of Sociology*
BSac	*Bibliotheca Sacra*
CBQ	*Catholic Biblical Quarterly*
CIL	*Corpus inscriptionum latinarum*
CP	*Classical Philology*
CQ	*Classical Quarterly*
CR	*Classical Review*
CSCA	*California Studies in Classical Antiquity*
CSSH	*Comparative Studies in Society and History*
CW	*Classical Weekly*
EvQ	*The Evangelical Quarterly*
EvT	*Evangelische Theologie*
Exp	*The Expositor*
ExpTim	*Expository Times*
GR	*Greece and Rome*
GRBS	*Greek, Roman and Byzantine Studies*
HBC	J.L. Mays *et al.* (eds.), *Harper's Bible Commentary*
Hesp	*Hesperia*
HSCP	*Harvard Studies in Classical Philology*
HTR	*Harvard Theological Review*
IDB	G.A. Buttrick (ed.), *Interpreter's Dictionary of the Bible*
IDBSup	*Interpreter's Dictionary of the Bible*, Supplementary Volume

ILS	*Inscriptiones latinae selectae*
Int	*Interpretation*
JAAR	*Journal of the American Academy of Religion*
JAC	*Jahrbuch für Antike und Christentum*
JBL	*Journal of Biblical Literature*
JHS	*Journal of Hellenic Studies*
JRH	*Journal of Religious History*
JRS	*Journal of Roman Studies*
JSNT	*Journal for the Study of the New Testament*
JSOT	*Journal for the Study of the Old Testament*
LCL	Loeb Classical Library
LSJ	Liddell–Scott–Jones, *Greek–English Lexicon*
NAB	New American Bible
NIDNTT	C. Brown, *The New International Dictionary of New Testament Theology*
NIV	New International Version
NJBC	R.E. Brown *et al.* (eds.), *The New Jerome Biblical Commentary*
NovT	*Novum Testamentum*
NTS	*New Testament Studies*
OCD	*Oxford Classical Dictionary*
PBSR	*Papers of the British School at Rome*
PCPhS	*Proceedings of the Cambridge Philological Society*
PP	*Past and Present*
RB	*Revue biblique*
RestQ	*Restoration Quarterly*
RevExp	*Review and Expositor*
REB	Revised English Bible
RSV	Revised Standard Version
SJT	*Scottish Journal of Theology*
SO	*Symbolae osloenses*
SQ	*Sociological Quarterly*
SR	*Sociological Review*
TAPA	*Transactions and Proceedings of the American Philological Association*
TDNT	G. Kittel and G. Friedrich (eds.), *Theological Dictionary of the New Testament*
TS	*Theological Studies*
TU	Texte und Untersuchungen
TynBul	*Tyndale Bulletin*
TZ	*Theologische Zeitschrift*
YCS	*Yale Classical Studies*
ZNW	*Zeitschrift für die neutestamentliche Wissenschaft*
ZTK	*Zeitschrift für Theologie und Kirche*

INTRODUCTION

What was the situation behind 1 Corinthians? Who made up the church at Corinth? How should we understand Paul's statement in 1 Cor. 1.26 where it says that not many of the Corinthians were wise, powerful or of noble birth? Was the church made up of poor and undistinguished people alone? Or were there also some especially rich and powerful patrons in the church? If the church was made up of both rich and poor people, Gentiles and Jews, then that means there were social and cultural differences in the church. If this was the case, how did the members relate to one another? Were they in conflict? If they were, who was involved and why? Or was there a kind of solidarity among some of the members? If there was, how and on what basis was it formed? How did the members of the church relate to the world outside? Did they continue to maintain their links with their pagan neighbours? If some did, who could they be and what could have been their reasons for doing so?

What was Paul's relationship with the church? How was he received by the Corinthians at the time of the writing of 1 Corinthians? Was he an authority recognized by the church? If his authority was being challenged by some people in the church, who were these challengers of Paul? Why would they want to challenge him? How did Paul respond to the situation in the church in 1 Corinthians? Did he propose a kind of patriarchalism which, in effect, would sustain the socially powerful against the socially powerless in the name of love? Did he preach a kind of egalitarian utopia in order to promote the liberation of the oppressed? Or, should the actual effect of Paul's theological response be understood in another way?

All of the above questions have been raised in social-historical studies on the church at Corinth. Although they concern basically relational problems in the church,[1] they are questions which can

---

1. N.A. Dahl, in his study of 1 Cor. 1–4, has not gone into the social situation in Corinth, yet he sees a relationship between personal matters and theological debates.

somehow be related to theological and social issues in Corinth. It is my intention to approach the problems in the church at Corinth from a social-historical perspective. Some of the social-historical studies on Corinth in the past three decades have suggested that patronage could have been an important context for understanding the problems in the church. It is this suggestion which I wish now to take further to see if it may shed further light on the situation in Corinth addressed by 1 Corinthians. In order to set the context for my study, I will first briefly review some of the more significant studies on the social setting of Corinth before I describe what I propose to do in this book.

Social-Historical Studies on Corinth

The immense interest scholars have taken in the Corinthian problem in the past has led to a great amount of literature on the subject. Given the limitations of this study, it is simply unrealistic to review all of it in this introductory chapter. Since I intend to attempt a social-historical investigation of some of the problems in Corinth, I hope the following survey will be able to show how my approach builds on some of the social-historical studies and differs from others. My survey will be divided into two parts. In the first part, I will briefly review some of the works on the social setting of Corinth done in the first half of this century which helped to lay the foundation for later studies. In the second part, I will discuss in more detail the merits and inadequacies of various models of interpretation which have been applied in the study of Corinth in recent years.

Some Early Studies
In the late nineteenth century and the beginning of this century, Marxists were among those who were interested in studying the social

---

He writes, 'In my essay I have explained the controversies reflected in 1 Cor. 1–4 in terms of the church policy and personal matters involved. This does not mean that I take the theological aspects to be of minor importance. But in actual practice theological debates are usually mixed up with questions of church policy and personal relations. I see no reason to assume that this was different at the time of Paul' ('Paul and the Church at Corinth according to 1 Corinthians 1.10–4.21', in *Christian History and Interpretation: Studies Presented to John Knox* [ed. W.R. Farmer, C.F.D. Moule and R.R. Niebuhr; Cambridge: Cambridge University Press, 1967], p. 331).

situation of the early Christians. In one of his studies on early Christianity, F. Engels compared the early Christian movement to the working-class movement of his day as a movement of the poor, the oppressed and the unpropertied.[1] K. Kautsky painted a similar picture in his study on early Christianity.[2] Interestingly enough, through a study of the newly found papyri, A. Deissmann also came to a similar conclusion,[3] despite the fact that he could not accept the materialistic interpretation of Christianity proposed by people like Kautsky.[4] Citing 1 Cor. 1.26-31 he gave an impressionistic description of the early Christian movement and described it as a movement of the 'lower class'.[5]

Looking at the early Christian movement from afar and in a broad perspective, the general description provided by Engels, Kautsky and Deissmann may indeed be justifiable. No wonder such a view still has its proponents today.[6] However, once we look at a particular church in a particular setting, like the one at Corinth, such a generalization may need to be qualified. In this respect, the work of E. von Dobschütz, a contemporary of Kautsky and Deissmann, is more impressive.[7] He repudiated the idea that the early Christian movement was made up of poor and uncultured people alone. Instead, he suggested that the church had some rich and cultured people too. The Christian community at Corinth serves his case well.[8] But the

1. F. Engels, 'On the History of Early Christianity', in *On Religion* (Moscow: Progress, 1975), pp. 275-300.
2. K. Kautsky, *The Foundations of Christianity* (New York: Russell & Russell, 1953 [1908]).
3. See A. Deissmann, *Light from the Ancient East* (Grand Rapids: Baker, 1965). The preface to the first German edition was written in 1908.
4. On Deissmann's critique of Kautsky, see *Light*, pp. 465-67.
5. *Light*, p. 144.
6. J. Gager, 'Shall We Marry Our Enemies? Sociology and the New Testament', *Int* 37 (1982), pp. 262-63.
7. E. von Dobschütz, *Christian Life in the Primitive Church* (London: Williams & Norgate, 1904), pp. 11-80. For a positive appraisal of the works of von Dobschütz, see L.E. Keck, 'On the Ethos of Early Christianity', *JAAR* 42 (1974), pp. 441-43.
8. So people like Stephanas were seen as rich benefactors to the church (von Dobschütz, *Life*, pp. 14, 57-58), and problems in the church, like those related to eating, disputes before the pagan court, and disorder in the observance of the Lord's Supper, were regarded as problems related either to the behaviour of the rich or to the difference between the rich and the poor (*Life*, pp. 24-25, 61-62, 66-67).

significance of von Dobschütz lies, most of all, in the perspective which guides his interpretation of the early Christian movement. What he intended to do was to free the study of early Christianity from dogmatic interests by focusing on the *historical reality* of the communities. In the preface to the German edition of his book, he set down the agenda of his study as follows:

> We must ask how far it was possible to realize the ideal in practice. How did things look in the early Christian communities? What was their actual moral condition? What was the individual's contribution to the moral life of the community?[1]

As far as his methodology is concerned, two things may be noted. First, in order to understand the early Christian movement, it is important to understand the historical context or the 'actual' condition, that is, the particular environment in which the Christian communities, like the one in Corinth, lived and worked. It is methodologically not acceptable simply to assume that the behaviour of the early Christians necessarily corresponded to the ideal which was set before them. Secondly, it is important to understand the contribution of the founder of a community in the building of its morals, since 'historical progress cannot be explained by forces originating in a collective way, but by eminent leaders or "heroes"'.[2] Indeed, according to von Dobschütz, 'the character of the single communities owes more to the founder than to the former situation of the individual members'.[3]

These views of von Dobschütz are still pertinent today for a study of the Christian community at Corinth. The need for a historical examination alongside theological and literary studies cannot be overemphasized. Since Paul's aim in writing 1 Corinthians was to nurture the church according to his perception of the Christian cause, there is a need to understand his message and to ascertain as far as possible its reception by the Corinthians.

That the church at Corinth was made up of both rich and poor people is accepted by many scholars today.[4] But it is necessary to refine von Dobschütz's approach at several points. First, with regard

1. *Life*, pp. vi-vii.
2. *Life*, p. xv.
3. *Life*.
4. See W.A. Meeks, *The First Urban Christians: The Social World of the Apostle Paul* (New Haven: Yale University Press, 1983), pp. 51-73.

to the goals of his study, von Dobschütz might have been a little over-optimistic about the possibility of getting back to the actual historical situation if by this he meant to write a kind of objective historical account.[1] Take Corinth as an example. What we have is only a one-sided account of the situation in the church provided by two canonical letters of Paul. Therefore, it should be stressed that any historical reconstruction of the situation in Corinth will at best remain a tentative one. Secondly, the work of von Dobschütz is mainly a study of literary materials. It may be helpful to supplement this with information provided by other sources and methods.[2] Thirdly, von Dobschütz's view of the prominence of Paul in the shaping of the community and his view of the Corinthian church as an almost innocent and immature community may represent more than anything else his value judgment only. The state of affairs in Corinth has to be evaluated more carefully in the light of information gleaned from 1 Corinthians.

Still, much can be learnt from von Dobschütz's study of early Christianity. Yet, for some reason, such social-historical study of the early Christian movement seems to have been disregarded by most scholars in the period between the two world wars. Only a few independent scholars were aware of the importance of the social context for an understanding of the early Christians. F.V. Filson called our attention to the context of house churches for understanding early Christian communities, and argued that the early Christian churches were made up of a broader constituency than was usually allowed.[3] With a good background in Graeco-Roman culture and apparently informed by new archaeological findings, J. Moffatt in his commentary on 1 Corinthians also showed some insights into the social

1. The possibility of achieving such a goal is highly questionable. On this, see M.I. Finley, *Ancient History: Evidence and Models* (London: Chatto & Windus, 1985), especially ch. 4. Cf. also R. Bultmann, 'Is Exegesis without Presuppositions Possible?', in *Existence and Faith* (ed. and trans. S. Ogden; New York: Meridian, 1960), pp. 289-96, and Gager, 'Shall We Marry Our Enemies?', pp. 259-60.
2. It just happens that developments in archaeology, sociology and anthropology have provided us with more information and conceptual tools with which to facilitate our understanding of life in the ancient world. There is no reason why these tools should not be used critically to help our study.
3. F.V. Filson, 'The Significance of the Early House Churches', *JBL* 58 (1939), pp. 105-12.

situation in Corinth.[1] However, the attention of scholarly debates in this period appears to be greatly dominated by the theological and philosophical issues posed by R. Bultmann.[2] After the Second World War, important and specific works on Corinth, such as *Gnosticism in Corinth* by W. Schmithals[3] and *The Origin of I Corinthians* by J.C. Hurd,[4] were still concerned solely with theological questions, such as possible Gnostic influence in Corinth or development in Pauline theology, and not with the social situation of the Corinthians.

Significant Studies since 1960

In the development of a social-historical method for the study of the New Testament, the year 1960 may be regarded as a watershed which marks off the old era from the new one. The main difference between the old era and the new one is in the way the issues are approached. As will be seen in the following discussion, after 1960, conscious efforts were made to employ different models of interpretation, which are either borrowed from or informed by theories of sociology or anthropology, in the study of the early Christian communities. This blooming of methodological flowers characterizes the studies in this new era.

E.A. Judge may perhaps be regarded as the herald of this new generation of New Testament social historians. Through his books and articles,[5] Judge has succeeded, to a large extent, in achieving his aim,

---

1. J. Moffatt, *The First Epistle of Paul to the Corinthians* (London: Hodder & Stoughton, 1938).
2. This concern is reflected most clearly in R.H. Fuller's review of Pauline studies in this period in *The New Testament in Current Study* (New York: Charles Scribner's Sons, 1962), pp. 54-69. It is an account about the challenge posed by Bultmann and responses to his position made by Käsemann, Dahl and Munck.
3. W. Schmithals, *Gnosticism in Corinth: An Investigation of the Letters to the Corinthians* (Nashville: Abingdon Press, 1972 [1956]).
4. J.C. Hurd, *The Origin of I Corinthians* (Macon: Mercer University Press, 2nd edn, 1983 [1965]).
5. So E.A. Judge, *The Social Pattern of the Christian Groups in the First Century: Some Prolegomena to the Study of New Testament Ideas of Social Obligation* (London: Tyndale Press, 1960); 'The Early Christians as a Scholastic Community', *JRH* 1 (1960–61), pp. 4-15, 125-37; 'Paul's Boasting in Relation to Contemporary Professional Practice', *ABR* 16 (1968), pp. 37-50; 'St Paul and Classical Society', *JAC* 15 (1972), pp. 19-36; 'Paul as a Radical Critic of Society', *Interchange* 16 (1974), pp. 191-203; '"Antike und Christentum": Towards a Definition of the Field:

which is to revive interest in the social context of early Christianity.¹ He has also provided stimulation for further research in the development of methodology and the raising of relevant issues.² Judge's works, such as *The Social Pattern of the Christian Groups in the First Century*, 'The Early Christians as a Scholastic Community' and 'Cultural Conformity and Innovation in Paul', may be seen as a continued response to a socialist or Marxist interpretation of Christian origins.³ The basic problem which Judge seeks to address is whether or not the early Christian movement was a movement of the lower classes.⁴ From the outset, Judge realizes that the problem is not only one of information, but also one of methodology. As far as his methodology is concerned, Judge strongly objects to the use of anachronistic models borrowed from modern-day theories of social classes, for, in his view, such models will do injustice to the unique historical situation in the first-century world. Instead, he proposes the following programme for study:

> We must ask what the patterns of contemporary society were, and how the constituency of the Christian groups was related to them... We need to know not only who they were, and what relation they had *as a group* to the social structure of their own communities, but what they existed for *as a group*, what activities they engaged in, and what their contemporaries would have made of them. This is, of course, purely a question of

A Bibliographical Survey', *ANRW* II.23.1 (1979), pp. 3-58; 'The Social Identity of the First Christians: A Question of Method in Religious History', *JRH* 11 (1980), pp. 201-17; *Rank and Status in the World of the Caesars and St Paul* (Christchurch: University of Canterbury, 1982); 'Cultural Conformity and Innovation in Paul: Some Clues from Contemporary Documents', *TynBul* 35 (1984), pp. 3-24.
  1. Judge, 'Social Identity', p. 202.
  2. Judge's influence is most evident in the works of G. Theissen and P. Marshall.
  3. Judge's earlier opponents are Kautsky and Kalthoff ('Early Christians', p. 5). In a recent article, he responds to G.E.M. de Ste. Croix ('Cultural Conformity and Innovation', pp. 3-4).
  4. Judge, 'Early Christians', p. 4. The question is not a new one. But it is still an issue for scholarly debate today. See, e.g., the exchange of views between J. Gager ('Shall We Marry Our Enemies?', p. 262) and A.J. Malherbe (*Social Aspects of Early Christianity* [Philadelphia: Fortress Press, 1983], esp. pp. 119-20). See also R. Scroggs's discussion, 'The Sociological Interpretation of the New Testament: The Present State of Research', *NTS* 26 (1980), pp. 164-79 and Judge's response in 'Social Identity'.

external appearances and social function. The *theological rationale of the church is not our concern*.[1]

As seen from his later publications, the details of the programme have undergone further development, but the basic perspective of the above approach appears to be more or less the same. For example, in an article, published in 1980, he writes,

> History walks a tightrope between the unique and the typical. If we explain everything by analogy, we deny to our forebears the individuality we take as a basic feature of our own humanity. The New Testament is conspicuously modern, and decidedly unclassical, in favouring the possibility of radical innovation—it is no doubt the prime source of our own attitudes in this matter. But we will never get the true measure of that until we can map out adequately the relationships of similarity and difference between the first churches and other *group phenomena* of their time.[2]

Two important features of Judge's approach have emerged. First, he places great emphasis on the importance of the context of the first-century world for an understanding of the early Christians. For, to Judge, only such a context can safeguard against a misinterpretation of early Christianity through the eyes of a modern interpreter. Secondly, one important aspect of his programme is a comparative study of the early Christian communities with contemporary 'social institutions' or groupings.

The first fruit of Judge's study programme was the publication of his *The Social Pattern of the Christian Groups in the First Century*. In this book Judge singles out three important institutions of the first-century world for study. They are *politeia*, *oikonomia* and *koinonia*. In relation to the Pauline community at Corinth, the context of a household bound together by the head of the house is especially significant. Like von Dobschütz, Judge is dissatisfied with the view which claims that the early Christian movement was one of the lower classes. But he goes further in defining it as 'a movement sponsored by local patrons to their social dependents'.[3] Based on this picture of the early Christian communities, he goes on to explore the external appearance of such communities as scholastic communities. Against such a background, Judge suggests that, to a contemporary observer,

1. Judge, 'Early Christians', p. 8.
2. Judge, 'Social Identity', p. 216.
3. Judge, 'Early Christians', p. 8.

Paul would look very much like a sophist.[1] He further paints a picture in which Paul was closely involved in patronal relations. He utilized the patronage of rich people.[2] While he was sponsored by rich patrons, he also had his own retinue.[3] In this context, a contemporary institution other than house groups begins to appear. The institution, or, depending on the context, quasi-institution, is patronage.

In Judge's later works, Paul's relationship to the patronage system of the Roman Empire is further defined, especially in the light of the Corinthian situation. Although Paul, Judge writes, 'was involved in relationships where he was in effect under patronage, or where he was himself in a position of patronage over other people', he 'clearly has no value to place upon patronal relations as such'.[4]

> The Corinthian letters show him in a head-on confrontation with the mechanisms by which it [the patronal system] imposed social power defined as moral superiority. His positive response to this collision was to build a remarkable new construction of social realities that both lay within the fabric of the old ranking system and yet transformed it by a revolution in social values.[5]

To Judge, Paul was not seeking to overthrow the household hierarchy, but to introduce a new set of values which challenged the contemporary value system.

Judge's study of Paul and the early Christians cannot be overlooked. He not only emphasizes that it is important to find a historical context for the interpretation of early Christianity, but has also demonstrated how the distinctiveness of Paul can only be brought out after he is placed firmly back into the context of his times. Although Judge's attempt to understand the early Christian communities as scholastic

---

1. What Judge attempts to do is 'to place Paul in his correct social class in terms of the impression his activities must have given to the contemporary observer' ('Early Christians', p. 125). Accordingly, he gives the following description of these 'sophists' or 'visiting professional preachers': 'They were all travellers, relying upon the hospitality of their admirers, all expert talkers and persuaders, all dedicated to their mission and intolerant of criticism' ('Early Christians', p. 126).
2. As many as 40 persons of substance who might have sponsored Paul are identified by Judge (see 'Early Christians', pp. 129-30).
3. Again, this group is made up of approximately 40 people (see Judge, 'Early Christians', pp. 131-34).
4. Judge, 'Paul as a Radical Critic', p. 196.
5. Judge, 'Cultural Conformity and Innovation', p. 23.

communities may be less persuasive, his depiction of the early Christian groups in terms of household groups is significant. But, to study the early Christians solely as a group phenomenon may not be without its limitations.[1] Such limitations may be evident when his model of interpretation is used to approach those problems in Corinth which cut across group boundaries and are often related to different groups at the same time, such as the settling of a dispute before the pagan court and the eating at table in an idol's temple.

The limitation of Judge's group study, in a way, has been countered by a different model, which builds more directly on another first-century phenomenon, that is, patronage. Judge may be correct in suggesting that Paul was in direct confrontation with the patronage system of his day in Corinth. In any case, Judge is surely right in pointing out the importance of patronage in holding the Roman Empire together.[2] However, Judge's use of patronage as a context for understanding early Christianity appears to be too formal and too limited. For example, in his analysis of the early Christians, wealth seems to be the most apparent factor in the making of patrons.[3] While there is no denying that wealth was a useful indicator of power in the ancient world, it should perhaps be pointed out that such an indicator has to be assessed in context. For there were differences even among the rich in those days. A more dynamic interpretive framework is probably needed to assess the relationship between patronage and the relational problems in Corinth. This is in no way a depreciation of the

---

1. To be fair, Judge himself seems to be aware of this problem. For instead of seeing the groups as distinct entities, he proposes to see the groups as 'a series of overlapping but not systematically related circles' (*Christian Groups*, p. iii).

2. Judge's early discussion of patronage is confined to *amicitia* and *clientela*. He writes:

> They (*amicitia* and *clientela*) are both forms of contract for political purposes, extra-legal, but invested with great sanctity by the force of immemorial tradition...*Amicitia* is a contract of political co-operation formed between members of the aristocracy of office... *Clientela* is a bond that tied members of the non-office holding classes to the political interests of one or other of the senatorial houses ('Early Christians', p. 6).

3. Judge's description of Paul's patrons is as follows: 'They all belong together as persons of substance, members of a cultivated social elite, and in particular as sympathizers with Jewish thought... They are the "devout and honourable" citizens of the Hellenistic states' ('Early Christians', p. 130).

Introduction

works of such a distinguished New Testament social historian as Judge. The household remains an important context for understanding the early Christian communities, and has been an important topic for scholarly research.[1] So is the institution of patronage.

Ten years or so after the publication of *The Social Pattern of the Christian Groups in the First Century*, the impact of Judge was observable in the works of a German scholar, G. Theissen. Building on the insights of both Deissmann and Judge, Theissen published a series of essays on the situation in Corinth.[2] If Judge is cautious in the use of sociological theories, Theissen is more daring. In his study on Corinth, Theissen first seeks to explain the conflicts in the church in terms of its 'internal stratification', that is, the contradiction between the rich and the poor.[3] Accepting the view that the church in Corinth was made up of both the rich and the poor, he goes on to show that the most visible people in the church were those who were of 'high social status'.[4] Theissen goes further to support his understanding of a stratified church by a brief study of the social-economic situation in Roman Corinth. In the light of such a background Theissen proceeds to show how much light a sociological approach can shed on two of the problems in the church. The first one concerns the controversy over the eating of meat offered to idols.[5] On this problem, the tension

---

1. E.g. R. Banks, *Paul's Idea of Community: The Early House Churches in their Historical Setting* (Exeter: Paternoster Press, 1980); D.C. Verner, *The Household of God: The Social World of the Pastoral Epistles* (Chico, CA: Scholars Press, 1983); L.M. White, '*Domus Ecclesiae—Domus Dei*: Adaptation and Development in the Setting for Early Christian Assembly' (Unpublished PhD dissertation, Yale University, 1983).

2. The English translation of these essays can be found in *The Social Setting of Pauline Christianity: Essays on Corinth* (ed. and trans. J.H. Schütz; Edinburgh: T. & T. Clark, 1982). References in the discussion below will be made to the above text. For detailed reviews of Theissen's works on Corinth, see Malherbe, *Social Aspects*, pp. 71-91; Schütz's 'Introduction', in *Social Setting*, pp. 1-23.

3. G. Theissen, 'Social Stratification in the Corinthian Community: A Contribution to the Sociology of Early Hellenistic Christianity', in Schütz (ed.), *Social Setting*, pp. 69-119.

4. Out of 17, Theissen is able to locate 9 people who belonged to the 'upper classes'. They are Aquila, Priscilla, Stephanas, Erastus, Sosthenes, Crispus, Phoebe, Gaius and Titius Justus.

5. Theissen, 'The Strong and the Weak in Corinth: A Sociological Analysis of a Theological Quarrel', in Schütz (ed.), *Social Setting*, pp. 121-43.

between the strong and the weak is not seen as one between Gentiles and Jews, but as one between the rich and the poor. The second occasion which reveals the social differences between the haves and the have-nots is the divisions at the Lord's table.[1] As to Paul's role in the church, Theissen, unlike von Dobschütz, sees Paul as a community organizer who sought to win the support of both the rich and the poor,[2] and preached a kind of love-patriarchalism in Corinth. On this love-patriarchalism, Theissen writes,

> In these congregations there developed an ethos obviously different from that of the synoptic tradition, the ethos of primitive Christian love patriarchalism. We encounter it particularly in the deutero-Pauline and Pastoral Letters, but it is already evident in Paul (namely, in 1 Cor. 7.21ff.; 11.3-16). This love-patriarchalism takes social differences for granted but ameliorates them through an obligation of respect and love, an obligation imposed upon those who are socially stronger. From the weaker are required subordination, fidelity, and esteem.[3]

To Theissen, it is this ethos which explains why the church later was accepted by Constantine. But also because of this ethos, there was no need for 'a struggle for equal rights'.[4]

Theissen obviously has done much to strengthen the case for a social-historical interpretation of early Christianity. An essentially functionalist view of social stratification becomes a lively and powerful tool of interpretation which helps to enlighten several facets of the problems in Corinth. But on closer examination, one can see some of the inadequacies of Theissen's approach. At this point, two questions may be raised, both of which concern his use of interpretive models. First, while reference to social stratification is able to explain the tensions within the church, it fails to account for another aspect of the relationships in the church, that is, what appears to be a kind of unified front in the church which stood against Paul. The most notable example is the church's stance in response to the case of immorality in 1 Corinthians 5. If the church was so divided, why did they show no clear differences over this case? Why did the church accept the man in

---

1. Theissen, 'Social Integration and Sacramental Activity: An Analysis of 1 Cor. 11.17-34', in Schütz (ed.), *Social Setting*, pp. 145-74.
2. Theissen, 'Legitimation and Subsistence: An Essay on the Sociology of Early Christian Missionaries', in Schütz (ed.), *Social Setting*, pp. 35-40.
3. Theissen, 'Social Stratification', p. 107.
4. Theissen, 'Social Stratification', p. 109.

their midst? To which group did the man belong? Was he a rich man? Or was he a poor man? Secondly, Theissen's description of Paul's response to the problems in Corinth as a kind of love-patriarchalism is successful only in emphasizing what seems to be the conservative outlook of Paul's reply. However, it has failed to take note of the radical implication of Paul's instructions in 1 Corinthians. For instance, if the immoral man in 1 Corinthians 5 whom Paul asked the church to remove from their midst was a powerful patron, would love-patriarchalism still be an adequate description of Paul's theological response in 1 Corinthians? Obviously, no one model can explain everything. We have to appreciate the special significance of Theissen's works which were undertaken at a time when the validity of a sociological interpretation of the New Testament had still to be justified. Nevertheless, the deficiencies in Theissen's models of interpretation, namely the overemphasis on the element of conflict inside the church and on the conservative outlook of Paul's theological response, do need to be taken into consideration in our research into the problems in Corinth.

If Judge influenced Theissen, it may have been in quite an indirect way. Judge's direct influence on P. Marshall is more evident. It may even be said that Judge's programme of study has materialized with a higher degree of sophistication in Marshall's study on the conflict between Paul and the Corinthians.[1] The goal of Marshall's study is 'to examine the causes of the hostility, the form it takes, and Paul's efforts to win back the Corinthians, in the light of Greco-Roman cultural traditions'.[2] The interpretive model behind his analysis is Marcel Mauss's model of gift exchange.[3] The basic import of the model is to suggest that the acceptance of gifts establishes friendship whereas the refusal of gifts creates enmity. Based on this model, Marshall first seeks to anchor his study firmly in the institution of friendship and enmity in the Graeco-Roman world. He then goes on to suggest that the Corinthians were hostile to Paul because he had violated the norms of friendship by refusing to accept their gift. The problem was

---

1. P. Marshall, *Enmity in Corinth: Social Conventions in Paul's Relations with the Corinthians* (Tübingen: Mohr, 1987). The book is an enlarged version of Marshall's PhD dissertation submitted in 1980.
2. *Enmity*, p. vii.
3. *Enmity*, p. 1. Cf. M. Mauss, *The Gift* (Glencoe: Free Press, 1954).

further complicated when later some outsiders were willing to accept the Corinthians' gift, and thus formed a coalition with the Corinthians in opposition to Paul. In addition to the study of gift exchange, Marshall also examines the use of the literary convention of invective in the opponents' attack against Paul and Paul's reply in 2 Corinthians. Marshall's study of the relationship between Paul and the Corinthians is illuminating. As far as the study of Corinth is concerned, he has made a convincing case for seeing the conflict between Paul and some of the Corinthians against the background of financial support. Marshall's use of friendship as a model for interpreting the conflicts between Paul and some of the Corinthians is also intriguing. The shift from the study of groupings to the study of relations is distinctive. In the meantime, Judge's call to set any study of the New Testament firmly in the contemporary context is also heeded by Marshall. So, while informed by anthropological insights, the focus of Marshall's study is still on the cultural conventions of friendship and enmity in the Graeco-Roman world.

There is much that we can learn from Marshall's approach. There is also, however, a kind of ambiguity in Marshall's interpretation which needs to be pointed out. It is important to note that friendship itself is a very ambiguous term. In the early Empire it denoted a wide range of relationships from a tie between equals to that between a patron and a client.[1] This ambiguity, however, is not clarified, and is evident in his definition of Paul's relations with the Corinthians when he writes,

> There are difficulties, though, in viewing Paul's relationship with his friends as patronal friendship, especially because of the implication of inequality in status. The absence of standard terms in regard to patronal friendship makes it hard to assess the level or nature of his relationship with them or theirs with the household churches. Even so, patronal friendship, I suggest, provides us with the best social context in which to view these relations and from which to assess the different way that Paul construes them. I shall argue in a later chapter that it is Paul who initiates the relationship, not simply as an itinerant stranger in need of hospitality,

---

1. See especially R.P. Saller, *Personal Patronage in the Early Empire* (Cambridge: Cambridge University Press, 1982), ch. 1; P. Garnsey and R.P. Saller, *The Roman Empire: Economy, Society and Culture* (London: Gerald Duckworth, 1987), pp. 151-52.

but that he deliberately entrusts himself to people who are his social equals or superiors, seeking their assistance for his efforts.[1]

So, could Paul have been a client of some rich patrons in the church or not? In Marshall's account, the way Paul approached the Corinthians gives the impression that he was. But, if Paul's opponents in the church were able to shake his authority, the very authority of the founder of the church, they perhaps could have been more powerful than Paul. If so, Paul and some of the Corinthians were possibly not equal in power. In which case, it is at least questionable whether Paul could have stood on equal grounds with the rich Corinthian opponents as their friend.

Marshall's failure to clarify the power differences among the 'friends' of Paul is perhaps the major weakness of his study. Unfortunately, for Marshall to resolve this problem by looking for some 'standard terms' for hints is difficult. This is because, under normal circumstances, it is natural for the patron especially to avoid referring explicitly to a relationship as a patron–client relation, lest the client is insulted in any way. To be fair, in demanding a clearer distinction between friendship and patronage, we may be asking too much of Marshall when the evidence is in itself unclear. Nevertheless, it still seems better, if possible, to take into account the power differences among the 'friends' of Paul when analysing their relationships with him.

Before I end this survey of significant social-historical studies on Corinth,[2] the works of W.A. Meeks[3] deserve to be mentioned. Meeks has not written a specific study on Corinth. However, *The First Urban*

---

1. Marshall, *Enmity*, p. 145.
2. Some other studies of individual problems in the church at Corinth in the light of its social-historical context which have not been mentioned in the above survey include R.F. Hock, *The Social Context of Paul's Ministry: Tentmaking and Apostleship* (Philadelphia: Fortress Press, 1980); D.E. Smith, 'Social Obligation in the Context of Communal Meals: A Study of the Christian Meal in 1 Corinthians in Comparison with Greco-Roman Communal Meals' (unpublished ThD dissertation, Harvard University, 1980); W. Willis, *Idol Meat in Corinth: The Pauline Argument in I Corinthians 8 and 10* (Chico, CA: Scholars Press, 1985). These and other theological studies on Corinth will be discussed at different points in this book.
3. W.A. Meeks, 'The Social Context of Pauline Theology', *Int* 37 (1982), pp. 266-77; *First Urban Christians*; *The Moral World of the First Christians* (London: SPCK, 1987).

Christians has helped to establish the validity of the social-historical approach to the study of the New Testament. Moreover, while some social historians have tended to put less emphasis on theological issues, Meeks has made an important contribution in recognizing a possible correlation between Paul's message of the cross and its acceptance by people who experienced 'status inconsistency'.[1] Having said that, however, it appears that part of his depiction of the life in local churches is not entirely applicable to the situation in Corinth. It is especially doubtful if Meeks's description of the Pauline communities as groups which are 'intimate and exclusive' and have 'strong boundaries'[2] is applicable to the church behind 1 Corinthians. This, in turn, suggests that we need to study the particular situation of different churches in the first-century world, like the one at Corinth.

Summary

The above survey of social studies on the problems in the Corinthian church is by no means exhaustive. It serves only to acknowledge some of the accomplishments of previous studies and to provide pointers for further research into the problems of the Corinthian church. Of these pointers, four are worth special mentioning. First, as Judge and Marshall have shown, it is important and possible to set the study of the New Testament, including the letters of Paul to the Corinthians, in the context of the first-century world. Secondly, there is no dispute that the church at Corinth was made up of both rich and poor people. But to find an appropriate description of the social identity of these Christians will perhaps continue to be a matter for debate. For, as Judge has rightly noted, the problem is not just one of information, but also of methodology.[3] Thirdly, with regard to the problems in the church at Corinth, Judge has established the church at Corinth as comprising household groups. Theissen has highlighted the conflicts in the church between the rich and the poor. Marshall has set the conflict

1. See especially Meeks, *First Urban Christians*, pp. 190-92.
2. *First Urban Christians*, p. 190.
3. Perhaps the problem will not be totally resolved as long as our discussions are closely tied up with the basic presuppositions of each interpreter and are confused by unclarified use of terms like 'upper class' or 'lower class', 'a cultivated social elite' and so forth (see, e.g., R.L. Rohrbaugh, 'Methodological Considerations in the Debate over Social Class Status of Early Christians', *JAAR* 52 [1984], pp. 519-46). Or is there a need to search for *one* single description of the early Christians?

between Paul and some of the Corinthians quite firmly in the convention of friendship and the exchange of gifts. But a more dynamic approach may be needed to illuminate the structuring of relationships in the church, and to make sense of other problems in the church, such as the behaviour of the immoral man, the settling of a dispute in court, the partaking of idolatrous feasts, and the practice of the rite of baptism for the dead. Fourthly, while patronage as an important phenomenon in the early Empire and one of the contexts for understanding the life of the early Christians is often assumed,[1] the implications of patronage for understanding the problems in the church at Corinth and Paul's theological response have not yet been fully explored.

In accordance with the four points above, I propose four tasks for this study of the Corinthian problem. First, the phenomenon of patronage will be investigated further to see if light can be shed on the problems in the church at Corinth. It may perhaps provide a plausible explanation for the co-existence of conflict and solidarity in the church. Secondly, since the particular historical context is important for understanding the early Christians, including those at Corinth, I will seek to reconstruct as far as possible the phenomenon of patronage in the specific situation in Corinth, the Roman colony.[2] Thirdly, since most models used to interpret the situation in Corinth are designed to answer particular questions, a usable model for interpreting the relational problems in the Corinthian church may have to be devised.[3] Fourthly, since some of the previous studies on Corinth could have misrepresented Paul's theological response to the situation in Corinth,[4] the relationship between the social context and Paul's

---

1. Apart from Judge and Marshall, Bruce Malina has also taken notice of the importance of patron client ties for understanding the Gospels (*The New Testament World: Insights from Cultural Anthropology* [Atlanta: John Knox, 1981], pp. 81-82).

2. While many scholars emphasize the importance of a study of the particular historical context, in the case of Corinth not enough effort has been spent on looking into the situation there. This is true even for the studies by Hock, Marshall and Willis. One of the few exceptions is Theissen.

3. Most models used are either too static for understanding the shifting relationship between Paul and the Corinthians or too simple for the differences which existed even within a certain 'class' or group of people in the Corinthian church.

4. E.g. Theissen's love-patriarchalism and Judge's de-emphasizing of the eschatological tenor of Paul's reply and advice.

theological response to it needs to be re-examined. At this point, I can state the purpose of this study.

Purpose

The purpose of this study is to investigate some of the behavioural problems in the church at Corinth in the light of the phenomenon of patronage. In the course of my investigation, the significance of some of the problems in the church, including particularly the immoral man's relationship with his stepmother, the settling of a dispute before a pagan judge, the partaking of idolatrous feasts and the rite of baptism for the dead, and the implication of Paul's theological response in 1 Corinthians for the patronal ties in the church, will be examined.

Method of Study

As stated before, my approach to the problems in 1 Corinthians is basically social-historical. Since the church at Roman Corinth was part of the early Roman Empire, a study of the church there may not differ much from a study of other social phenomena in the Graeco-Roman world. Regarding the study of history, especially ancient history, M.I. Finley, an eminent ancient historian, has some invaluable advice to offer. Finley suggests that it is unrealistic to claim that it is possible to write *objective, scientific* history because our data are fragmentary and accidental in nature. Hence the ancient historian has to accept his limitations and find ways to control his discourse. One way to do it is to use a model. Finley writes,

> The ancient historian... can resort to a second-best procedure through the use of non-mathematical models, thereby controlling the subject of his discourse by selecting the variables he wishes to study. A model has been defined as 'a simplified structuring of reality which presents supposedly significant relationships in a generalized form. Models are highly subjective approximations in that they do not include all associated observations or measurements, but as such they are valuable in obscuring detail and in allowing fundamental aspects of reality to appear. This selectivity means that models have varying degrees of probability and a limited range of conditions over which they apply.'[1]

---

1. Finley, *Ancient History*, p. 60.

Introduction

He then goes on to comment on the usefulness of modelling:

> It is the nature of models that they are subject to constant adjustment, correction, modification or outright replacement. Non-mathematical models have few if any limits to their usefulness... there is virtually nothing that cannot be conceptualized and analyzed by non-mathematical models—religion and ideology, economic institutions and ideas, the state and politics, simple descriptions and developmental sequences. The familiar fear of a priorism is misplaced: any hypothesis can be modified, adjusted or discarded when necessary. Without one, however, there can be no explanation; there can be only reportage and crude taxonomy, antiquarianism in its narrowest sense.[1]

Finley's comment points right at the heart of the problems involved in writing ancient history. His insight seems to be equally applicable to the study of biblical history if one wants to make such a distinction.

Take, for example, this study of the historical situation in the Corinthian church. We are faced with a similar problem. All we have are two canonical letters from Paul which were written with the aim of guiding the Corinthians to the goal which Paul saw as appropriate. There is no other record to help us assess the *real* situation. Every account of the situation has to depend on Paul's own witness. Archaeology can help to shed light on isolated aspects of the situation in the colony. But we can never expect to have all our questions answered by these findings. In the light of such limitations, Finley's suggestion to make use of modelling appears to be an attractive one.

As a matter of fact, the possibility of using models to facilitate New Testament interpretation has been explored by some New Testament scholars in recent years.[2] B. Malina is one of them. In one of his discussions, he proposes the following criteria for a good model:

> (1) it should be a cross-cultural model, accounting for the interpreter as well as the interpreted in some comparative perspective; (2) it should be of a sufficient level of abstraction to allow for the surfacing of similarities that facilitates comparison; (3) the model should be able to fit a larger sociolinguistic frame for interpreting texts; (4) it should derive from experiences that match what we know of the time and place conditioned biblical world as closely as possible; (5) the meaning it generates should be irrelevant but understandable to us and our twentieth century United States

---

1. Finley, *Ancient History*, p. 66.
2. See Gager, 'Shall We Marry Our Enemies?', pp. 256-65; B. Malina, 'The Social Sciences and Biblical Interpretation', *Int* 37 (1982), pp. 229-42.

society; (6) the application of the model should be acceptable to social scientists.[1]

Not everyone will agree with all the criteria set by Malina.[2] But granting that these criteria can provide a kind of guideline, which model should we use?

In my opinion, patronage, as a model, meets most of the above requirements well. For patronage was a first-century phenomenon, but is still with us today.[3] It has been shown that patronage can be used as a model of analysis.[4] It has actually been used in studies of relations in Republican Rome and the early Empire which involve the interpretation of texts.[5] Hence, I propose to use patronage as a model to help explain several of the problems inside and outside the church in Corinth.

Patronage

What is patronage? How do we know patron–client ties exist? What are some of the characteristics of patron–client relations? After almost 40 years of studies in different parts of the world social anthropologists, social scientists and political scientists[6] agree that patron–client

---

1. Malina, 'Social Sciences and Biblical Interpretation', p. 241.
2. From a Chinese point of view, the usefulness of the fifth one is highly questionable.
3. The fact that patronage did not die with Western modernization is what gives rise to a renewed interest in the study of patronage among sociologists and anthropologists (see S.N. Eisenstadt and L. Roniger, *Patrons, Clients and Friends: Interpersonal Relations and the Structure of Trust in Society* [Cambridge: Cambridge University Press, 1984], pp. 3-4).
4. See, e.g., C.H. Landé, 'Introduction: The Dyadic Basis of Clientelism', in *Friends, Followers and Factions: A Reader in Political Clientelism* (ed. S.W. Schmidt, L. Guasti, C.H. Landé and J.C. Scott; Berkeley: University of California Press, 1977), pp. xiii-xxxvii; R. Lemarchand, 'Comparative Political Clientelism: Structure, Process and Optic', in *Political Clientelism: Patronage and Development* (ed. S.N. Eisenstadt and R. Lemarchand; London: Sage, 1981), pp. 7-32.
5. See L. Roniger, 'Modern Patron–Client Relations and Historical Clientelism: Some Clues from Ancient Republican Rome', *AES* 24 (1983), pp. 63-95; Saller, *Personal Patronage*.
6. Eisenstadt and Roniger, *Patrons, Clients and Friends*, pp. 43-47, 50-162.

relations can be described as ties with the following common features.[1]

1. *A patron–client relation is an exchange relation.* In a patron–client relation the patron gives the client what he needs, and in turn gets from the client what he wants. In this respect, a patron–client relation is not unlike other exchange relationships, for example, friendship. Through such a relation, different kinds of resources can be simultaneously exchanged. Very often, the favours granted by the patron are immediately tangible items. Depending on the context, they may be farming land for tenants, economic aid, a job or promotion, and/or protection against the encroachment of hostile forces, legal or illegal.[2] The clients usually pay back more intangible goods. They may, for example, publicize the good name of the patron to the people in the community. They may support the patron in the political process by, for instance, voting in his favour. They may also serve as informants to the patron.[3]

2. *A patron–client relation is an asymmetrical relation.* It is this feature which marks a patron–client relation off from a friendship tie.[4] The patron and the client are not equal in terms of power. Such inequality is usually the result of differences in the ability to have access to scarce resources. These resources may be different things in different settings. They may be material[5] or spiritual.[6] The patron is a person who holds a key position over the access to such resources in a certain setting. Because the client is denied direct access to such resources, he is forced either to depend on the patron for the provision of such resources or to seek the mediation of the patron, who

1. Adapted mainly from Eisenstadt and Roniger, *Patrons, Clients and Friends*, pp. 48-49.
2. E.g. J. Boissevain, 'Patronage in Sicily', *Man* ns 1 (1966), pp. 8-33.
3. E.R. Wolf, 'Kinship, Friendship and Patron–Client Relations in Complex Societies', in Schmidt *et al.* (eds.), *Friends, Followers and Factions*, p. 174.
4. The patron–client relation has been appropriately described as 'lop-sided friendship' (J.A. Pitt-Rivers's term quoted in Wolf, 'Kinship, Friendship, and Patron–Client Relations in Complex Societies', in Schmidt *et al.* (eds.), *Friends, Followers and Factions*, p. 174).
5. See discussion above.
6. M. Kenny, 'Patterns of Patronage in Spain', in Schmidt *et al.* (eds.), *Friends, Followers and Factions*, pp. 355-59; M. Bloch and S. Guggenheim, 'Compadrazgo, Baptism and the Symbolism of a Second Birth', *Man* ns 16 (1981), pp. 376-86.

then becomes a broker, in order to get to the resources. To a certain extent the strength of a patron–client tie can also be measured by the degree of difficulty in getting to the needed resources. If the patron's power to monopolize is weakened or is robbed by a more powerful patron,[1] it is likely that the strength of the ties between the patron and the client will be weakened and that the client may turn to establish a relationship with a new patron.

3. *A patron–client relation is usually a particularistic and informal relation.* Resources are usually channelled to specific individuals or groups of individuals and are not meant to be bestowed universally. This element of particularity is pivotal to giving a sense of solidarity between the patron and the client. Without this particularistic quality, the relation may be weakened.

4. *A patron–client relation is usually a supra-legal relation.* It is usually not fully legal, often opposed to the official laws of the country, and is based on mutual understanding. Hence, it is often a subtle relationship.

5. *A patron–client relation is often a binding and long-range relation.* It is a relation which carries a strong sense of interpersonal obligation. For example, if the client fails to support the patron, hostile feeling can be generated and action may sometimes be taken by the patron to censure the client.

6. *A patron–client relation is a voluntary relation.* In theory, at least, the relation is established voluntarily and can be abandoned voluntarily. Of course, under certain circumstances, a client may have no other choice but to turn to the patron for help.

7. *A patron–client relation is a vertical relation.* It binds the patron and individual clients or networks of clients together, often to the exclusion of other patrons. Such a relation tends to discourage horizontal group organization and the solidarity of clients. In time of crises a client may have to serve his leader and become a member of a faction. But because there can often be competition between patrons,

---

1. On the changes of patronal relations in Malta, see J. Boissevain, 'When the Saints Go Marching Out: Reflections on the Decline of Patronage in Malta', in *Patrons and Clients in Mediterranean Societies* (ed. E. Gellner and J. Waterbury; London: Gerald Duckworth, 1977), pp. 81-96.

room is sometimes left for the clients to manipulate for their own benefit.[1]

From these characteristics we may see two paradoxes existing in a patron–client relation. The first one is the peculiar combination of inequality and seeming mutual solidarity. The second one is the combination of potential coercion and mutual obligation. At the same time, it should also be pointed out that there can be variations in patron–client ties. In the light of the situation of the Roman Empire, clearly not all of the above characteristics are applicable. For example, the ties between the patron and his freedmen or freedwomen in the early Empire were not supra-legal relations, but were sanctioned by law. So in the use of patronage as a model we need to take into consideration the particularity of the evidence. The model is only meant to provide a framework for interpretation and understanding. Hopefully, through the use of patronage as a heuristic tool, we can come to a better understanding of the situation in Corinth.

Networks
Having set up a theoretical framework for interpretation, I can go on to explain my method of analysis. According to Weingrod there are two ways to study patronage.[2] For anthropologists, to study patronage is to study how persons of unequal powers seek to attain their goals through personal ties. To political scientists, to study patronage is to study how political party leaders seek to win votes and to turn public resources to their own ends by bestowing different kinds of favours. For a study of relations and problems in a community like the church at Corinth, it seems more appropriate to adopt the former approach.

In this study, I will also attempt to use networks as a guiding concept to help analyse the relational structure and problems in the Corinthian church.[3] As a metaphor a network has been in use for a

1. J. Boissevain, 'Factions, Parties, and Politics in a Maltese Village', in Schmidt *et al.* (eds.), *Friends, Followers and Factions*, pp. 279-87. Cf. also M. Kenny, *A Spanish Tapestry: Town and Country in Castile* (Bloomington: Indiana University Press, 1962), p. 136.
2. A. Weingrod, 'Patrons, Patronage, and Political Parties', in Schmidt *et al.* (eds.), *Friends, Followers and Factions*, pp. 323-25.
3. For discussions of the theory of networks, see J.C. Mitchell, 'The Concept and Use of Social Networks', in *Social Networks in Urban Situations* (ed. J.C. Mitchell; Manchester: Manchester University Press, 1969), pp. 1-50; J. Boissevain and

long time as an impressionistic description of the interrelatedness of social relationships.[1] In the past two decades, however, this concept has been taken one step further and used as an analytical tool. As such, a network has been defined by one network analyst as

> A specific set of linkages among a defined set of persons, with the additional property that the characteristics of these linkages as a whole may be used to interpret the social behaviour of the persons involved.[2]

In the light of this definition, the aim of network analysis is to study the relationship between the patterns of ties in a defined social field so as to understand the behaviour of those involved in that field.

In a recent explication of the working principles of network analysis, B. Wellman claims that network analysis is the basic and most direct way to study a social structure.[3] Instead of seeing the world and society in fixed social categories and groupings, network analysts see the world or society as an unbounded network of ties which cuts across different social categories and groupings. Instead of treating individuals as members of a social category, assuming that members who belong to one category will all behave in a similar way, network analysts see individuals in the light of their structural positions in a network or networks. Based on this conception of society, network analysts seek to understand how network structures constrain social behaviour and social change. The following working principles of

---

J.C. Mitchell (eds.), *Network Analysis* (The Hague: Mouton, 1973); F.V. Price, 'Only Connect? Issues in Charting Social Networks', *SR* 29 (1981), pp. 283-312; B. Wellman, 'Network Analysis: Some Basic Principles', in *Sociological Theory* (ed. R. Collins; San Francisco: Jossey-Bass, 1983), pp. 155-200.

For some classic studies using networks, see J.A. Barnes, 'Class and Committees in a Norwegian Island Parish', *Human Relations* 7 (1954), pp. 39-58; Boissevain, 'Patronage in Sicily', pp. 8-33; A. Mayer, 'The Significance of Quasi-Groups in the Study of Complex Societies', reprinted in *Social Networks: A Developing Paradigm* (ed. S. Leinhardt; New York: Academic, 1977), pp. 293-318.

1. See, e.g., A.R. Radcliffe-Brown, 'On Social Structure', reprinted in *Social Networks: A Developing Paradigm*, pp. 221-32. For its application in New Testament study, see, e.g., Meeks, *First Urban Christians*, p. 30; *idem*, *Moral World of the First Christians*, p. 111.

2. Mitchell, 'The Concept and Use of Social Networks', p. 2.

3. Wellmann, 'Network Analysis', p. 157. The following discussion is based mainly on this article.

network analysis may be highlighted to sensitize our awareness in this study of the situation in the Corinthian church.

1. *Ties are often asymmetrically reciprocal, differing in content and intensity.* The contents which flow through personal ties can be information, material goods, or power. While ties are usually reciprocated, in reality they are seldom symmetrical in intensity and in the amount and kinds of resources that flow through the links.
2. *Ties link network members indirectly as well as directly; hence ties must be analysed within the context of larger network structures.* While some ties, such as friendship ties, may be formed voluntarily, others, like kinship, neighbourhood or even patron–client ties, may not. The significance of such involuntarily formed ties should not be overlooked.
3. *The structuring of social ties creates non-random networks; hence network clusters, boundaries and cross-linkages arise.* Individuals are connected to multiple social networks. Some of these ties can form clusters. While cross-linkages give access to external resources and provide the basis for coalitions, internal linkages allocate resources within a cluster and provide the basis for solidarity.
4. *Cross-linkages connect clusters as well as individuals.* The nodes of a network may be individual persons, clusters of ties, groups and other units. The linkages of some members in clusters with outside resources may have important consequences for the structure of ties within clusters.
5. *Asymmetric ties and complex networks distribute scarce resources differentially.* Because some members in a network control the access to scarce resources, while others do not, resources are distributed differently. This difference in social location can lead to the formation of hierarchy.
6. *Networks structure collaborative and competitive activities to secure scarce resources.* The need to compete for resources encourages the rise of collective political activity which, in turn, may lead to social structural change and redistribution of access to resources.

These working principles will serve only as guidelines in this study of the situation in St Paul's Corinth. For our use of network analysis cannot be total because, unlike anthropologists and sociologists who can collect first-hand information for their studies through participation, observation or sending out questionnaires, New Testament historians will never be able to obtain information through those channels. Thus, while the interpretation is informed by the above working principles, I do not pretend that I can give a scientific account of the actual situation in Corinth in the first century. I do hope that these guiding principles can help us to read afresh the few pieces of information preserved in a letter of Paul to the Corinthians.

It may also be mentioned that this study of the relationships in Corinth differs from the work of some of the network analysts at two other points. First, I do not intend to pursue, as some network analysts do, a quantitative study. The focus of this study remains the quality of the relationships and the problems in the church at Corinth. Secondly, while network analysts are more interested in the structure of relational ties and many of them, not without reason, tend to put less emphasis on human intention in the shaping of the relationships, this emphasis is not accepted in this study. 1 Corinthians was written with the intention of changing a situation according to the ideal of the author. It is important for New Testament students to bring this subjective element into their analysis.

Plan of Study

As applied to this study of the church at Corinth, I will seek to analyse one particular type of network, namely, patron–client ties, and its implications for our understanding of the relationships and problems in the church at Corinth.

Since New Testament historians have stressed that New Testament studies using sociological models should first be set securely in the first-century context and network analysts have suggested that it is important to study local networks with reference to broader networks, so, in Chapter 1, I examine the structure of relationships in Corinth, the Roman colony. Through such an examination I hope to see whether patronage provided an important means by which social relationships in Roman Corinth were structured. Although the study of patronage in Chapter 1 is not exhaustive, it is hoped that it will be adequate to provide a context for understanding some of the problems in the church at Corinth.

In Chapter 2, I seek to ascertain a pattern of relational ties in the church at Corinth at the time of the writing of 1 Corinthians. Through such a study, I hope to understand the nature of the relationships in the church. Then the relationship between patronage and two of the problems in the church, namely the controversy over Paul's refusal to accept financial support from the Corinthians and the divisions at the Lord's table, are discussed.

In Chapter 3, I seek to make sense of other problems in the church in the light of the patronal background. They include in particular the church's acceptance of the immoral man who lived with his stepmother, the settling of a dispute before the pagan court, and the Corinthian rite of baptism for the dead.

In Chapter 4, Paul's response to the situation in the church in 1 Corinthians is examined to bring out its implications for the patronal ties in Corinth.

Chapter 1

PATRONAGE IN ROMAN CORINTH

On a monument made in the middle of the first century AD in Corinth, the following words were inscribed to honour Julius Spartiaticus, a man of influence, an important patron to the tribe of Calpurnia and a contemporary of Paul:

> Gaius Julius, Son of Laco,
> Grandson of Eurycles, [of the tribe] Fabia, Spartiaticus,
> Procurator of Caesar and Augusta
> Agrippina, Tribune of the Soldiers, Awarded a Public Horse
> By the Deified Claudius, Flamen
> Of the Deified Julius, Pontifex, Duovir Quinquennalis twice,
> Agonothete of the Isthmian and Caesar-
> Augustan Games, High-Priest of the House of Augustus
> In Perpetuity, First of the Achaeans.
> Because of his Virtue and Eager
> And all-encompassing Munificence toward the Divine House
> And toward our Colony, the Tribesmen
> Of the Tribe Calpurnia
> [Dedicated this] to their Patron.[1]

From the relationships recorded in the above inscription, a rough picture of how social relationships were organized in Roman Corinth is displayed before our eyes. While Spartiaticus was a patron to one of the tribes in Corinth, he himself was under the Roman emperor, an even more powerful man. Do we see here a chain of patron–client

---

1. A.B. West, *Latin Inscriptions 1896-1926. Corinth: Results*, VIII.2 (Cambridge, MA: Harvard University Press, 1931), no. 68. The translation is adapted from D.C. Braund, *Augustus to Nero: A Sourcebook on Roman History, 31 BC–AD 68* (London: Croom & Helm, 1985), no. 469 and R.K. Sherk, *The Roman Empire: Augustus to Hadrian* (Cambridge: Cambridge University Press, 1988), no. 164B.

ties? Can it be inferred that patron–client ties made up an important part of social relationships in first-century Corinth? If so, how then did patronage function in Roman Corinth? According to one political scientist, patron–client ties tend 'to arise within a state structure in which authority is dispersed and state activity limited in scope, and in which considerable separation exists between the levels of village, city and state'.[1] Assuming that such an assertion is true, it would appear that the ancient Roman Empire with its vast territories and great regional differences, and possibly conflicts of interests too, might be an ideal breeding-ground for patron–client ties. Significantly, one ancient historian actually suggests that patronage was the secret to the integration of the Roman Empire.[2]

1. Weingrod, 'Patrons, Patronage and Political Parties', in Schmidt *et al.* (eds.), *Friends, Followers and Factions*, p. 325. This assertion has been supported by a study of the structure of the classic Chinese state which in many ways was comparable to the Roman State (see O. Lattimore, *Inner Asian Frontiers of China* [Boston: Beacon Press, 1962]). For a comparison between Chinese and Roman bureaucracy, see Saller, *Personal Patronage*, Appendix 3A, pp. 111-16.

2. G.E.M. de Ste. Croix writes, 'Patronage, indeed, must be seen as an institution the Roman world simply could not do without' (*The Class Struggle in the Ancient Greek World* [London: Gerald Duckworth, 1981], p. 364.) Although not all would agree with the view of de Ste. Croix, not a few have recognized the influence of patronage in the Roman society on politics, legal proceedings and literary activities.

(a) On patronage and politics, see R. Syme, *The Roman Revolution* (Oxford: Oxford University Press, 1939); L.R. Taylor, *Party Politics in the Age of Caesar* (Berkeley: University of California Press, 1949); G.E.M. de Ste. Croix, 'Suffragium: From Vote to Patronage', *BJS* 5 (1954), pp. 33-48; E. Badian, *Foreign Clientele (264-70 BC)* (Oxford: Clarendon Press, 1958); G. Bowersock, *Augustus and the Greek World* (Oxford: Clarendon Press, 1965); E.M.I. Edlund, 'Invisible Bonds: Clients and Patrons through the Eyes of Polybius', *Klio* 59 (1977), pp. 129-36; de Ste. Croix, *Class Struggle*; Saller, *Personal Patronage*; Garnsey and Saller, *Roman Empire*.

(b) On patronage and legal proceedings, see J.M. Kelly, *Roman Litigation* (Oxford: Clarendon Press, 1966); J.A. Crook, *Law and Life of Rome* (London: Thames & Hudson, 1967); M. Gelzer, *The Roman Nobility* (Oxford: Basil Blackwell, 1969), pp. 70-86; P. Garnsey, *Social Status and Legal Privilege in the Roman Empire* (Oxford: Clarendon Press, 1970).

(c) On patronage and literary activities, see G. Bowersock, *Augustus and the Greek World*, pp. 30-41; *idem*, *Greek Sophists in the Roman Empire* (Oxford: Clarendon Press, 1969); R. Saller, 'Martial on Patronage and Literature', *CQ* 33

The institution of patronage has also helped to explain how the Roman rulers were able to rule such an enormous empire with the minimal number of officials.[1] As a Roman colony,[2] Corinth was already influenced by Rome in language,[3] architecture[4] and city administration.[5] If patronage was an important phenomenon in the early Empire, it would be reasonable to expect Corinth to be influenced by Rome even in this aspect of its social life.

In this chapter, I will investigate to see if patronage provided one of the important ways through which social relationships were organized in Roman Corinth. I will begin by analysing some of the networks of relationships in Corinth, which can roughly be seen as a hierarchy made up of the emperor, Roman officials, local notables and the populace. Then I will show how a kind of patronal hierarchy may be seen

(1983), pp. 246-57; N. Rudd, *Themes in Roman Satires* (London: Duckworth, 1986), pp. 126-61.
 (d) On the relationship between patrons and freedmen, see A.M. Duff, *Freedmen in the Early Roman Empire* (Oxford: Clarendon Press, 1928); S. Treggiari, *Roman Freedman during the Late Republic* (Oxford: Clarendon Press, 1969).
 1. Saller, *Personal Patronage*, pp. 205-206.
 2. Corinth was rebuilt as a Roman colony by the decree of Julius Caesar in 44 BC, and was named *Colonia Laus Julia Corinthiensis* in his honour (Strabo, 8.6.23; 17.3.15; Appian, *Roman History* 8.20.136; Plutarch, *Caesar* 57; Pausanias, 2.1.2; Dio Cassius, 43.50.3-5). See also O. Broneer, 'Colonia Laus Julia Corinthiensis', *Hesp* 10 (1941), pp. 388-90; J.H. Kent, *The Inscriptions, 1926-1950. Corinth: Results*, VIII.3 (Princeton: American School of Classical Studies at Athens, 1966), no. 130.
 3. The official language in Corinth, especially in the early days, was probably Latin. Out of 104 texts found and dated as prior to the reign of Hadrian, 101 are in Latin (Kent, *Inscriptions*, pp. 18-19).
 4. Roman road patterns were built on top of the old Greek city (C.K. Williams and O.H. Zervos, 'Corinth, 1981: East of the Theater', *Hesp* 51 [1982], pp. 118, 128). A forum was built southwest of the old civic centre (J. Wiseman, 'Corinth and Rome I: 228 BC–AD 267', *ANRW* II.7.1 [1979], pp. 512-13). An altar, the style of which resembles that of the *Ara Pacis*, might have been erected in the reign of Augustus (R.L. Scranton, *Monuments in the Lower Agora and North of the Archaic Temple. Corinth: Results*, I.3 [Princeton: American School of Classical Studies at Athens, 1951], pp. 140-41).
 5. The local government, which consisted of an assembly of citizen voters, a city council and annual magistrates, looks like a replica of the civic government of Republican Rome (A. Bagdikian, 'The Civic Officials of Roman Corinth' [MA thesis, Vermont, 1953], pp. 9-18; Kent *Inscriptions*, pp. 23-24).

in the structure of relationships in different institutions, such as the association and the household. Lastly, I will explore the improper influence of patronage on the execution of justice in the Roman court. Hopefully, these studies will in the end help to shed light on some of the problems in the Corinthian church as reflected in 1 Corinthians.

Patronage and Society

As defined before, a patron–client tie is basically an asymmetrical exchange relationship. The parties on both ends of such a tie are unequal in the control of resources, and so differ in terms of power and status. They are bound together mainly because their tie can serve their mutual interests through the exchange of resources. If the above are some of the characteristics of patron–client ties, one would expect such ties in the Roman Empire to be somewhat similar. As will be discussed below, it seems that similar ties could indeed be found at work in different strata of Roman society, ranging from the relationship between the emperor and his hand-picked officials to that between a patron and his freedmen. The influence of patronage in the political scene at Rome is aptly described by G.E.M. de Ste. Croix:

> At Rome election from below became less and less important, even in the last years of the Republic, and early in the Principate it came to occupy only a minor place... A Roman emperor made most of the top appointments himself from among men whom he would personally know. He, on the recommendation of his immediate subordinates, or those subordinate themselves, would appoint to the less exalted posts; and so the process went on, right down the line to the humblest local officials.[1]

Naturally, the situation at Rome might not be the same as that of Corinth. For this reason, I want to take a closer look at the situation in Corinth.

The Emperor

If the Roman emperor was comparable to the patron of the entire Empire,[2] in some ways, he was the patron of Corinth too. That he was

---

1. *Class Struggle*, pp. 364-65.
2. In another way, the Roman emperor can be regarded as a middleman between the gods and mankind. He was first of all a man. An emperor like Augustus gave the impression that he was dependent upon the help of the gods. In return for his

able to bring peace and order to a vast Empire naturally would inspire reverence and awe. Not surprisingly, in some parts of the Empire, especially in the Greek east, such reverence for the Roman rulers was expressed by showering them and members of the imperial family with honorific titles like 'patron', 'benefactor', 'saviour' and 'son of a god', which suggest a greatly superior status.[1] In Corinth, some of

successes, thanksgivings were offered to the gods (*Res Gestae* 4.2). Temples were built for Apollo, Mars and other gods (*Res Gestae* 19–21). Prayers had to be offered for the health and safety of Augustus by priests and ordinary citizens (*Res Gestae* 9). Divine honours were not accepted by emperors like Tiberius (V. Ehrenberg and A.H.M. Jones, *Documents illustrating the Reigns of Augustus and Tiberius* [Oxford: Clarendon Press, 2nd edn, 1955], no. 102b = Braund, *Augustus to Nero*, no. 127) and Claudius (Smallwood, *Documents*, no. 370 = Braund, *Augustus to Nero*, no. 571. However, because an emperor like Augustus was able to bring peace and order, he won himself a special place in the hearts of his people, especially those in the East (e.g. Ehrenberg and Jones, *Documents*, no. 98 = Braund, *Augustus to Nero*, no. 122). A man or woman in the street might see the emperor as the man of men, even a god. Consequently, in the realm of human affairs, his will would possibly be regarded highly by both the leaders and the inhabitants of a local community, like those in Corinth. As the focus of our attention in this part of our discussion is on human relationships, I thus choose to begin by looking at the patronal image of the emperor in Corinth.

1. Just to give some examples:

(a) 'Patron': Marcus Agrippa (Ilium [Braund, *Augustus to Nero*, no. 67]); Lucius Caesar, son of Augustus (Pisa [Ehrenberg and Jones, *Documents*, no. 68 = Braund, *Augustus to Nero*, no. 62]);

(b) 'Benefactor': Marcus Agrippa (Myra [Ehrenberg and Jones, *Documents*, no. 72 = Braund, *Augustus to Nero*, no. 66]); Augustus (Myra [Ehrenberg and Jones, *Documents*, no. 72 = Braund, *Augustus to Nero*, no. 66]); Tiberius (Myra [Ehrenberg and Jones, *Documents*, no. 88 = Braund, *Augustus to Nero*, no. 107]);

(c) 'Saviour': Marcus Agrippa (Myra [Ehrenberg and Jones, *Documents*, no. 72 = Braund, *Augustus to Nero*, no. 66]); Augustus (Asia [Ehrenberg and Jones, *Documents*, no. 98 = Braund, *Augustus to Nero*, no. 122]; Gytheum [Ehrenberg and Jones, *Documents*, no. 102a = Braund, *Augustus to Nero*, no. 127]); Tiberius (Myra [Ehrenberg and Jones, *Documents*, no. 88 = Braund, *Augustus to Nero*, no. 107]);

(d) 'Son of a god' or 'god': Augustus (Gytheum [Ehrenberg and Jones, *Documents*, no. 102 = Braund, *Augustus to Nero*, no. 127]); Tiberius (Cyprus [Ehrenberg and Jones, *Documents*, no. 134 = Braund, *Augustus to Nero*, no. 164]); Caligula (Didyma [Smallwood, *Documents*, no. 127 = Braund, *Augustus to Nero*, no. 181]); Claudius (Volubilis [Smallwood, *Documents*, no. 407a = Braund, *Augustus to Nero*, no. 680a]).

these titles, even the title 'patron',[1] were also found in some of the inscriptions dedicated to the emperors or members of the imperial house.[2]

Was the image of the Roman emperor in Corinth comparable to that of a supreme or even quasi-divine patron? If it was, how was such an image projected? In what ways was the Roman emperor such a patron? To get a better picture of the Roman emperor as a supreme patron, the ultimate centre of power granting favours and expecting loyalty and honour in return, I suggest the need to look further into the life situation in the colony and the relationships between the emperors and the local leaders rather than to study the occurrences of the word 'patron' in the inscriptions. The image of the Roman emperor as one who dominated the life of the colony could hardly be overlooked by the people in Corinth. The name of the colony, *Colonia Laus Julia Corinthiensis*, stood as a constant reminder of the grace of Julius Caesar who helped to refound the colony. The names of the voting tribes or local political divisions would also remind people of the imperial presence in Corinth. Some of these names are Agrippia,

---

1. Between 18–12 BC, Marcus Agrippa was honoured as a patron of the tribe Vinicia (West, *Latin Inscriptions*, no. 16 = Ehrenberg and Jones, *Documents*, no. 73 = Braund, *Augustus to Nero*, no. 69). But it is actually possible that Agrippa was a patron of the colony (West, *Latin Inscriptions*, p. 15). At a later time, Diocletian was honoured as a patron by his freedman (Kent, *Inscriptions*, no. 67).

It is apparent that there is a lack of explicit references in Corinth to the early Roman emperors as patrons. But this should not necessarily lead to the conclusion that they could not and cannot be regarded as such. Two points should be considered here. First, it should be noted that patronage is an ambiguous phenomenon. Hence, the existence of such a tie might not necessarily be represented in words. Secondly, more important, the mere title 'patron' might not be enough to represent the enormous power and honour embodied by a Roman emperor. Perhaps that is why divine titles were given to some of the emperors instead.

2. The title θεοῦ υἱός was used to designate Augustus (B.D. Meritt, *Greek Inscriptions, 1896–1927. Corinth: Results*, VIII.1 [Cambridge, MA: Harvard University Press, 1931], no. 19). The title *divus* was also given to Julius Caesar (Kent, *Inscriptions*, no. 50) and Augustus (Kent, *Inscriptions*, no. 52).

Titles such as 'saviour' and 'benefactor', and other grander ones, were used in inscriptions made at a later date. So Hardian was named as 'saviour and benefactor' (Kent, *Inscriptions*, no. 102); C. Vibius Afinius Trebonianus Gallus (c. AD 252) was honoured by the city as 'our master the greatest and most god-like Emperor' (Kent, *Inscriptions*, no. 116).

Atia, Aurelia, Calpurnia, Claudia, Domitia, Hostilia, Livia, Maneia, Vatinia and Vinicia.[1] It is clear that these tribes were named after members of the imperial families or close friends and associates of Augustus.[2] When Paul walked down the streets of Corinth, other symbols which conveyed the presence and power of the Roman emperor could also be seen. Coins which circulated in the market bore the images of the emperors.[3] Imperial images of Augustus and his sons were erected.[4] A Roman temple, or Temple E, which was built probably in the reign of Claudius[5] for the cult of the imperial family,

1. Agrippia (West, *Latin Inscriptions*, no. 110); Atia (West, *Latin Inscriptions*, no. 86); Aurelia (West, *Latin Inscriptions*, no. 97); Calpurnia (West, *Latin Inscriptions*, no. 68); Hostilia (West, *Latin Inscriptions*, no. 109); Maneia (West, *Latin Inscriptions*, no. 56); Vinicia (West, *Latin Inscriptions*, no. 16); Domitia (Kent, *Inscriptions*, no. 249); Livia (Kent, *Inscriptions*, no. 259); Vatinia (Kent, *Inscriptions*, no. 222). On the identification of the tribe of Claudia, see J. Wiseman, 'The Gymnasium Area at Corinth', *Hesp* 41 (1972), p. 37.

2. Aurelia and Calpurnia were names of the mother and the wife of Julius Caesar. Atia and Livia were names of the mother and the wife of Augustus. The tribe Vatinia could be named after P. Vatinius, legate and friend of Caesar. The tribe of Agrippia was named in honour of Marcus Agrippa. M. Vinicius, consul in 19 BC, a personal friend of Augustus was probably remembered by the tribe of Vinicia. It is to be expected that the other three tribes were also named for close friends and associates of Augustus. Later, in either the reign of Tiberius and Claudius, the tribe of Claudia was added. See West, *Latin Inscriptions*, no. 110 and commentary; Kent, *Inscriptions*, nos. 23 and 249 and commentary; Wiseman, 'Corinth and Rome I', pp. 497-98.

3. For a discussion on coins found in Corinth, see K.N. Edwards, *The Coins, 1896–1929. Corinth: Results*, VI (Cambridge, MA: Harvard University Press, 1933). Coins which bear the images of the Roman emperors and some members of the imperial family are as follows: Augustus, nos. 28, 30, 32, 34, 35; Agrippa, no. 36; Tiberius, nos. 40, 43; Livia, nos. 41, 42; Caligula, nos. 45, 46, 47; Claudius, nos. 50, 51; Nero, nos. 54, 55, 56, 57, 59, 61, 62, 63, 64.

4. F.P. Johnson, 'The Imperial Portraits at Corinth', *AJA* 30 (1926), pp. 158-76; *idem*, *Sculpture, 1896–1923. Corinth: Results*, IX.1 (Cambridge, MA: Harvard University Press, 1931), pp. 70-78; E.H. Swift, 'A Group of Roman Imperial Portraits at Corinth', *AJA* 25 (1921), pp. 142-59, 248-65, 337-63; B.S. Ridgway, 'Sculpture from Corinth', *Hesp* 50 (1981), pp. 429-35.

5. Wiseman, 'Corinth and Rome I', p. 519. Cf. S.E. Freeman, *Architecture. Corinth: Results*, I.2 (ed. R. Stillwell, R.L. Scranton and S.E. Freeman; Cambridge, MA: Harvard University Press, 1941), pp. 168-79. D.W.J. Gill has suggested that the temple might have been built prior to 38/39 AD ('Roman Corinth: A Pluralistic

1. Patronage in Roman Corinth

stood at the west end of the forum, witnessing to the transcending status of the Roman rulers.[1] In addition, there were, of course, many other monuments and inscriptions which were made to honour the emperors.[2]

If the above symbols conveyed the message that the Roman emperors were powerful masters over the colony, one episode in the history of first-century Corinth would serve to demonstrate further how their power could affect the fate of the people in Greece. In AD 67 freedom was granted to them by Nero.[3] Through such an action, the image of the emperor as an unsurpassing benefactor or patron to his people in Achaia almost certainly would strike deep into the hearts and minds of the people there.[4] But because such magnificent benefaction was based solely on the extemporaneous will of the powerful benefactor, it should be understood that there was absolutely no guarantee of how long it would last. The capricious nature of these powerful benefactions

Society?' [1989 Tyndale New Testament/Biblical Archaeology Study Groups Paper], p. 10).

1. Most scholars regard Temple E as the Temple of Octavia, the sister of Augustus (Wiseman, 'Corinth and Rome I', p. 522; C.K. Williams's view quoted in V.P. Furnish, *II Corinthians* [Garden City: Doubleday, 1984], p. 19; Gill, 'Roman Corinth', pp. 10-11). But Freeman prefers to see the temple as the Temple of Jupiter Capitolinus ('Temple E', *Architecture*, I.2, pp. 179-236).

2. From Julius Caesar to Nero, all had inscriptions dedicated to them in Corinth: Julius Caesar (Kent, *Inscriptions*, no. 50); Augustus (Kent, *Inscriptions*, nos. 51, 52, 53, 69); Tiberius (Kent, *Inscriptions*, no. 72); Claudius (Kent, *Inscriptions*, nos. 74, 75, 77, 79); Nero (Kent, *Inscriptions*, nos. 80, 81).

3. The speech of Nero and a decree of Akraephia in Boeotia have been preserved (Smallwood, *Documents*, no. 64 = Braund, *Augustus to Nero*, no. 261; cf. Suetonius, *Nero*, p. 24). See also A. Momigliano, 'Nero', in *Cambridge Ancient History*, X (ed. S.A. Cook, F.E. Adcock and M.P. Charlesworth; Cambridge: Cambridge University Press, 1934), pp. 735-36.

4. The responses of the people in Greece are noteworthy. For they fitted in well with the principles of patronage. In return for such a generous benefaction the decree at Boeotia hailed Nero as a great lord and benefactor or, in their words, 'the lord of the whole world' (ὁ τοῦ παντὸς κόσμου κύριος) (Smallwood, *Documents*, no. 64, l. 31) and 'a benefactor of Greece' (εὐεργετεῖν τὴν Ἑλλάδα) (Smallwood, *Documents*, no. 64, l. 35). Accidentally or not, Nero was able to win all the prizes at different games in Greece like the Isthmian games (Suetonius, *Nero* 23–24). Most striking of all, the Boetians decreed that Nero should be worshipped at the altar dedicated to Zeus, and that his statue be placed among their ancestral gods in the temple of Apollos Ptoos.

was revealed several years later when the freedom granted by Nero was nullified by Vespasian.[1] The force of the imperial power was the same, but its effect on the life of the people in Greece was very different.

For different reasons, whether to honour the benevolent rule of the imperial house or otherwise, many celebrations organized in Corinth were related to the Roman emperors. Some of them were occasional while others were recurrent. One of the occasional events which probably called for celebrations, as it did elsewhere,[2] was the coronation of the new emperor.[3] Other occasional events which concerned the Roman emperors were celebrated as well. A cult was founded to celebrate the safety of the emperor, possibly at the time when Sejanus's plot against Tiberius was discovered.[4] Another was established to celebrate Claudius's victories in Britain.[5]

Apart from these occasional events, there were the recurrent festivals. As in other parts of the Roman world, the birthdays of the Roman rulers were often celebrated,[6] and it is highly likely that such dates were also celebrated in Corinth. Above all, the most important celebration which emphasized the power and glory of the Roman rulers was probably the holding of the imperial games at the same

---

1. Suetonius, *Vespasian* 8.4; Pausanias, 7.17.4.

2. When Claudius became emperor in AD 41, the Alexandrians sent envoys to express their desire to honour him (Smallwood, *Documents*, no. 370 = Braund, *Augustus to Nero*, no. 571).

3. In the reign of Caligula, envoys were sent from Achaea in AD 37 to express the loyalty of the League of Achaeans to the new emperor with a proposal to honour him in different parts of Achaea. The programme included the offering of sacrifices for the safety of the emperor, the holding of festivals and the setting up of his statues in various places, including Isthmia (Smallwood, *Documents*, no. 361 = Braund, *Augustus to Nero*, no. 564).

4. West, *Latin Inscriptions*, no. 110 = Ehrenberg and Jones, *Documents*, no. 113 = Braund, *Augustus to Nero*, no. 140.

5. See West, *Latin Inscriptions*, nos. 86-90. Cf. also no. 11.

6. In Forum Clodii, Etruria, sacrifices were offered on the birthday of the emperor (Ehrenberg and Jones, *Documents*, no. 101 = Braund, *Augustus to Nero*, no. 126). In 9 BC, as an attempt to honour Augustus, it was proposed that the calendar in Asia should be changed so that time began with his birthday, that is, 23 September (Ehrenberg and Jones, *Documents*, no. 98 = Braund, *Augustus to Nero*, no. 112). See also W.F. Snyder, 'Public Anniversaries in the Roman Empire', *YCS* 7 (1940), pp. 226-35.

1. *Patronage in Roman Corinth* 47

time as the famous biennial Isthmian games.[1] By the time Paul visited Corinth, two new programmes were already added alongside the Isthmian games to sing praises to the imperial house. They were the Caesarea and the 'imperial contests'. The Caesarea was the first programme added in honour of Augustus[2] c. 30 BC after the battle of Actium.[3] Its first three contests included an encomium of Augustus, an encomium of Tiberius, and a poem in honour of Livia.[4] A second series of contests or the 'imperial contests' was added later, possibly in the reign of Tiberius,[5] to honour the reigning emperor.[6] The programme of these 'imperial contests' is not clear. Kent suggests that, like that of the Caesarea, it was primarily thymelic and changed with the change of emperor.[7]

---

1. For a general discussion of the imperial cult in the early Empire, see especially L.R. Taylor, *The Divinity of the Roman Emperor* (Middletown, CT: American Philological Association, 1931); A.D. Nock, 'Religious Developments from the Close of the Republic to the Death of Nero', in *Cambridge Ancient History*, X, pp. 481-89; I.S. Ryberg, *Rites of the State Religion in Roman Art* (Memoirs of the American Academy in Rome, XXII; Rome: American Academy in Rome, 1955); Bowersock, *Augustus and the Greek World*, pp. 112-21; idem, 'Greek Intellectuals and the Imperial Cult', in *Le culte des souverains dans l'empire romain* (ed. E. Bickerman; Geneva: Vandoeuvres, 1972), pp. 179-206; M.K. Hopkins, *Conquerors and Slaves: Sociological Studies in Roman History*, I (Cambridge: Cambridge University Press, 1978), pp. 197-242; S.R.F. Price, *Rituals and Power: The Roman Imperial Cult in Asia Minor* (Cambridge: Cambridge University Press, 1984). For references to the imperial cult in Corinth, see West, *Latin Inscriptions*, nos. 14-16, 81; Kent, *Inscriptions*, nos. 152, 153, 156, 209, 210, 213, 218, 224, 272. Cf. also Kent, *Inscriptions*, pp. 28-30.

2. See West, *Latin Inscriptions*, no. 81 and commentary.

3. The date of the introduction of the Caesarea was not recorded. But it is possible that the Caesarea was first established c. 30 BC, shortly after the battle of Actium (West, *Latin Inscriptions*, p. 65; Kent, *Inscriptions*, p. 28).

4. Meritt, *Greek Inscriptions*, no. 19; Kent, *Inscriptions*, p. 29, no. 153 and commentary.

5. Kent, *Inscriptions*, p. 28.

6. In honour of Tiberius, the contests were called the *Tiberea Caesarea Sebastea* (Kent, *Inscriptions*, nos. 153, 156). In the time of Claudius, the name of the contests was changed to *Isthmia et Caesarea et Tiberea Claudiea Sebastea* (West, *Latin Inscriptions*, no. 82). By the time of Nero, the title became *Neronea Caesarea et Isthmia et Caesarea* (West, *Latin Inscriptions*, nos. 86-90). See Kent's discussion, *Inscriptions*, pp. 28-29.

7. Kent, *Inscriptions*, pp. 28-29.

Through these celebrations, occasional and regular, the images of the Roman rulers as powerful lords and benefactors could and probably would be enhanced. Superficially or not, the emperor as a superior man was probably honoured and acknowledged, at least by the organizers of the different festivals, if not by the participants in the celebrations. The fact that the imperial games were added on to the Isthmian games, especially in the first half of the first century, is also suggestive. It certainly indicates that, for some reason, the local leaders or the organizers of the games were keen to honour or to express their gratitude to their Roman masters. Indeed, many of the Corinthians would have reason to be grateful to some of the Roman rulers who would look almost like life-givers. For it was Julius Caesar who gave Corinth a chance to develop. Under Augustus, the colony was able to enjoy a long period of peace and prosperity.[1]

Having said this, it must be pointed out that, because the sources which we have, such as the inscriptions, were mainly related to the rich and the successful, it is not easy, though not impossible, to assess the attitude of the common crowd towards the Roman emperors. By the same token, our sources allow us to understand a little better why many of the local notables were eager to express their loyalty to the imperial house. In this respect, the story of the family of C. Julius Eurycles in Spartan Greece may be cited as an exemplary case to highlight the power of the emperor as the supreme patron in the Greek east and the instrumental nature of the relationship between the emperor and the local rulers and notables.

C. Julius Eurycles,[2] the famous Spartan dynast, probably did not come from a respected family. His father was alleged to be a pirate.[3] But because he helped to bring victory to Octavian at Actium, he was able to win the *philia* of Augustus. Consequently he was granted

---

1. In the reign of Augustus, Corinth enjoyed a time of great prosperity. In fact, many were so rich that they were able to build many buildings and to give them as gifts to the colony. For a list of the donors, see Kent, *Inscriptions*, p. 21.
2. For detailed discussions of the Euryclids, see G. Bowersock, 'Eurycles of Sparta', *JRS* 51 (1961), pp. 112-18; *idem*, *Augustus and the Greek World*, pp. 59-60; P. Cartledge and A. Spawforth, *Hellenistic and Roman Sparta: A Tale of Two Cities* (London: Routledge, 1989), pp. 97-104.
3. Plutarch, *Antony* 67. The island of Cythera, which was given to Sparta, was perhaps the base which his father once used. See Polybius, 4.6.

1. *Patronage in Roman Corinth* 49

Roman citizenship and the control of Sparta c. 30 BC.[1] In return for such benefactions he founded the imperial cult in Sparta as an expression of his loyalty to the imperial house.[2] After securing his friendship with the emperor he set about to fulfil his dream which was to regain control over Laconia. Some time between 7 and 2 BC he started to take action by stirring up civil disturbances throughout the province of Achaea.[3] For this he was twice brought to trial before Augustus by his opponents in Sparta[4] and was finally banished. Eurycles was probably dead by 2 BC.[5]

After the death of Eurycles, his descendants continued to enjoy power and prestige in Greece in the early Empire. In an inscription from Gytheum (or Gytheion),[6] dated c. AD 15, the proposal to honour the imperial house was followed by another proposal to stage thymelic performances in honour of the deceased Eurycles, the benefactor, and his son Laco, the guardian, for their benefactions. This suggests that, by the end of the Principate of Augustus and the early reign of Tiberius, Laco, the son, was in a position comparable to that of his father, a good friend of Augustus. Ironically, like his father Eurycles, the same prestigious Laco was soon deprived of his power by Tiberius.[7] It is not clear why Tiberius took this action. But there is reason to believe that it could possibly be related to the proposed worship of Laco in Gytheum.[8] In Corinth, a certain Laco, a procurator of Claudius, was honoured on an inscription.[9] As to the identification of

1. Bowersock, 'Eurycles', p. 112; Cartledge and Spawforth, *Sparta*, p. 98.
2. Cartledge and Spawforth, *Sparta*, p. 99.
3. Bowersock, 'Eurycles', pp. 113-16.
4. One of them was a descendant of Brasidas who still was not a Roman citizen (Plutarch, *Moralia* 207F). This may suggest that conflict and competition among local notables might be related to the uneven distribution of favour by the imperial house. The lack of Roman citizenship may partly explain why the family of Brasidas attacked Eurycles.
5. Bowersock, 'Eurycles', p. 114; Cartledge and Spawforth, *Sparta*, p. 101.
6. Ehrenberg and Jones, *Documents*, no. 102a = Braund, *Augustus to Nero*, no. 127.
7. Strabo 8.5.5; Tacitus, *Ann.* 6.18. See also West, *Latin Inscriptions*, pp. 47-48.
8. For Tiberius's reaction to the proposal of the people in Gytheum, see Ehrenberg and Jones, *Documents*, no. 102b = Braund, *Augustus to Nero*, no. 127.
9. West, *Latin Inscriptions*, no. 67 = Smallwood, *Documents*, no. 263 = Braund, *Augustus to Nero*, no. 468.

this Laco, scholars differ.[1] If, as many have suggested, this Laco was the son of Eurycles, it would mean that he probably benefited from the change of emperor and was once again able to enjoy the favour of the imperial master by the time of Claudius, if not in the reign of Caligula.[2] In any case, like his father Eurycles, Laco might have helped to institute the worship of Livia in Sparta.[3] That this was in any way related to his reinstatement is, however, not clear.

By the time of Claudius, the third generation of the Euryclids was able to befriend the Roman ruler. The most representative example was a grandson of Eurycles, namely Spartiaticus.[4] As a procurator of Caesar and Augusta Agrippina, Spartiaticus was by now part of the imperial system.[5] He was also awarded the equestrian rank. The reason why Spartiaticus was able to enjoy power and prestige is not clear. It is quite likely that the past ties between his family and the imperial house formed an important basis for his rise to power. Perhaps not by mere accident, like other members of his family, he also held many priestly posts besides his political offices. He was *flamen* of the deified Julius, *pontifex*, and high priest of the House of Augustus in perpetuity. Such explicit and unequivocal expressions of loyalty to the imperial house might also have helped him a great deal. Of course, his enormous wealth might have been another reason for his winning the favour of the ruler in Rome.[6] As to the later years of

1. There are basically two interpretations: (a) many see this Laco as the Spartan dynast, the son of Eurycles, reinstated by Claudius (West, *Latin Inscriptions*, pp. 47-48; M.P. Charlesworth, 'Gaius and Claudius', in *Cambridge Ancient History*, X, p. 682; Syme, *Roman Revolution*, p. 506; Cartledge and Spawforth, *Sparta*, p. 102). (b) Bowersock disagrees and suggests that this Laco was a different man, presumably the son of the Spartan dynast Laco. He bases his argument on two points. First, the filiation of the procurator is not linked directly to Eurycles. Secondly, the dynast would be old by the time of Claudius ('Eurycles', p. 117).
2. Laco was likely to be reinstated by Caligula rather than Claudius (West, *Latin Inscriptions*, p. 48; Cartledge and Spawforth, *Sparta*, p. 102).
3. According to Cartledge and Spawforth, it was either after Livia's death in AD 29 or her official deification in AD 42 (*Sparta*, pp. 102-103, 205-206).
4. An inscription which was made to honour him in Corinth is listed at the beginning of this chapter. Cf. also Meritt, *Greek Inscriptions*, no. 70.
5. The recruitment of people like Spartiaticus into the imperial system has been interpreted by Syme as a subtle move by Claudius to establish trustworthy clients without arousing unnecessary opposition (*Roman Revolution*, p. 506).
6. According to Dio Cassius, 59.9, in the reign of Caligula people from good

1. Patronage in Roman Corinth 51

Spartiaticus not much is known. An anecdote, recorded in Musonius,[1] suggests that he was banished in the reign of Nero.[2] If so, this is indeed ironical. For it means that after the death of his friendly emperor Claudius he fell from grace under the new emperor, Nero. The Euryclid was once more overwhelmed by the power of the Roman emperor, an even more powerful man.

In the rise and the fall of the Euryclids, one of the decisive factors, if not the most decisive factor, in determining their fate seems to be their relationships with the Roman emperors. The emperors were the ones who raised them up, and they were also the ones who knocked them down. So, Augustus first installed Eurycles from among his contemporaries, and later brought him down because of his misbehaviour. Laco was reinstated by the end of the reign of Augustus, but he was soon deposed by Tiberius. Under Claudius, the fate of the Euryclids turned upwards again. Spartiaticus was able to enjoy the imperial favour, but he may have been knocked down later under Nero, just like his forefathers. Could such ups and downs be accidental? I am not suggesting that all the important appointments in the early Empire were the products of personal patronage. But the history of the Euryclids does point to the possibility that patronage played an important part in the placement of local rulers and/or important Roman officials in at least a certain part of Greece, namely Sparta and Corinth. It also serves to highlight the Roman emperor as the supreme, though somewhat capricious, patron in those days. Hence it might be essential to maintain a good relationship with him if one wanted to climb high on the power ladder and to stay there. Against such a background one can perhaps better understand why the imperial cult was strongly promoted in first-century Corinth.

---

family and with wealth were chosen to fill the equestrian rank. This may be another factor, among others, contributing to the rise of Spartiaticus (cf. West, *Latin Inscriptions*, p. 52). That Spartiaticus was a man of great wealth is suggested by his being able to serve as the *agonothete* of the Isthmian and Caesarean games which required great outlay of capital (Kent, *Inscriptions*, p. 30; Wiseman, 'Corinth and Rome I', p. 500).

1. Stobaeus, *Anthologium* 3.40.9 = C.E. Lutz, 'Musonius Rufus: The Roman Socrates', *YCS* 10 (1947), p. 70.
2. Cartledge and Spawforth suggest that the date was no later than AD 61 (*Sparta*, p. 103).

Roman Officials

The role of a Roman official within the hierarchical structure of the Roman Empire has to be defined in context.[1] We can again take Spartiaticus as an example. In relation to Claudius he would look not unlike a friend or a client. As a procurator of Caesar in his province, however, he would assume the role of a broker or mediator, representing the interests of his superior in a locality. But at a local level, because he had access to the emperor, was apportioned a certain amount of power, and possessed enormous wealth, he probably would have become an authority to be honoured and respected. No wonder he was named as the patron of a tribe in Corinth.[2] To illustrate

---

1. In a simplified way, one may suggest that the hierarchical structure of the early Empire was made up of the emperor (the supreme patron), officials of the government or local leaders (mediators), and the community (clients). Such a structure can be seen in some of the inscriptions which recorded events in the reign of Claudius. Two examples may be given. (a) In AD 44, M. Valerius Severus, a local magistrate who once helped Claudius to suppress a rebellion, successfully secured Roman citizenship, exemption from imperial taxes for 10 years and other rights for the city of Volubilis in Mauretania from the emperor (Smallwood, *Documents*, no. 407b = Braund, *Augustus to Nero*, no. 680b). (b) In AD 48–49, through the work of Marcus Valerius Iunianus, member of Claudius's household, the Dionysiac performers were able to get their rights confirmed by Claudius (Smallwood, *Documents*, no. 373b = Braund, *Augustus to Nero*, no. 580b).

2. It is not immediately evident what sort of benefaction was given by Spartiaticus to the tribe of Calpurnia. Could it be benefaction related to his official duties as an imperial procurator? (On the duties and power of the procurator, see H.F. Jolowicz, *Historical Introduction to the Study of Roman Law* [Cambridge: Cambridge University Press, 2nd edn, 1952], pp. 348-50; *OCD*, pp. 881-82; F. Millar, 'Some Evidence on the Meaning of Tacitus *Annals XII*.60', *Historia* 13 [1964], pp. 180-87; idem, 'The Development of Jurisdiction by Imperial Procurators: Further Evidence', *Historia* 14 [1965], pp. 362-67; P.A. Brunt, 'Procuratorial Jurisdiction', *Latomus* 25 [1966], pp. 461-89; Saller, *Personal Patronage*, pp. 166-67). Or could it be benefaction related to his wealth? In any case, even though the Euryclids might be dependent upon the favours of the emperors, they were without doubt important patrons or benefactors to other cities and Corinth. Eurycles and Laco were so important that in Gytheum a cult was founded to honour them (Ehrenberg and Jones, *Documents*, no. 102a = Braund, *Augustus to Nero*, no. 127). In Corinth, Spartiaticus probably was also an important benefactor as *agonothete* of the Isthmian and Caesarean games. The baths of Eurycles represent another kind of benefaction made by one of the later Euryclids, probably in the Hadrian period (Kent, *Inscriptions*, no. 314 and commentary).

1. Patronage in Roman Corinth 53

further the different roles of a Roman official in a province, that is, as a middleman between the emperor and the local people, I will look at P. Memmius Regulus an important governor in Achaea in the late thirties and the early forties.[1] Since Achaea was part of an imperial province from AD 15 to 44, its governor was appointed by the emperor to represent him in the province.[2] His power and term of office were naturally defined by the emperor. In that case, it is reasonable to expect that the emperor most probably would appoint only those who were loyal to him. It is also likely that the appointee would also work to please the emperor as well as to secure his present position and a better prospect in the future.[3] Is this what we see in the career of P. Memmius Regulus, the legate of the Roman emperor in Achaea?

P. Memmius Regulus was not of particularly distinguished ancestry.[4] He began his career in the reign of Tiberius as *quaestor*. He then became *praetor*. In the autumn of AD 31 he was made consul.[5] Later he was appointed as the governor of Achaea, Moesia and Macedonia. He held the post from AD 35-44, that is, for eight years and under three emperors, Tiberius, Gaius and Claudius.[6] In AD 47, he was proconsul of Asia.[7] He died in the reign of Nero in AD 61. Memmius was able to earn favour and trust[8] from most of his superiors, that is, the emperors. In this respect, Memmius Regulus was not unlike Eurycles,

1. West, *Latin Inscriptions*, no. 53.
2. The governor of an imperial province was called a legate and was usually chosen from the rank of ex-praetor and ex-consul (F. Millar, *The Roman Empire and its Neighbours* [London: Duckworth, 2nd edn, 1981], pp. 54-55; Garnsey and Saller, *Roman Empire*, p. 22). For a discussion of the provincial officials in Corinth, see Bagdikian, 'Civic Officials', pp. 4-6.
3. Garnsey and Saller, *Roman Empire*, pp. 34-36. Note F. Millar's warning against drawing too clear a line between the imperial provinces and the senatorial provinces ('The Emperor, the Senate and the Provinces', *JRS* 56 [1966], pp. 156-66).
4. Tacitus, *Ann.* 14.47.
5. Ehrenberg and Jones, *Documents*, no. 217 = Braund, *Augustus to Nero*, no. 388.
6. Dio Cassius 58.25. See also West, *Latin Inscriptions*, pp. 29-31.
7. Ehrenberg and Jones, *Documents*, no. 218 = Smallwood, *Documents*, no. 225 = Braund, *Augustus to Nero*, no. 389; L.R. Dean, 'Latin Inscriptions from Corinth, III', *AJA* 26 (1922), p. 456.
8. Tacitus, *Ann.* 14.47.

the Spartan dynast. But he differed from the latter at one crucial point, that is, Memmius Regulus was able to rise steadily to power and to remain in power until he died. How did he manage to do it despite his undistinguished background? A brief review of some of the episodes in his life may help to provide a partial answer and to highlight the unequal exchange relationship between the emperor and his subordinate.

Under Tiberius[1] he showed himself to be a loyal friend of the emperor by helping him to strike down the mighty opponent Sejanus. When Caligula came to power, he proposed to marry Regulus's rich and perhaps beautiful wife, Lollia Paulina. Regulus complied with the demand of the emperor, and even personally escorted her to Rome.[2] Equally noteworthy was the development of the imperial cult in Achaea under his governorship. Probably with his encouragement, a larger *koinon* was formed to promote the cult. Games were held in honour of the imperial house and envoys were sent to see Caligula with a proposal to express the loyalty of Achaea to Rome.[3] It is thus not surprising that he held priestly titles like *sodalis Augustalis*,[4] Arval brother[5] and one of the seven for feast.[6] Interestingly enough,

---

1. Tacitus, *Ann.* 5.11; 6.4. See also M.P. Charlesworth, 'Tiberius', in *Cambridge Ancient History*, X, pp. 637-38; B. Levick, *Tiberius the Politician* (London: Thames & Hudson, 1976), pp. 177-78.
2. Dio Cassius 59.12. Cf. Suetonius, *Gaius* 25. See also J.H. Oliver, 'Lollia Paulina, Memmius Regulus and Caligula', *Hesp* 35 (1966), pp. 150-53.
3. Smallwood, *Documents*, no. 361 = Braund, *Augustus to Nero*, no. 564. See also West, *Latin Inscriptions*, pp. 30-31.
4. A *sodalis Augustalis* or a 'Fellow of the priesthood of (the deified) Augustus' was a member of a chosen group of eminent Romans whose function was to superintend and promote the imperial cult. The *sodales Augustales* were first founded by Tiberius after the death of Augustus. Claudius instituted the *sodales augustales Claudiales* and later emperors organized similar *sodales*. For further discussion, see Taylor, *Divinity*, p. 230; Kent, *Inscriptions*, p. 84; Sherk, *Roman Empire*, p. 266.
5. The *fratres Arvales* was a priestly college in Rome, responsible for offering worship for the well-being of the imperial house. The college was made up of 12 members. The reigning emperor was always a member. The others were chosen from the most distinguished senatorial families by cooption (*OCD*, p. 447). Memmius Regulus held this title since at least AD 38 (West, *Latin Inscriptions*, p. 29; R. Syme, *Some Arval Brethren* [Oxford: Clarendon Press, 1980], p. 67).
6. The *septemviri epulones* were priests who organized the banquet of Jupiter and

his later years in Rome were also spent actively offering sacrifices for the emperor with other Arvales brothers.[1] Such preparedness to demonstrate his loyalty to the imperial house and to serve the emperors at whatever cost may to a large extent account for his steady rise to power without being deposed later on.

The position of P. Memmius Regulus as a node in the patronage structure of the early Empire would not be fully understood if we looked only at his relationship with the Roman emperors without at the same time considering his relationship with the people he governed, especially those in Achaea. From the very many inscriptions made in honour of P. Memmius Regulus in Corinth[2] and other places in the Greek east,[3] it looks probable that Regulus was well-supported and well-connected in the region.[4] However, though he was named as a patron in Ruscino, Narbonensis,[5] such a title is not found on the inscription which honoured him in Corinth. Nonetheless, his image as a patron in the region is still visible in some of the benefactions he bestowed. In the reign of Caligula made the risky attempt to delay the delivery of the statue of Zeus at Olympia to Rome.[6] Whether he might have dispatched other kinds of benefactions, such as helping to promote provincials[7] or making legal decisions in favour of his

---

other banquets at various festivals. Many of them were formerly the partisans of the emperors (Sherk, *Roman Empire*, p. 266).

1. Smallwood, *Documents*, nos. 16-22. Cf. N. Lewis and M. Reinhold, *Roman Civilization* (2 vols.; New York: Harper & Row, 1951, 1966), II, pp. 554-55.

2. West, *Latin Inscriptions*, no. 53.

3. E.g. Delphi (Smallwood, *Documents*, no. 225 = Braund, *Augustus to Nero*, no. 389); Athens (P. Graindor, 'Inscriptions attiques d'époque romaine', *BCH* 51 [1927], p. 269, no. 36).

4. West, *Latin Inscriptions*, p. 30.

5. Ehrenberg and Jones, *Documents*, no. 217 = Braund, *Augustus to Nero*, no. 388. It may be added that Roman officials could be requested to serve as patrons of certain towns to represent their interests in Rome (e.g. *ILS*, no. 6106 = Sherk, *Roman Empire*, no. 193). Actually, a kind of patron–client agreement was sometimes made between a Roman official and his client communities. For samples of these agreements, see Ehrenberg and Jones, *Documents*, no. 354 = Braund, *Augustus to Nero*, no. 668 (Brixia, AD 28); Smallwood, *Documents*, no. 413 = Braund, *Augustus to Nero*, no. 686 (Hippo Regius, North Africa, AD 55).

6. Josephus, *Ant.* 19.8-10. See also Charlesworth, 'Gaius and Claudius', in *Cambridge Ancient History*, X, p. 664.

7. Saller, *Personal Patronage*, pp. 169-75.

clients,[1] is not clear. Apparently he had helped quite a number of people in Corinth to secure Roman citizenship. P. Memmius Cleander,[2] a prominent leader in Corinth in the sixties, was probably one of them.

Just as the emperor was courted by some of his officials because he had the power to promote or depose them, there are also indications that some Roman officials at a local level were also befriended by cities and local notables. In an inscription which was made possibly in AD 52/53 the governor Aquillius Florus Turcianus Gallus was honoured by two *duoviri*, namely Ti. Claudius Anaxilas and Ti. Claudius Dinippus.[3] Such a good relationship between a government official and local elites is intriguing. Presumably it was one which would benefit both parties. For the officials, the support of the local notables would be needed, among other things, to protect them from any future troubles, such as complaints about their maladministration.[4] For the local elites, they would be in a more advantageous position than other people in the pursuit of ambitions, be it power, honour or material benefit, for themselves or their home towns,[5] if they could have a good relationship with the Roman officials or, even better, with the emperor himself. In order to secure the favour of local Roman officials, gifts were sometimes exchanged, despite the fact that it was

---

1. Saller, *Personal Patronage*, pp. 152-54; Millar, *Roman Empire*, pp. 63-64; Garnsey and Saller, *Roman Empire*, pp. 151-52.
2. Smallwood, *Documents*, no. 62 = Braund, *Augustus to Nero*, no. 262. P. Memmius Cleander was the *duovir quinquennalis* at the time of Nero's visit in AD 67. He probably received his Roman citizenship during Regulus's time in Greece (West, *Latin Inscriptions*, p. 31; Kent, *Inscriptions*, p. 26). On the Memmi in Sparta, see Cartledge and Spawforth, *Sparta*, p. 163.
3. West, *Latin Inscriptions*, no. 54 and commentary.
4. Eulogies from some local people could help to cover up a governor's offences against the law in court (P.A. Brunt, 'Charges of Provincial Administration under the Early Principate', *Historia* 10 [1961], pp. 212-17).
5. Here some comparable cases can be given. (a) To bring glory to their town and perhaps to themselves too, some of the people in Prusa cultivated their relationship with the proconsuls, but Dio negotiated directly with the emperor (Dio Chrysostom, *Or.* 45.2-3). (b) Through the recommendation of Pliny, the governor of Bithynia, one of his friends was able to secure from Trajan the privileges granted to parents with three children (*Ep.* 10.94). Pliny also made recommendations for the promotion of his friend and his friend's son (*Ep.* 10.26, 87).

illegal for Roman officials to receive gifts from the provincials.[1] If the local notables were eager to establish 'friendly' relationships, patronal relations in a local community could only be reinforced.

In Corinth the good relationship between government officials and the Gellius family is quite obvious. It is possible that the Gellii were granted citizenship early in the first century BC through the work of an important Roman official in Achaea, L. Gellius Poplicola.[2] By the time Caligula came to power, a member of the Gellius family, Menander, was possibly the head who led the embassy to express the loyalty of the Achaeans to the new emperor.[3] If so, it is quite possible that Menander was a good friend of P. Memmius Regulus and that they worked closely together in the promotion of the imperial cult in the region. This desire to link up with important officials was demonstrated again by two Gellii in the early second century, L. Gellius Menander and L. Gellius Justus.[4] Not a few monuments were erected by them in honour of important officials.

In the light of the relationships discussed above, the relationships between the emperor and some of his officials in Corinth can best be seen as patron–client ties. It looks as if one of the important keys with which to open the door to the advancement of personal ambitions in the early Empire was to become a faithful and beloved friend of the emperor. Not insignificantly, a similar kind of tie appears to have existed between some of the Roman officials and some of the local notables in Corinth. Does that mean that if an ambitious local notable could not have direct access to the emperor, he would at least achieve something by becoming a faithful and beloved friend of a friend of the emperor? If such were some of the relationships linking Corinth to Rome, what about the relationships within the local community in

1. The prohibition in the law did not deter Julius Bassus, praetorian proconsul of Bithynia and *amicus* of Domitian, from receiving such gifts on occasions like his birthday. The whole scandal was later revealed in a court case handled by Pliny (*Ep.* 4.9).
2. West, *Latin Inscriptions*, p. 79, no. 93.
3. West, *Latin Inscriptions*, p. 78; T.R. Martin, 'Inscriptions at Corinth', *Hesp* 46 (1977), pp. 193-95. For a view which objects to the above identification, see J.H. Oliver, 'Panachaeans and Panhellenes', *Hesp* 47 (1978), pp. 185-95.
4. Kent, *Inscriptions*, nos. 124, 125, 135, 137. See also W.R. Biers and D.J. Geagan, 'A New List of Victors in the Caesarea at Isthmia', *Hesp* 39 (1970), pp. 79-93.

Corinth? If the governor of an imperial province was chosen by the emperor, who would have control over positions of power and honour locally? Could any one have influence over the selection of local leaders? Who were some of the local notables in Corinth? How did they rise above other people? What made them so different?

Local Notables
In the politics of a local community the *decuriones* would probably represent the powerful people in a town.[1] They were often the local aristocrats, men of great wealth and often men who had once served as local magistrates. The authority of such people might even be higher than that of the administering officials, including the *duoviri*, who were elected by the assembly of citizens. They could request that matters relating to public accounts and public lands and buildings be referred to them for investigation or decision. The right to give honorary titles to benefactors of the city was under their control. Appeal against the *duovir*'s verdict could be directed to them. Furthermore, they might even be able to exercise influence over the recruitment of new council members, if not the actual election of magistrates.[2] Under such circumstances, it would be natural for the magistrates to try to please the *decuriones*.[3]

Because Corinth was a Roman colony, it is conceivable that the power of the people in the local council in Corinth would have been as powerful as those elsewhere.[4] Can it then be surmised that, apart from winning the support of the populace, an ambitious person in Corinth, especially one from a less distinguished background, who wanted to be

1. W.T. Arnold, *The Roman System of Provincial Administration to the Accession of Constantine the Great* (rev. E.S. Bouchier; Oxford: Basil Blackwell, 3rd edn, 1914), pp. 245, 251-52; Garnsey and Saller, *Roman Empire*, pp. 114-15. For a sample of a colonial charter, see F.F. Abbott and A.C. Johnson, *Municipal Administration in the Roman Empire* (Princeton: Princeton University Press, 1926), no. 26 = Lewis and Reinhold, *Roman Civilization*, I, pp. 420-28.

2. *Decuriones* were usually recruited from ex-magistrates. The ones responsible for such recruitment were the *quinquennales* who served as local censors (Arnold, *Provincial Administration*, p. 254). Cf. Abbott and Johnson, *Municipal Administration*, pp. 78-79; C.P. Jones, *The Roman World of Dio Chrysostom* (Cambridge, MA: Harvard University Press, 1978), pp. 97-98.

3. G.H. Stevenson, *Roman Provincial Administration* (Oxford: Basil Blackwell, 1939), p. 171.

4. Bagdikian, 'Civic Officials', pp. 9-18.

elected to the local magistracy, or even to become a local councillor, would also have to cultivate his relationship with such powerful superiors? This seems quite possible, even though we do not have clear evidence to say for sure. Nevertheless, we do know who some of the local notables were and what services they had contributed to the colony. A study of their careers may help to throw light on their rise to power.

As mentioned above, well-connected and unusually rich families like the Euryclids were already very active in the politics of Corinth in the first century AD. That such were the famous people in Corinth already indicates that good family background and wealth were important in the making of a local notable.[1] But in Corinth wealth appears to have been an especially important pre-condition. For if a person was especially rich, even though that person was not of distinguished family, there might still be a chance that he could make a name for himself.[2] So rich freedmen in Corinth were not barred from holding such offices as *aedilis* and *duovir*, even though, in other places, they were excluded from the magistracies and the local council.[3] One such freedman was Erastus, a figure who interests students of the New Testament greatly. He was made an *aedilis* of the colony,[4] probably after his promise to lay the pavement outside the theatre.[5]

Another rich freedman in Corinth who succeeded in making himself prominent in the first half of the first century AD was Babbius Philinus.[6] If the imperial temple in the west end of the forum was a witness to the majesty and power of the Roman ruler, the buildings

1. According to Pliny, such were the people the Roman government wanted to help govern the common crowd (Pliny, *Ep.* 10.79.3).
2. It should be noted that there was a basic property requirement to be met before one could hold civic office (Millar, *Roman Empire*, p. 82). As Corinth was a well-known and rich city, it is likely that the amount required would not be inconsiderable. Moreover, to compete for local honours in first-century Corinth, one probably would have to do more than simply meeting the basic requirement.
3. Duff, *Freedmen*, p. 137.
4. Kent, *Inscriptions*, no. 232. Kent identifies this Erastus, a freedman, with the Erastus of Rom. 16.23 (*Inscriptions*, pp. 99-100).
5. Bagdikian, 'Civic Officials', p. 17.
6. West, *Latin Inscriptions*, nos. 2, 3, 98-101, 130, 131, 132; Kent, *Inscriptions*, nos. 155, 241. For evidence that Babbius Philinus probably was a freedman, see West, *Latin Inscriptions*, p. 108.

donated by Babbius Philinus around the city could be seen as indications of his power and wealth. The most notable piece of architecture was the Babbius monument, a circular structure set on the northwest corner of the *agora*, just outside the site where Temple E would later be built.[1] Possibly the fountain next to it, a dedication to Poseidon, was also donated by Babbius. In addition, the reconstruction of the southeast building too might be due to the generosity of Babbius and his son.[2] Presumably because of these gifts he was voted not only to the office of *aedilis*, but also of *duovir*. It should also be noted that Babbius held two other priestly offices, *pontifex* and a priest of Neptune.[3] So his wealth was able to win him some honours and power. But not insignificantly, for some reason, he had not been able to get the highest honour, that is, the agonoteheship of the Isthmian games.[4] The fact that he was a freedman may help partly to explain his failure to obtain further advancement, despite his tremendous wealth. If that was the reason, it may suggest that although in the competition for local honours wealth was important, perhaps there was still a limit to what wealth could do at that time. Whether it also means that the way to further advancement was controlled by men of higher ranks, however, is moot.

Unlike Babbius Philinus, L. Castricius Regulus, probably one of the unusually distinguished leaders in Corinth, was one who was awarded the highest honour.[5] In fact, not only was he one of the *agonothetai* of the Isthmian games, but also the one who brought the management of the games back to Corinth, some time between 7 BC and AD 3.[6] Needless to say, he was an extremely rich man. He was so rich that he

---

1. Scranton, *Monuments*, pp. 17-32; Wiseman, 'Corinth and Rome I', p. 518. See also West, *Latin Inscriptions*, no. 132; Kent, *Inscriptions*, no. 155.
2. West, *Latin Inscriptions*, no. 122; Kent, *Inscriptions*, no. 323. See also Wiseman, 'Corinth and Rome I', p. 514.
3. West, *Latin Inscriptions*, nos. 2 and 3. Such combination of political and priestly roles has already been seen in the career of people like Spartiaticus and Memmius Regulus and will also be seen in the career of many of the local notables in Corinth.
4. The *agonothetes* of the Isthmian games was the highest honour the colony could bestow (Kent, *Inscriptions*, p. 30; Wiseman, 'Corinth and Rome I', p. 500).
5. Kent, *Inscriptions*, no. 153 and commentary; Edwards, *Coins*, p. 7.
6. After 146 BC, the Isthmian games were under the control of the Sicyon (Pausanias 2.2.2; cf. Wiseman, 'Corinth and Rome I', p. 496).

not only paid for the expenses of the games,[1] but also put in money to repair the sanctuary at Isthmia and to give a banquet of celebration for all the inhabitants of the colony upon the completion of the repair work. With such magnificent benefactions it would be unthinkable if he was not rewarded with appropriate honours in Corinth. Unsurprisingly, during his politically active period from c. 10 BC to AD 23, he was able to hold most of the important municipal offices which included *aedilis, praefectus iure dicundo, duovir, duovir quinquennalis, agonothetes* of the Isthmian and the Caesarean games and *agonothetes* of the *Tiberea Caesarea Sebastea*. But the climax of his career as the *agonothetes* of *Tiberea Caesaera Sebasta* in AD 23 is most interesting. For in the games of that year, not only was the reigning emperor honoured, but more significantly, Livia was honoured as divine Julia Augusta with the introduction of a poetry contest in her honour. In other words, she was deified in Corinth before her death in AD 29, even before her formal deification in AD 42.[2] Why was such an action adopted? Does this gesture suggest that even such a rich and eminent benefactor to the colony as Castricius Regulus had to express his goodwill to the imperial house? What benefits would it bring?

Whatever the significance of such an action was, this concern to honour the imperial house and to demonstrate one's loyalty to it appears to be quite common among local notables in the first half of the first century. For a similar but slightly different action was devised by T. Manlius Juvencus, another *agonothetes* and a young contemporary of L. Castricius Regulus.[3] Like Castricius Regulus, Juvencus started as an *aedilis* and ended up being the *agonothetes* of the Isthmian and Caesarean games. The most distinctive mark of his career was his close relationship with the imperial family. Having served as an *aedilis*, he was chosen to be a *praefectus iure dicundo*, possibly representing Tiberius.[4] As *agonothetes* of the Isthmian and Caesarean games, he was the first man to schedule the Caesarean games, the games which honoured the imperial house, ahead of the Isthmian

---

1. Kent, *Inscriptions*, p. 30; Wiseman, 'Corinth and Rome I', p. 500.
2. Kent, *Inscriptions*, p. 73.
3. West, *Latin Inscriptions*, nos. 81, 86; Kent, *Inscriptions*, no. 154. Cf. Edwards, *Coins*, p. 5.
4. See discussion in West, *Latin Inscriptions*, pp. 65-66.

games, the traditional games. Had he learned from the example of Castricius Regulus? Why did these two distinguished leaders do such things? Could there be a connection between such actions and the advancement of personal interests?

Interestingly enough, such apparent affection for the imperial rule was seen again in the actions of another popular and important figure in the colony, namely Tiberius Claudius Dinippus.[1] Dinippus served as *cura annonae* or curator of the grain supply three times. That suggests strongly that he was a very rich patron of the colony.[2] We know that there were several famines in the reign of Claudius, and that the one in AD 51 was especially serious.[3] Dinippus probably became an important benefactor to the city in this period. This would make him a contemporary of Paul. With such pivotal benefactions it was inevitable that Dinippus was made *duovir*, then *duovir quinquennalis* (c. AD 52/53) and *agonothetes* of *Neronea Caesarea* and of the Isthmian and Caesarean games (c. AD 55).[4] Like Babbius Philinus, Dinippus also held some priestly roles. He was an *augur*, that is, a member of an honourable priesthood in the Roman empire. But most fascinating of all, he was a priest of the cult of Britannic Victory, a peculiar cult in Corinth which was probably established to honour the victories of the Claudian campaign in Britain. But the cult was a rather short-lived one, and did not reappear at a later time. Hence, it is likely that Dinippus was the first and only priest of this Claudian cult.[5] Such an interesting phenomenon leads us back to the question which puzzles

---

1. West, *Latin Inscriptions*, nos. 86-90; Kent, *Inscriptions*, nos. 158-63. Cf. also L.R. Dean, 'Latin Inscriptions from Corinth', *AJA* 22 (1918), pp. 189-90. So far, at least, ten inscriptions with the same cursus and the same order have been recovered. They possibly were made by different tribes in Corinth. The sheer number of inscriptions made in his honour suggests that this man was no ordinary leader. It is also noteworthy that one inscription was authorized by a decree of the local senate (West, *Latin Inscriptions*, no. 89).

2. These curators were appointed in times of threatened or actual famine with a responsibility to relieve the needs of the city, either by purchasing grain or by handing out money, often out of their own resources (West, *Latin Inscriptions*, p. 73; Bagdikian, 'Civic Officials', pp. 18-19; P. Garnsey, *Famine and Food Supply in the Greco-Roman World: Responses to Risk and Crisis* [Cambridge: Cambridge University Press, 1988], pp. 230-31).

3. Tacitus, *Ann.* 12.43; Suetonius, *Claudius* 18.

4. West, *Latin Inscriptions*, pp. 72-73.

5. West, *Latin Inscriptions*, p. 72.

1. *Patronage in Roman Corinth* 63

us: why did Dinippus found such a cult? Why did local notables in Corinth, not just Dinippus but others too, have to find ways to honour the imperial house?

Based on this examination of the lives of some of the local notables in Corinth, we gain the following impression of the way relationships were organized in the larger community at Corinth. The populace had to look to the rich to provide them with entertainment like games, to bring a better environment and honour to the city through new buildings, and at times to provide food relief. Honourable offices[1] and honourable titles like 'patron'[2] were usually offered to the benefactors in return for their benefactions. There might even be privileges for them to enjoy.[3] Hence, it is almost inevitable that the rich people were often the powerful people in Corinth.

However, in first-century Corinth, especially in the first half of the century, there were apparently many rich people in the colony. It is thus possible to postulate that there would be competition among them. And if one wanted to get ahead of other competitors, something more than wealth perhaps was needed. Good family background of course was a helpful factor. But since most of the distinguished notables were eager to honour the imperial house in one way or another, I suggest that, like other government officials and provincial leaders, a connection with the Roman authorities was another thing which might

---

1. 'Pay and be honoured'. The principle of reciprocity is clearly seen in the benefaction of Erastus. For he apparently was made an *aedilis* after promising to pave the road outside the theatre. The same principle is seen again in the works of Babbius Philinus. On his monument, the following words were inscribed: '[Gnaeus Babbius Philinus], aedile and pontifex, [had this monument erected at his own expense] and he approved it in his official capacity as duovir' (Kent, *Inscriptions*, no. 155; West, *Latin Inscriptions*, no. 132). Was this a way to perpetuate his name, even to congratulate himself?

2. Cornelius Pulcher, an *agonothetes* in the reign of Trajan, was honoured as the patron of the Corinth perhaps because he helped to relieve a famine (West, *Latin Inscriptions*, no. 71).

3. In other places, statues or even shrines might have been built for the rich patrons (Ehrenberg and Jones, *Documents*, no. 114 = Braund, *Augustus to Nero*, no. 141; Smallwood, *Documents*, no. 65 = Braund, *Augustus to Nero*, no. 265). When they went to watch public games, they should have special seats reserved for them (Ehrenberg and Jones, *Documents*, no. 105 = Braund, *Augustus to Nero*, no. 130). Cf. Dio Chrysostom, *Or.* 41.2; 44.2-4.

have given an ambitious person the leading edge.¹ By the same token, there is reason to believe that the support of influential men in the city council might also be sought by men who wanted to climb the ladder of power in Corinth, especially if they did not have a particularly good background.² If this was the situation, can we say that proper public relations, part of which would probably be patron–client relations, were an important factor contributing to one's success in the pursuit of fame and power?

In short, patronage was probably *one* of the ways through which the society in Corinth, if not Roman society at large, was organized. Because of such relations, people at different levels, from the emperor down to a citizen in a town, were linked together, even though their interests might not be the same. Such relations might also be one of the important channels through which scarce resources, such as powerful positions in the imperial government or local government were distributed.

Patronage and Institutions

If patronage was such a pervasive phenomenon in Corinth one naturally would wonder how far such relationships might have been established within the society as a whole. Would there be some influence on the structuring of relationships in contemporary institutions, like association and household? One is also tempted to ask if patronage might also have exerted some improper influences on the legal system which supposedly should uphold the cause of justice. In this section, I will examine the relationship between patronage and these institutions.

Patronage and the Associations
Rome was suspicious of clubs or associations,³ but associations, legal⁴

---

1. It does not rule out the possibility that some of the notables could be sincere in their honouring of the imperial house.
2. Cf. Dio Chrysostom, *Or.* 45.7-8; 50.3.
3. See Trajan's reply to Pliny's request for organizing an association of firefighters (*Ep.* 10.34).
4. The poor were allowed to form associations, provided that they met once a month (*Digest*, 47.22.1 = Sherk, *Roman Empire*, no. 177A).

or illegal,[1] were still organized.[2] Many of the associations were formed by people who worked in the same trade.[3] That there were associations in Corinth at the turn of the first century AD, if not earlier, is suggested by a monument erected by the Association of the Lares of the imperial house in the early second century.[4]

Members of this Corinthian association, under the leadership of two of its outstanding members,[5] met to offer worship to the Lares of the imperial house. Presumably sacrifices and meals formed an important part of their activities.[6] The two outstanding members were Titus Flavius Antio[chus], a freedman of the emperor, and Tiberius Claudius Primigenius, probably a freedman's son. Even though no special title was given to them, they apparently were responsible for erecting the monument, and therefore it is not impossible, though not certain, that their role in the club was comparable to that of leader, if not patron. If so, the structure of the association can be seen as a hierarchical structure. There were the deities, the patrons or leaders, and the members. Perhaps not accidentally, as will be shown below, the

---

1. Tacitus, *Ann.* 14.17.

2. My purpose here is not to give a detailed study of the phenomenon of associations in the Roman Empire, but to show that the structure of many of these associations was similar to a patronal hierarchy. For further studies on associations, see, e.g., S. Dill, *Roman Society from Nero to Marcus Aurelius* (London: Macmillan, 1905), pp. 251-86; M.N. Tod, *Sidelights on Greek History* (Oxford: Basil Blackwell, 1932), pp. 71-96; K. Hopkins, *Death and Renewal: Sociological Studies in Roman History*, II (Cambridge: Cambridge University Press, 1983), pp. 211-17.

3. For example, the association of band-players (*ILS*, no. 4966 = Sherk, *Roman Empire*, no. 177B); the association of mule-and-ass-drivers (*ILS*, no. 7293 = Sherk, *Roman Empire*, no. 177C); the association of hay merchants (*ILS*, no. 1577 = Sherk, *Roman Empire*, no. 177E).

4. Kent, *Inscriptions*, no. 62. The presence of such an association gives further support to my suggestion above that the imperial house was highly honoured in Corinth. According to Kent, the members of the association were likely to be freedmen in the colony (*Inscriptions*, p. 35). If so, it would mean that the imperial rulers were honoured not only by the local ruling classes, but also by the freedmen.

5. Kent, *Inscriptions*, p. 35.

6. While incense, wine and flowers were used in the worship of the Genius of an individual *paterfamilias*, a victim was sacrificed to the Genius Augusti (Ryberg, *Rites of the State Religion*, pp. 55, 62). On the development of the cult of Lares Augusti, see Taylor, *Divinity*, pp. 184-85.

underlying structure of many other associations resembles that of a patronal hierarchy.

Perhaps because the law allowed people to form associations for the sake of religion, many associations were formed in honour of one or more deities.[1] These deities can be compared to a sort of divine patron. Under them were their human counterparts, the patrons. In the early Empire, it was not uncommon for associations to invite rich men or men of influence to serve as patrons.[2] That rich and powerful men liked to sponsor clubs and associations is quite understandable, for it must have been an extremely pleasant experience when they were honoured or praised by the members for their benefactions.[3] An association was actually founded to perpetuate the name of a rich man.[4] On the other hand, the ordinary members would also like to have influential and rich men as their patrons, giving them protection and benefaction.[5] The structure of a patronal hierarchy with the patron deities at the top, rich and powerful men as patrons and leaders in the middle, and ordinary members at the bottom is most clearly revealed in an often quoted inscription from Lanuvium which recorded the by-laws of a burial society.[6]

---

1. For example, Silvanus was honoured by the carpenters (*CIL*, 13.1640) and the woodcutters (*ILS*, no. 3547), Annona and Ceres were adopted by the grain-measurers (*ILS*, nos. 3816, 6146). Sometimes the *genius* of its patron was honoured (*CIL*, 5.7469). See Duff, *Freedmen*, pp. 116-17; R. MacMullen, *Roman Social Relations, 50 BC to AD 284* (New Haven: Yale University Press, 1974), pp. 82-83.

2. In Ostia, Gnaeus Sentius Felix was such a rich and powerful patron (*ILS*, no. 6146 = Sherk, *Roman Empire*, no. 182). He was not only elected to hold important municipal offices, like *aedilis*, *quaestor* of the Ostian treasury, and *duovir*, but also honourable posts, like patron of different groups and clubs.

3. One association proposed that a bronze tablet with the resolution of the association to elect a certain man as patron inscribed should be placed in the patron's house if he accepted the post and, presumably, supported the association (*ILS*, no. 7216 = Lewis and Reinhold, *Roman Civilization*, II, p. 276).

4. A college of Aesculapius and Hygia was founded by a rich lady called Salvia Marcellina to commemorate her deceased husband (*ILS*, no. 7213; Dill, *Roman Society*, p. 262).

5. It was not unheard of that an association could get so poor that it had to dissolve (*ILS*, no. 7215a = Lewis and Reinhold, *Roman Civilization*, II, pp. 276-77). On the use of patrons to secure interests of the association in the Republic, see M. Gelzer, *Roman Nobility*, p. 92.

6. *CIL*, 14.2112 = *ILS*, no. 7212 = Lewis and Reinhold, *Roman Civilization*, II,

1. Patronage in Roman Corinth 67

With the approval of the Roman Senate, the society was founded in the name of its deities Diana and Antinous.[1] They met in the temple of Antinous where the inscription containing the by-laws of the society was found. In honour of the patron deities their birthdays were celebrated with worship followed by a banquet. Like many other associations, it also had a prominent man as its patron. He was Lucius Caesennius Rufus who happened to be the patron of the municipality. He promised to make an endowment to the society. Under the protection of such a patron, the association could probably be sure that they could meet without interruption. With his endowment the members could have some more money to spend on their feasts. To repay and perhaps also to exploit further the generosity and kindness of the patron, it was proposed that the birthdays of the patron and his family members, including the patron's father, mother and brother, should also be celebrated by banquets. Thus the way the patron was honoured strikes an interesting parallel with the way the patron deities were honoured. Likewise, the honouring of the patron along with his family members also calls to mind the honouring of the emperor and members of the imperial family.

The society had its own administrative officials. They were elected by the members. The chief official was called *quinquennalis*. Since such a person had to provide oil for the society in the public bath before they feasted on the birthdays of Diana and Antinous, the chosen person probably was a relatively rich man. While he was in office he had an attendant. It was within his power to make certain decisions regarding the burial of deceased members. He was also given the honour of conducting worship on festive days in white clothing, offering incense and wine. Presumably these steps were taken to emphasize the difference between the leading official and the ordinary members. Such a difference would look even clearer in the dining hall. The *quinquennalis* was eligible to receive a double portion of the food, and

---

pp. 273-75 (AD 136). For further discussion, see Dill, *Roman Society*, pp. 259-61; Macmullen, *Roman Social Relations*, pp. 78-79; R.L. Wilken, *The Christians as the Romans Saw Them* (New Haven: Yale University Press, 1984), pp. 36-39; Garnsey and Saller, *Roman Empire*, pp. 156-57.

1. It is worth pointing out that Antinous was not exactly a god, but a deified man. He was a favourite of Hadrian and was given divine honours after his death in AD 130. Perhaps as a custom, good wishes for the well-being of the imperial house were also expressed in the inscription.

even his helper had a share and a half. Members were forbidden to use abusive language in speaking to the leader, and were also forbidden to move around, lest they caused disturbances. It is possible, though not certain, that the difference in rank might also be reflected in the seating arrangement. That there was such a difference should not be surprising. For in contrast to the patron and the leading official who put in large sums of money to the association, a person who wanted to join the association and to enjoy himself only had to pay a relatively small sum for the entrance fee and an amphora of good wine, plus a monthly fee.

From the above picture of the organization of the association in Lanuvium it is perhaps not difficult to see that the structure resembles a kind of patronal hierarchy. In this respect the association was not unlike a mirror of the larger political structure of the day. The special treatment the patron and leading members received was also in line with the reciprocal principle which undergirded the patronage system. But the parallels between the two seem to go beyond the way relationships were structured in the association. For the title given to the chief official, *quinquennalis*, was actually an honourable office in a municipal government.[1] Whether such a borrowing of terms was intentional or not, the similarity in structure between the association and the political system is simply too striking to be overlooked. Perhaps they just reinforced one another.

Patronage and the Household
If a certain form of patronal structure underlay the structuring of relationships in an association, can it be demonstrated that a similar kind of structure also undergirded relationships in a Roman household? Interestingly enough, the two institutions sometimes overlapped with one another when a society was formed in a large household with the head of the household as its patron.[2] Nevertheless, even without

1. Sherk, *Roman Empire*, p. 265; cf. also Stevenson, *Roman Provincial Administration*, pp. 149, 172. Other titles of offices in local government which were given to officials in associations are *magistri*, *praefecti* and *quaestores* (Dill, *Roman Society*, pp. 269-71).

2. In one case, a burial society met in the house of Sergia Paullina in Rome (*CIL*, 6.9148; Meeks, *First Urban Christians*, p. 31). In another case, a Bacchic association was formed in a large household near Rome with more than 300 members (second century AD). It was headed by Pompeia Agrippinilla, wife of Gavius Squilla

1. *Patronage in Roman Corinth* 69

referring to such formal organization in a household, it still seems possible to see a kind of patronal hierarchy behind certain relationships in a Roman house. To demonstrate this I shall examine the relationships which involved Trimalchio, one of the most interesting figures in Petronius's *Satyricon*.

Trimalchio was the host of a dinner party. He was a freedman,[1] that is to say, he had a patron over him.[2] He became rich through trade. So it was appropriate for him to adopt Mercury, the god of trade, as his patron deity.[3] As a rich man he had his own clients. A teacher of rhetoric, Agamemnon, seems to have been like a client figure.[4] Even if Agamemnon was not a client of Trimalchio, when Trimalchio eventually freed his own slaves, he would become a patron to his freedmen.[5] If such relationships were typical, then relationships in a Roman household, from the householder's patron deity down to freedmen, can perhaps be seen as made up of a series of patronal relations, in either ascending or descending order. Against this background, it may be said that similar hierarchical relationships would probably also be found in a first-century Corinthian household.

Let us now turn away from relationships which linked up the human with the divine and look more closely at the relationships between a householder and those under his authority. As the head of a household, a man like Trimalchio was without doubt a patron figure.

(consul in AD 150). She was also one of the priestesses (Lewis and Reinhold, *Roman Civilization*, II, pp. 572-73). As such, she was permitted to perform sacrifice, to have revenue from offerings, to preside at initiations, to conduct processions and to lead the *thiasos* outside of the city for the celebration of orgies. In her honour, a statue was made. For further discussion, see A. Vogliano, 'La grande iscrizione Bacchica del Metropolitan Museum, I', *AJA* 37 (1933), pp. 215-31; F. Cumont, 'La Grande Inscription Bachique du Metropolitan Museum, II', *AJA* 37 (1933), pp 232-63; C. Alexander, 'Abstract of the Articles on the Bacchic Inscription in the Metropolitan Museum', *AJA* 37 (1933), pp. 264-70.

1. Petronius, *Satyricon* 57.
2. *Satyricon* 52.
3. Petronius, *Satyricon* 29, 77. Mercury was believed to be the one who helped to push him into the office of *sevir*, that is, a municipal office responsible for the imperial cult (J.P. Sullivan, *Petronius: The Satyricon; Seneca: The Apocolocyntosis* [Harmondsworth: Penguin Books, rev. edn, 1986], p. 188). It is also worth noting that lares of the household were also worshipped by Trimalchio (*Satyricon* 29).
4. *Satyricon* 46, 48.
5. *Satyricon* 71.

The image of a householder as patron may be seen on occasions where he assumed the role of a priest to the whole house, securing divine cooperation and blessings for the whole house.[1] But such an image is seen even more clearly in his relationships with three groups of people. They were his freedmen, his literary friends and those who sought his help, financial or otherwise. All of them were in one way or another the clients of the householder, whether formally or informally. I will first look at the patron's relationship with his freedmen or freedwomen.

When slaves in a household were manumitted by their masters, in name they were freed persons. But in reality, they were neither totally free from the domination of nor equal in status to their patron. So even though the relationship between a freedman and his former master was compared to that between a son and a father,[2] it was one way of saying that the freedman was still under the power of the patron, just as the son was under the power of the father. Against this background, the taking of the *praenomenon* and *nomen* of the patron by the freedman may be understood as a symbol of the patron's power, however shadowy, over the rest of the freedman's life. It would, in a very subtle way, remind the freedman that he owed his freedom (or new life?) to his patron. So he should be grateful to him and honour him. That such a response was sanctioned by law is most striking.[3]

But there was other legislation made to protect the interests of the patron. On the one hand, a freedman was not allowed to act in such a way as to harm his patron.[4] Under this condition, unless the freedman had special permission from the *praetor*, he was not allowed to bring certain cases against his patron.[5] So, in actual effect, it meant that a

---

1. R.M. Ogilvie, *The Romans and Their Gods* (London: Hogarth Press, 1969), p. 100.
2. *Digest* 37.15.9: 'By freedman or son the person of patron or father should always be honoured and held sacred' (Duff, *Freedmen*, p. 36). See also T.C. Sandars, *The Institutes of Justinian* (London: Longmans, 1952), p. 21.
3. It has been suggested that ungrateful freedmen could be punished in the early Empire (Suetonius, *Claudius* 25; Dio Cassius 60.13; Sandars, *Institutes*, pp. 60-61).
4. Crook, *Law and Life*, pp. 51-55.
5. *Digest* 2.4.4; Sandars, *Institutes*, p. 500; Duff, *Freedmen*, pp. 37-40; Garnsey, *Social Status*, p. 182.

1. Patronage in Roman Corinth   71

freedman would hardly be able to bring his patron to court, even if he had suffered injustice. On the other hand, a freedman had a duty to continue serving his former master.[1] It is noteworthy that the right of the patron was extended even to the property of the freedman for, according to law, the patron was entitled to have a share in the freedman's legacy.[2] Of course, as one party in an exchange relationship, a patron, in theory, also had some obligations to fulfil.[3] But the unequal relationship between a patron and his freedman should be quite obvious.

Because such a relationship was so unequal and appears to be very oppressive, it would not be surprising that a freedman might murder his patron.[4] But the element of conflict in the relationship between a patron and his freedmen can also be exaggerated. For there is evidence to show that some of the relationships were not at all bad.[5] Some of the positive gestures shown by freedmen towards patrons and vice versa may perhaps be used to illustrate the paradoxical nature of patronal relations. Inequality seems to have been accepted. But life

    1. A patron could demand a freedman to provide different kinds of services, such as taking care of his children, attending to his friends, even to help the patron if he was in poverty. For further details, see Duff, *Freedmen*, pp. 40-46.
    2. Sandars, *Institutes*, pp. 21, 63-64. In the time of the Republic, a patron could claim half of the estate from the legacy of his freedman. In the time of Paul, the freedman had to have three actual descendants to bar the patron from sharing equally with the one or two descendants if the estate was worth 100,000 sesterces. If the descendants were not actual descendants, the patron could claim half of the estate. See W.W. Buckland, *A Textbook of Roman Law* (Cambridge: Cambridge University Press, 3rd edn, 1968), p. 597; Duff, *Freedmen*, pp. 43-44; Crook, *Law and Life*, pp. 53-54.
    3. For example, a patron had the right to act as a *tutela* to protect the interests of a freedwoman, no matter how old she was, or a freedman under 20 years of age, giving them legal advice and guiding them in the handling of their property. Likewise, if a freedman was really in need, a patron was obliged to feed him. And if a freedman was murdered, a patron was required to help to bring the murderer to justice. For further discussion, see Duff, *Freedmen*, pp. 43, 48-49.
    4. Lewis and Reinhold, *Roman Civilization*, II, p. 256.
    5. Some patrons left legacies to their freedom (*ILS*, no. 8271 = Sherk, *Roman Empire*, no. 180; Lewis and Reinhold, *Roman Civilization*, II, p. 257). Some freedmen were buried with their patrons in the same tomb (Lewis and Reinhold, *Roman Civilization*, II, p. 257; Duff, *Freedmen*, p. 101). On the other hand, inscriptions were made by freedmen in honour of their patrons (*ILS*, no. 5010 = Lewis and Reinhold, *Roman Civilization*, II, pp. 259-60).

was made easier to bear with the bestowal of favours. If a slave wanted to have a better future, at least for his descendants, seeking manumission, even if it meant being under the power of a patron, might still appear to be the one way which actually would give him some control over his life.

A second group of people who clustered around a rich patron were the literary friends or men with special skills, such as philosophers or even religious persons. The fact that it was common for some satirists to denounce their colleagues for associating themselves with the rich and the powerful and for flattering them suggests how common it was for literary men to attach themselves to rich houses.[1] Ironically, many of the famous satirists themselves actually were clients of rich patrons.[2] On the matter of courting rich houses, philosophers seemingly were not far behind.[3] Like the satirists, some of them also debated over the problem of receiving gifts from the rich patrons.[4] Besides poets and philosophers, religious figures such as soothsayers might also be among the followers of a rich and powerful patron.[5] With regard to the specific situation in Corinth, especially in the first half of the first century, we have to admit that clear and concrete evidence is lacking. However, since Corinth was such a rich city at that time, there is reason to believe that literary clients or the like would seek refuge under some rich patrons.[6]

1. Horace, *Ep.* 1.19.35; Persius, *Prologue, Satires* 1; Pliny, *Ep.* 5.19.
2. Horace, *Satires* 2.6.40-41; *Ep.* 1.7; Persius, *Satires* 1.108-109; Martial, *Epigrams* 1.20; 3.60; Pliny, *Ep.* 3.21; Juvenal, *Satires* 5.
3. Tacitus, *Ann.* 16.32; *Hist.* 4.10. Cf. Dio Chrysostom, *Or.* 77/78.34-35.
4. So in the Socratic letters, those philosophers who found shelter under the roofs of the rich houses became a type to be attacked by the ascetic Cynics (*Ps.-Socratic Ep.* 8, 9).
5. A *duovir* and an *aedilis* of a town were allowed to keep a soothsayer as their assistant (Abbott and Johnson, *Municipal Administration*, no. 26, LXII = Lewis and Reinhold, *Roman Civilization*, I, p. 421). It is tempting to see the magician Elymas as a client to the proconsul of Cyprus Sergius Paulus (Acts 13.8). The identity of Elymas as a client would help to explain, to a small extent, Elymas's reaction to Sergius Paulus's interest in the message of Paul and Barnabas. He withstood them perhaps because he did not like competition coming from the two missionary workers (cf. F.F. Bruce, *The Acts of the Apostles* [London: Tyndale Press, 2nd edn, 1952], p. 257; I.H. Marshall, *The Acts of the Apostles* [Grand Rapids: Eerdmans, 1980], p. 257).
6. Cf. Philostratus's apology for Apollonius's stay in a household in Macedonia

1. Patronage in Roman Corinth 73

Unlike the patron–client relation between the former master and his freedman which was formal and sanctioned by law, the patronal nature of the relation between a rich patron and his literary friends was much more informal and subtle. Very often, because of practical needs, such relationships were sought by poets or philosophers, whether they liked it or not. A literary client needed a patron for, with the support of a rich and prominent host, a client would have been able to gain at least some material benefits, such as food and financial support.[1] Apart from these tangible things, literary clients might also be able to get other intangible benefits such as opportunities to display their talents which ultimately might win them fame.[2] In a different way, the patron too needed the companionship of his literary friends. For with a group of literary men around him, the dignity of the patron, as a cultured man, would be enhanced.[3] They could be sure that there would always be people to applaud their actions,[4] not to mention literary works which praised their benevolence and virtues.[5]

Having said this, it should be noted that differences and inequalities between the patron and the literary clients would always exist. These features of their relationship were usually unfolded on two occasions, namely, the dinner party and the morning salutation. While the dinner table was a place for the patron to show off his wealth, to congratulate himself and to reward the services of his clients,[6] it was also the place where the clients had to fulfil their duty, even if it meant inconve-

---

(*Lives of the Sophists*, 600; Hock, *Social Context*, pp. 53-55).
  1. A literary friend could be invited to dinners (Horace, *Satires* 2.7.32-42; Martial, *Satires* 3.60; Juvenal, *Satires* 1.52.5; *Ps.-Socratic Ep.* 9). Or he could be given gifts in the form of money (Persius, *Prologue*; Martial, *Epigrams* 10.75; Juvenal, *Satires* 1.128; *Ps.-Socratic Ep.* 9; Pliny, *Ep.* 3.21.3), clothing (Persius, *Satires* 1.54; *Ps.-Socratic Ep.* 9), even land (Horace, *Satires* 2.6; Juvenal, *Satires* 9.59). He could also be taken on journey with the patron (Horace, *Satires* 2.6.40-41).
  2. Pliny, *Ep.* 8.12.
  3. Petronius, *Satyricon* 48, 55.
  4. Such actions might be a speech in the forum (Martial, *Epigrams* 6.48; Juvenal, *Satires* 1.128), a recitation (Martial, *Epigrams* 4.49; 10.4, 10; Juvenal, *Satires* 1.52), even wit at the dinner table (Petronius, *Satyricon* 34-35, 41, 48).
  5. Horace, *Satires* 2.6; Persius, *Satires* 1.50-56; Pliny, *Ep.* 3.12.
  6. Juvenal, *Satires* 5.12-15.

nience for themselves.¹ Food first bore witness to their unequal positions. It was not uncommon for the satirists to protest against the serving of inferior food and wine to the clients when good food and good wine were reserved for the host and his honourable friends.² Seating arrangements told the same story.³ The place of honour or the third position in the middle couch, sometimes next to the host, was reserved for the chief guest.⁴ Ordinary clients understandably would have to occupy less honourable positions,⁵ and so would the freedmen.⁶ Slaves and the poor simply had to dine on pallets or sitting upright.⁷ But the difference between the patron and his clients went further than these arrangements. For in order to be a successful client, one had to follow the golden rule, that is, to please the patron and try to accommodate oneself to his opinion.⁸

Before the rich patron and some of his client-guests could recover from the tiresome party the night before, they had to get up early to fulfil their duties at the morning salutation.⁹ Receiving the salutation of his clients, the patron could once more satisfy his desire to be superior and different both before his peers and his inferiors. Paying their visits to the patron, some poor clients could get limited financial help to support their wretched lives.¹⁰ But it should be stressed that

---

1. Horace, *Satires* 2.7.32-34; cf. Juvenal, *Satires* 5.15-23.
2. Martial, *Epigrams* 3.49, 60; 6.11; Juvenal, *Satires* 5.24-25. Note also Pliny's apparent distaste for such a practice (*Ep.* 2.6).
3. For more discussions of the Roman seating arrangement, see 'Triclinium', in *A Dictionary of Classical Antiquities: Mythology, Religion, Literature and Art* (rev. H. Nettleship and J.E. Sandys; London: Swan Sonnenschein, 1894), p. 653; J.E. Sandys (ed.), *A Companion to Latin Studies* (Cambridge: Cambridge University Press, 3rd edn, 1921), pp. 206-207; *OCD*, pp. 1093-1094.
4. N. Rudd, *Horace: Satires and Epistles; Persius: Satires* (Harmondsworth: Penguin Books, 1979), p. 122.
5. Juvenal, *Satires* 5.15-18.
6. Sullivan, *Petronius*, p. 189 n. 9.
7. *OCD*, p. 1094.
8. Horace, *Ep.* 1.18; Seneca, *De Ira* 3.8.6; 3.35.
9. Martial, *Epigrams* 10.82; Juvenal, *Satires* 1.95-138; Seneca, *De Brev. Vit.* 14.4; Pliny, *Ep.* 3.12.2. See also J.P.V.D. Balsdon, *Life and Leisure in Ancient Rome* (London: Bodley Head, 1969), pp. 21-24.
10. By attending the door of the rich a poor client might get a *sportula* which is either a basket of food or some money to buy food for the day (Juvenal, *Satires* 1.128).

probably not all the clients were treated in the same way. In a reference to the custom of morning salutation Seneca suggested that friends or clients were classified and treated accordingly by patrons in the great houses.[1] The closest friends were seen in private, the less close friends in company with others, and the rest were seen *en masse*. That may be why some clients complained that they did not get to see the patron while others did.[2] Although some might complain, the same people perhaps would come again the next morning. Why did people still hang around the doors of the great houses if they did not like doing so?

Some might do it out of a sense of duty as faithful clients.[3] But others had to do it because of necessity. The latter group of people made up the third group of clients under an influential patron. Who were these people? What did they want? They were those who sought the help of a patron in different matters. Some wanted the support of an important patron in the pursuit of a public career.[4] Others needed the help of a patron in legal matters.[5] That there were people who sought legal help from an important patron is interesting. Why did people need such help? And from great patrons? These questions lead naturally into our next topic, namely the relationship between patronage and the legal system.

Patronage and the Lawcourt

Did patronage have anything to do with legal proceedings in the early Empire? That formal support was lent by Roman laws to protect the patrons at the expense of the freedmen or freedwomen already suggests something about the orientation of the Roman legal system in relation to patronage. But, in another way, the institution of patronage could work to protect the weak.[6] Indeed, that was probably the reason

---

1. Seneca, *De Ben.* 6.34.2.
2. Seneca, *De Const.* 10.2; Juvenal, *Satires* 1.100-101. To solve this problem, the advice of experienced clients was to bribe the servants or to wait for the patrons on the street (Horace, *Satires* 1.9.56-58; Juvenal, *Satires* 3.189).
3. Martial, *Epigrams* 10.28.
4. Martial, *Epigrams* 12.26; Seneca, *De Brev. Vit.* 14.3; 20.1; Plutarch, *Moralia* 814D.
5. Seneca, *De Brev. Vit.* 11.4.
6. It is noteworthy that the term *patronus* refers to a legal representative before court (*OCD*, p. 791). Cf. Gelzer, *Roman Nobility*, p. 70.

why some people sought the help of their patron. How did this work? Who were these people? What sort of help did they need?

It should first be noted that going to court in the Roman Empire could be a costly business. It was not cheap to employ a barrister.[1] In ordinary civil law-suits both parties had to pay bail before they appeared in court on another day.[2] To make an appeal one also had to pay a sum which would be forfeited if the case was lost.[3] Besides, if the case could not be heard in one's town, the plaintiff had to pay for his journey to bring the case in the defendant's forum. Worse still, if the case could not be heard immediately, he had to pay for his own lodging.[4] Because large sums of money might be required to take legal action, the relatively poor would need the help of a rich patron to survive the harassment of a powerful opponent, and sometimes even a rich man might need an even richer patron to get him out of trouble. Actually the relatively poor and less powerful might do better if they could avoid involving themselves in legal disputes. But if, for one reason or the other, such a person was being drawn into a legal dispute, he or she would perhaps find it difficult to survive without the support of a considerate patron. This was so not only because of economic reasons, but for practical reasons too. For it was not unheard of that the court was used by the strong to trample the relatively weak and less powerful. In a case related by Dio Chrysostom a poor and innocent huntsman was accused of using the public land without paying taxes. He would be in trouble if there were no good people to speak on his behalf.[5] In the face of such adverse conditions the poor and the less powerful would do well to seek refuge under a

---

1. In AD 47, the maximum fee a barrister could ask from his client was fixed at 10,000 sesterces. Before that, a client could pay up to 400,000 sesterces (Tacitus, *Ann.* 11.5-7). We can compare this with the rate of pay at that time: a clerk for the *duovir* in a colony in Spain, 1,200 sesterces (Lewis and Reinhold, *Roman Civilization*, I, p. 421); members of the praetorian guard after 16 years of service, 20,000 sesterces (Dio Cassius 55.23).
2. Crook, *Law and Life*, pp. 75-76. For a detailed discussion of the procedure involving civil cases, see Garnsey, *Social Status*, pp. 181-218.
3. Tacitus, *Ann.* 14.28.
4. On this and other expenses, see Crook, *Law and Life*, pp. 95-97.
5. Dio Chrysostom, *Or.* 7.21-63. See also Jones, *Roman World*, pp. 56-61.

powerful patron.¹ Otherwise, they could easily fall prey to the strong and the powerful.

The protection provided by a strong patron, however, represents only one side, naturally the brighter side of the story. For, as already implied in the above discussion, patronage could work in another way, that is, to protect the strong and to oppress or even destroy the weak.² Such improper influences of patronage on justice may be seen at work both in Rome and in the provinces. In the days of Augustus, perhaps earlier, there were already people exploiting their friendship with men of influence and power, such as the emperor and members of the imperial family, to their advantage.³ Cases related to Urgulania, Augusta's friend, in the time of Tiberius are also suggestive.⁴ Because of her friendship with Augusta, she was described by Tacitus as one who stood above the law. When she was summoned by Lucius Piso, an official who was indignant about the corruption in court, to stand trial, she was able to refuse to cooperate. In another case, when she was asked to give witness to the senate, she again disobeyed. That legal justice could be seriously impeded by personal connections can be seen again in one of the actions taken by Tiberius.⁵ It has been suggested that Tiberius's purpose in sitting in court beside the magistrate and reminding the jury of the sanctity of the law was to prevent justice from being corrupted by bribery and personal influence. Tiberius's action suggests that it was probably common for powerful men to exert influence on the decision of the judge. Ironically, Tiberius's action might have reinforced such a malpractice.⁶

If the court in Rome could be corrupted, one can imagine what the situation in the provinces might have been. It has been shown that the loose structure of an assize could give room for informal influences,

---

1. Ascyltus's words can perhaps represent more or less a popular view regarding the use of court in the early Empire: 'What use are laws where money is king, where poverty's helpless and can't win a thing?' (Petronius, *Satyricon* 14). The translation is by Sullivan.
2. According to Kelly, in the late Empire, *gratia* was a synonym for corruption, just as *potentia* was an equivalent for oppression. He also suggests that the seed of the problem was already sown in the early Empire (*Roman Litigation*, p. 55).
3. Suetonius, *Augustus* 56.
4. Tacitus, *Ann.* 2.34.
5. Suetonius, *Tiberius* 33; Tacitus, *Ann.* 1.75.
6. De Ste. Croix, *Class Struggle*, pp. 366-67.

like status and bribery, to interfere with the proper hearing of cases so that those of the less important litigants could be overlooked.[1] The possible negative influence of the personal factor on the administration of justice is echoed again in the accusations which were brought against Dio Chrysostom, whether such accusations were true or not, claiming that he had abused his friendship with a proconsul which led to the downfall and the torturing of his enemies.[2] That the court could be controlled by not just one or two officials, but a whole network of powerful men is also spotlighted by one of the cases which Pliny the Younger reported in his letters.[3] If even Pliny sometimes had to act cautiously when prosecuting some of the strong men, an ordinary advocate would have to be extra-vigilant.[4]

Perhaps the cases which involved Paul as reported in the book of Acts[5] may illumine further possible connections between the personal factor and the handling or sometimes mishandling of justice in the provinces. According to Acts[6] there was no charge against him which merited death or imprisonment when he was detained in Jerusalem. But he was imprisoned in Caesarea.[7] When Paul was in prison, the author of Acts suggests that Felix, the governor, expected him to pay a bribe.[8] Since nothing was forthcoming and perhaps with the intention of granting a favour to the Jewish leaders, Paul was left in prison for two more years.[9] With the coming of a new governor, Festus, the

---

1. G.P. Burton, 'Proconsuls, Assizes and the Administration of Justice under the Empire', *JRS* 65 (1975), pp. 100-102. Cf. also Saller, *Personal Patronage*, pp. 150-54.
2. Dio Chrysostom, *Or.* 43.11. See Jones, *Roman World*, p. 102. Against this background, it is understandable how Jesus' death could be seen as Pilate bowing to the pressure exerted by the High Priest, the Sanhedrin and popular demand (Millar, *Roman Empire*, pp. 63-64).
3. Pliny, *Ep.* 2.11; cf. 3.9.
4. In one case, an advocate, Tuscilius Nominatus, employed by the people of Vicetia to fight against a senator Sollers, did not attend, because he was afraid of the power of his opponent (Pliny, *Ep.* 5.4, 13).
5. On the reliability of Acts for information related to the social background of the Graeco-Roman world, see Nicholls's view quoted by Judge ('Social Identity', p. 208).
6. Acts 23.29; 25.25-27; 26.30-32.
7. Acts 23.35; 24.1-2.
8. Acts 24.26.
9. Acts 24.27.

religious leaders in Palestine seem to have known what they should do. They first tried to secure the favour of Festus, and then pressed him to bring Paul to Jerusalem to be killed.[1] Apparently Festus was also eager to win the favour of the local leaders, so he asked Paul if he would like to go up to Jerusalem.[2] As a last resort Paul could only appeal to stand before Caesar. In contrast, the outcome of Paul's earlier encounter with Gallio in Corinth is completely different.[3] When the Jews brought their case against Paul before the proconsul, Gallio, he refused to hear their case, even before Paul opened his mouth to speak for himself. Why? The reason given by Gallio is fair enough. He did not want to involve himself in an arbitration on a controversy within a Jewish sect. But the possibility that Gallio's refusal to hear the case might have been due not only to the nature of the case, but also partly to the weak Jewish influence in Corinth should not be ruled out.[4] If this interpretation is acceptable, then Paul's escape in Corinth may not necessarily have been because Gallio was a fairer judge, but could partly have been because Jews in Corinth fared worse.

As to the people responsible for the administration of justice at Corinth we know little. Presumably important cases were heard by the governor. But the governor had to travel in a circuit to hear cases at other centres in the province and so he could hardly handle all the cases himself. Some powers of jurisdiction were in the hands of the

1. Acts 25.3.
2. Acts 25.9.
3. Acts 18.12-17.
4. It is not clear how big the Jewish population in Corinth was. The two pieces of evidence which tell of a Jewish presence in Corinth, namely an inscription bearing the words, 'Synagogue of the Hebrews' and a marble impost with three seven-branched candlesticks engraved, are probably of late origin (Furnish, *II Corinthians*, p. 21). With regard to Jewish influence on Corinth, another piece of information from the same episode is telling. After Gallio refused to hear the case, the author of Acts tells us that he drove the Jews away and took no notice when Sosthenes, the synagogue-ruler, was beaten up. If what some scholars have suggested is right, that is, that those who hassled Sosthenes were the local people in Corinth (H. Conzelmann, *Acts of the Apostles* [Philadelphia: Fortress Press, 1987], p. 154; Bruce, *Acts*, p. 348; E. Haenchen, *The Acts of the Apostles* [Oxford: Basil Blackwell, 1971], pp. 536-37, 541), then even if there was a sizeable Jewish community in Corinth, possibly the Jews there would have been looked down upon by the Gentile community at large or even become targets of racial prejudice.

city authorities. As in other cities, the *duoviri* and the *aediles* were the magistrates in Corinth.[1] Ordinary civil cases probably were heard by the *duoviri*.[2] It is also possible that cases relating to the market place and commercial transactions would be brought to the *aediles*.[3] But the quality of their jurisdiction is hard to assess. It is not unheard of that the local courts were actually used for personal gain[4] or for knocking down one's opponents.[5] If Acts' account of Paul's imprisonment in Philippi is trustworthy, it shows once again how rough justice could be apportioned easily by the local magistrates. According to Acts 16.16-24, after Paul cast out the spirit of divination from a slave girl, and thus destroyed her master's source of profit, he and Silas were dragged to appear before the authorities, the *duoviri*.[6] This time Paul was in an unfavourable situation as a foreigner and a Jew. The crowd was against him. Possibly because of the pressure from the local people, the *duoviri* ordered the *lictores* to have Paul stripped, whipped and put into prison, without first making sure if he was a Roman citizen.

I do not mean to suggest that there was no justice whatsoever in the Roman world, but it may perhaps be said that patronage did have an important role to play in the Roman court. While it might provide help for the weak, it could also work to destroy and ruin people. If this were so, it would provide another case which suggests that patronage was quite a pervasive phenomenon in Roman society and exerted a strong influence on the lives of the people at that time.

Conclusion

As one who lived and worked in the early Roman Empire Seneca should have some first-hand information concerning patron–client relations. Let us listen to what he has to tell us regarding the interpersonal relationships in his day:

1. Jolowicz, *Historical Introduction*, pp. 48, 307-308, 324, 341-42, 359.
2. Bagdikian, 'Civic Officials', p. 14.
3. Bagdikian, 'Civic Officials', p. 17.
4. Dio Chrysostom, *Or.* 43.6, 10; 46.8.
5. Dio Chrysostom, *Or.* 46.8; 43.6. See Jones, *Roman World*, p. 99.
6. Acts 16.20 uses the term στρατηγός, literally *praetor*, who actually was a *duovir* of a Roman colony (BAGD, p. 770; Haenchen, *Acts*, p. 496).

> Look at those whose prosperity men flock to behold; they are smothered by their blessings. To how many are riches a burden! From how many do eloquence and the daily straining to display their powers draw forth blood... To how many does the throng of clients that crowd about them leave no freedom! In short, run through the list of all these men from the lowest to the highest—this man desires an advocate, this one answers the call, that one is on trial, that one defends him, that one gives sentence; no one asserts his claim to himself, everyone is wasted for the sake of another. Ask about the men whose names are known by heart, and you will see that these are the marks that distinguish them: A cultivates B and B cultivates C; no one is his own master.[1]

Such a picture of interconnected patron–client relationships serves well to sum up the results of the above study on Corinth. At this point we can say with some confidence that patronage provided *one* of the ways through which relationships in Corinth would have been organized. The relationship complexes in the community, which involved the common people, the local notables, the Roman officials, and in a way the emperor, may also be seen as interlocking nets of patrons and clients.

It is worth mentioning that patronage, as manifested in the early Empire including Corinth, appears to be a two-faced phenomenon. Some of the patron–client relations, such as those between a governor and a city or those between a former master and his freedmen, were formal and legal relations. But some, such as those between the emperor and some of his officials and those between a rich patron and his literary friends, were not formal but quite subtle relations. Yet even though the terminology of patronage might not have been used in describing these less formal relations, it should not be denied that they could have existed. Through such ties, whether formal or informal, resources were exchanged.

Such exchanges might also have been guided by a kind of reciprocal ethics. The patron was expected to provide protection and favours which might not have been accessible through other channels. In return, he could expect to get power, honour, support and perhaps more benefits. So the emperor established his loyal officials in his provinces who would support him and served his interests. The local notables used their wealth to take care of the common crowd who voted them to honourable offices and special privileges. Likewise, the

---

1. Seneca, *De Brev. Vit.* 2.4 (LCL).

patrons of the associations and the heads of individual households were also able to enjoy special privileges and powers because of their positions in the respective groups. Even the court where the ideal of a just society was supposedly to be upheld could become one of the contexts for similar exchanges. The pervasiveness of the patronage system can thus be seen.

In the light of the specific situation in first-century Corinth, one particular aspect of the phenomenon of patronage deserves our special attention. That is the possible impact of patron–client relations on the local politics. While in first-century Corinth honour and power, whether political or religious, were sought by the ambitious men, the way to fame was probably marked by strong competition. That is to say, in order to climb the ladder of power and honour, one would have to do more than fulfil the basic property requirements. Hence it was essential for those who did not come from a good family background, like freedmen, to have proper personal connections. For the seats of honour were probably in the hands of the ruling elites under the system of cooption. One of the necessary and honourable things to do was to cultivate relationships with men of influence and, if possible, the Roman authorities. Perhaps that is why many of the local notables were at the same time priests of the imperial cult.

Significantly enough, it seems that the values and structure of the patronal society were also reflected in institutions, such as associations and households. In such contexts it is of particular interest to note that patronal relations can be seen as projected beyond the realm of human relations into that of human–divine relations. So even though a rich householder could be the patron of many, he himself would need the protection of a patron god.

If patronage formed such an important part of life in Roman Corinth, it would be most unrealistic to expect the Christians there to be wholly untouched by its influence and to behave in a completely new way immediately after their conversion. On the contrary, it is most likely that patronage would become the background for understanding the relational ties in the church and some of the problems Paul discussed in 1 Corinthians. I will turn now to examine the relationships in the Corinthian church.

Chapter 2

THE CHURCH IN ROMAN CORINTH

In Chapter 1, I attempted to show that, in a way, social relationships in Roman Corinth, from emperor to freedmen, may be seen as networks of patron–client ties through which power, honours and favours were exchanged, and that patronage can be found at work in different levels of the society. Moreover, while wealth might often wield influence in Corinth, it appears that other factors such as personal connections were of equal importance in the making of a local notable. Against this background, it would be natural to ask if the convention of patronage might have influenced the behaviour of members of the Christian community at Corinth. But before I examine whatever impact the convention of patronage might have had on the church at Corinth, it will be helpful first to consider a broader question which pertains to the relationships in the church, especially at the time when 1 Corinthians was being written.

The Corinthian Network

At this point, perhaps, I should explain briefly a methodological consideration. It is necessary to point out that our understanding of the situation behind 1 Corinthians will always remain partial. We are handicapped by the nature of the evidence. The problem we face and some of the attempts to provide a solution are well summed up by Fiorenza. She writes,

> Since many things are presupposed, left out, or unexplained in a speech/letter, the audience must in the process of reading 'supply' the missing information in line with the rhetorical directives of the speaker/ writer. Historical critical scholars seek to 'supply' such information generally in terms of the history of religions, including Judaism, while preachers and bible-readers usually do so in terms of contemporary

values, life, and psychology. Scholarship on 1 Corinthians tends to 'supply' such information about Paul's 'opponents' either with reference to the symbolic universe of contemporary Judaism, of pagan religion, especially the mystery cults, philosophical schools, Hellenistic Judaism, or developing Gnosticism. The studies of the social setting or 'social world' of Pauline Christianity in turn, do not utilize ideological, doctrinal models of interpretation, but supply the missing information in terms of 'social data' gleaned from the Pauline corpus, Acts, and other ancient sources, which in turn, are organized in terms of sociological or anthropological models.[1]

I do not presume that I can supply more accurate information regarding the situation in Corinth. But it is my intention to apply the analytical concept of networks to the problem of the relationships behind 1 Corinthians. I hope that, through such a study, the situation behind 1 Corinthians can be appreciated anew.

One of the working assumptions of network analysis is that linkages in a defined set of ties may be used to interpret the behaviour of the people involved.[2] In other words, if we want to ascertain the nature of the relationships in the Corinthian church at the time when 1 Corinthians was being written, we can do so by analysing the pattern of relational ties which involved the Corinthians at that stage.[3] To start from the above assumption, we will have to define the 'field' of our study. The network of ties behind 1 Corinthians naturally involved many people in and outside the church.[4] Paul apparently is a significant person in relation to the Corinthians. For although Paul was not in the church (1 Cor. 16.5-9), he was still closely connected to

1. E.S. Fiorenza, 'Rhetorical Situation and Historical Reconstruction in 1 Corinthians', *NTS* 33 (1987), pp. 389-90.
2. Mitchell, 'The Concept and Use of Social Networks', in *Social Networks*, p. 2.
3. It would be even better if we had enough information to help us ascertain the shifting relationships between Paul and the Corinthians from the founding of the community to the writing of 1 Corinthians. But since no unambiguous data are available, I confine this study to the situation at the stage when 1 Corinthians was written.
4. It should be marked that the constituents of the church apparently had changed when 1 Corinthians was written. For when Paul wrote 1 Corinthians, he was no longer in Corinth (1 Cor. 16.5-9). Some of the people, including Aquila and Prisca/Priscilla (1 Cor. 16.19; Acts 18.18), Timothy (1 Cor. 4.17; 16.10-11; 2 Cor. 1.19; Acts 18.5, 18) and Silvanus (2 Cor. 1.19; Acts 18.5, 18), who had been in the church earlier were also not in the church.

2. The Church in Roman Corinth

the church through letters (1 Cor. 5.9) and his messengers, like Timothy (1 Cor. 4.17; 16.10-11). He also received oral information (1 Cor. 1.11; 5.1; 11.18), and might even have received written information (1 Cor. 7.1, 25; 8.1; 12.1; 16.1, 12) concerning the situation in the church at Corinth.[1] Next, there are those who were in the church. Those baptized by Paul when he first visited Corinth presumably still made up part of the church. In 1 Corinthians, Crispus, Gaius and Stephanas are mentioned explicitly by Paul (1 Cor. 1.14-16). We should also include Apollos in our study. For we know that Apollos came to work in Corinth for some time after the departure of Paul and before the writing of 1 Corinthians (1 Cor. 3.5-9; Acts 18.24–19.1),[2] and that some people in Corinth apparently looked forward to his next visit (1 Cor. 16.12). It is also natural to surmise that the church would have attracted some new members during the period between the departure of Paul and the writing of 1 Corinthians (1 Cor. 3.5).[3] If there were such new people in the church, they should not be neglected—however, we are not able to ascertain who they might have been. But we do come across some other names in 1 Corinthians. They are Fortunatus and Achaicus (1 Cor. 16.17) and Chloe's people (1 Cor. 1.11).[4] Another interesting figure whose name is not mentioned in 1 Corinthians but in Romans 16 might also have been related to the Corinthian church. He is Erastus (Rom. 16.23).[5] Lastly, we should not neglect people, such as the pagan judge (1 Cor.

---

1. Hurd, *I Corinthians*, pp. 48-49, 114-209.
2. Hurd, *I Corinthians*, p. 98.
3. Commenting on 1 Cor. 3.5, G.G. Findlay writes: 'Some Cor. had been converted through Apollos' ('St Paul's First Epistle to the Corinthians', in *The Expositor's Greek Testament*, II [Grand Rapids: Eerdmans, 1988], p. 788. Cf. also White, *'Domus Ecclesiae—Domus Dei'*, p. 564 n. 185).
4. Sosthenes is named as the joint author of 1 Corinthians. The name is too common to be certain about his identity (Meeks, *First Urban Christians*, p. 215 n. 27), though some identify him as the Sosthenes of Acts 18.17 (W.F. Orr and J.A. Walther, *1 Corinthians* [Garden City: Doubleday, 1976], p. 142).
5. There are other names mentioned in Rom. 16 which could have been related to the church at Corinth. They include Lucius (Rom. 16.21), Jason (Rom. 16.21), Sosipater (Rom. 16.21), Tertius (Rom. 16.22) and Quartus (Rom. 16.23). But not much certain is known about these people (Theissen, *Social Setting*, pp. 94-95). We know, however, that Phoebe probably was a prominent leader in the church of Cenchreae (Rom. 16.1-2). But it is not immediately clear if Phoebe was related directly to the church at Corinth.

6.1), who were not part of the church, but were somehow connected to the church. Such were the people whom we know were connected to the Corinthian church.

From the above survey, it is clear that we are not fully informed concerning the people who made up the Corinthian network at the time when 1 Corinthians was being written. Neither do we have information about the 'frequency' or the 'density' of the ties involved. Hence we face here another problem of insufficient information. Moreover, we will never be able to live among the Corinthians to observe how often they met one another. Therefore, I do not presume that the study below is network analysis in the strict sense. I also want to emphasize once again that what I attempt to do is to highlight, based on what we can know about the Corinthian situation, the orientation of the relational ties in the church so that a picture of the relationships in the church behind 1 Corinthians can emerge.

Before I proceed any further, it is appropriate to give a brief explanation of other preliminary matters concerning the study in this chapter. First, the pattern of relational ties which links up members of the Christian community at Corinth and its implications are our basic concerns, even though statements which may reveal the background of individuals and the quality of the relationships in the church will be used to facilitate the reconstruction. Secondly, since the situation behind 1 Corinthians is what we seek to understand, 1 Corinthians is of primary importance as a source of information. The integrity of 1 Corinthians is assumed.[1] Relevant information from other undisputed letters by Paul, including 2 Corinthians, 1 Thessalonians, Philippians, Philemon, Galatians and Romans, may also be made use of where applicable. Acts will also be consulted for background information concerning various individuals related to the church.[2]

---

1. Although the integrity of 1 Corinthians is questioned from time to time (e.g. Schmithals, *Gnosticism in Corinth*, pp. 90-96), the majority of scholars still accept the basic unity of 1 Corinthians (e.g. H. Conzelmann, *I Corinthians* [Philadelphia: Fortress Press, 1975], pp. 2-4; C.K. Barrett, *A Commentary on the First Epistle to the Corinthians* [London: A. & C. Black, 2nd edn, 1971], pp. 12-17).

2. The problem with using information in the book of Acts for the construction of the situation related to Paul is acknowledged (J.C. Hurd, 'Pauline Chronology and Pauline Theology', in Farmer, Moule and Niebuhr [eds.], *Christian History and Interpretation*, pp. 225-48). But G. Bornkamm regards Acts 18.1-17 as a reliable source of information for understanding the situation in Corinth (*Paul* [London:

2. The Church in Roman Corinth

The study in this chapter will be divided into two sections. In the first section, I hope first to ascertain the nature of the relationships in the church at the time of the writing of Corinthians. Then, in the second section, I will explore two of the problems in the church, namely the controversy over financial support (1 Cor. 9) and the divisions at the Lord's table (1 Cor. 11.17-34), which some scholars strongly suggest could be related to the phenomenon of patronage.

Personal Relations in the Church

With regard to the relationships in the Corinthian church behind 1 Corinthians, two related issues have often been discussed by biblical commentators. The first concerns the relationships inside the church, and the second the relationship between Paul and the Corinthians. As far as the problem of the relationships inside the church is concerned, the issue has often been discussed with reference to the problem of 'parties' in the church. Some scholars, Barrett[1] for instance, following the lead of Paul's statement in 1 Cor. 1.12, propose that there were 'parties' in the church.[2] However, the presence of some of the 'parties', the Christ party in particular, is difficult to ascertain.[3] Munck therefore argues that there was no 'party' in the church at all.[4] But the way Paul responds to the Corinthians has convinced most scholars that Munck has probably overstated his case, and that there probably was some kind of division in the church.[5] Meeks, for example, postulates the existence of two opposing fronts. There were those who were for Paul and those for Apollos.[6] N. Dahl also contends that

---

Hodder & Stoughton, 1969], p. 68). Cf. M. Hengel, *Acts and the History of Earliest Christianity* (London: SCM Press, 1979).
   1. C.K. Barrett, 'Christianity at Corinth', in *Essays on Paul* (London: SPCK, 1983), pp. 4-6.
   2. Theissen also seems to assume the existence of 'parties' in the church (*Social Setting*, p. 54).
   3. The presence of a Cephas party is also dubious. For a helpful discussion of the problem of 'parties' in Corinth, see Hurd, *I Corinthians*, pp. 96-107.
   4. J. Munck, *Paul and the Salvation of Mankind* (London: SCM Press, 1969), p. 167.
   5. E.g. Conzelmann, *I Corinthians*, p. 34; G.D. Fee, *The First Epistle to the Corinthians* (Grand Rapids: Eerdmans, 1987), p. 47.
   6. Meeks, *First Urban Christians*, p. 117.

the church was probably divided, but only between those who were for Paul and those who were against him.[1] This in turn raises the question about Paul's relationship with the church at Corinth. On this matter Dahl further surmises that the sending of a delegation with the church's letter to Paul might have precipitated opposition in the church against Paul.[2] But, based on the fact that the Corinthians still sought Paul's advice on various problems relating to the church, Hurd argues that though Paul's relationship with the church might be strained, his authority as an apostle was not challenged by the church.[3] So was the church at Corinth divided? Were there people in the church who were against Paul? These are the questions which will be studied in this section.

The Corinthians
Before I proceed to examine the relational indicators behind 1 Corinthians, it may be helpful to know something about the social background of the people whom we know made up the Corinthian church and, if possible, their relations with Paul. According to Paul, 'the first fruits' at Corinth were Stephanas and the members of his household (1 Cor. 16.15). They were among those baptized personally by Paul (1 Cor. 1.16). As such, it is readily understandable that they would have a special affection for Paul. Building on the work of E.A. Judge, P. Marshall has pointed out that, in the undisputed letters of Paul, enemies may be condemned but were never referred to by name.[4] In the light of this convention, Stephanas could hardly be an opponent of Paul. On the contrary, since he was commended explicitly by Paul (1 Cor. 16.15-18), he apparently was a supporter of Paul in the church. In view of the fact that Stephanas was a householder and was able to render services to the church there (1 Cor. 16.15),[5] it may

1. Dahl, 'Church at Corinth', pp. 313-35. As noted by Dahl, this two-party view goes back to F.C. Baur.
2. Dahl, 'Church at Corinth', p. 323.
3. E.g. Hurd, *I Corinthians*, pp. 108-13.
4. Marshall, *Enmity*, pp. 341-48. Cf. Judge, 'Paul's Boasting', p. 41.
5. 'The saints' probably refers to the Christian community at Corinth, and not to the Jerusalem saints (Findlay, 'First Epistle to the Corinthians', p. 950; Barrett, *First Corinthians*, p. 394; Fee, *First Corinthians*, pp. 929-30). The service Stephanas offered to the church might have taken the form of using his home as a

2. The Church in Roman Corinth

be inferred that he was a man of independent means[1] and a patron or a leader of the church.[2] But there is no evidence to suggest that he was especially rich[3] or socially powerful or of distinguished background.[4] As implied by the idea of 'the first fruits', Stephanas and members of his household were not the only people in Corinth who came to accept Paul's proclamation. Crispus may be another one (Acts 18.8). In any case he is another person who was baptized personally by Paul (1 Cor. 1.14). So he too would have a reason to support Paul. The fact that Crispus is referred to by name in 1 Corinthians should, at least, suggest that he probably was not regarded by Paul as his enemy. However, if Crispus was a strong supporter of Paul at the time when 1 Corinthians was being written, it is not immediately clear. In 1 Corinthians the background of Crispus is not stated. Many commentators assume that he was the Crispus of Acts 18.8.[5] If so, then he possibly used to serve in the capacity of a synagogue ruler. As a householder and a former leader of the Jews, it is very likely that he would be one of the leaders in the church. It is also quite understandable that Crispus is regarded by many scholars as a person of 'high social status'.[6] It should be granted that, since Crispus was a synagogue ruler, he was probably a person of wealth and might have enjoyed high prestige among his own people. But if, as Acts 18.17 seems to suggest, a synagogue ruler could be beaten up by the colonists, one wonders how prestigious and powerful Crispus was among the colonists. Moreover, one also wonders what kind of effect his turning to the new faith might have on Crispus. Would he still be respected by the Jews in Corinth?[7] Would he be cut off from his

place of worship (Moffatt, *First Corinthians*, p. 278; Fee, *First Corinthians*, p. 930).
1. Theissen, *Social Setting*, p. 87; Findlay, 'First Epistle to the Corinthians', p. 950.
2. Meeks, *First Urban Christians*, pp. 58, 78, 119.
3. Malherbe has rightly warned that the power and influence of Stephanas in the church may have been over-estimated by Theissen (*Social Aspects*, p. 73 n. 27).
4. Meeks further suggests that Stephanas was possibly not as wealthy as Crispus and Gaius on the one hand, and not as notable as Erastus on the other (*First Urban Christians*, p. 58).
5. E.g. Barrett, *First Corinthians*, p. 47; Theissen, *Social Setting*, pp. 73-74.
6. Theissen, *Social Setting*, p. 75; Meeks, *First Urban Christians*, p. 57.
7. According to Acts 18.17, Crispus apparently was soon replaced by Sosthenes as the ruler of the synagogue.

power and economic base?¹ In short, Crispus's status still looks quite ambiguous.

Gaius, like Stephanas and Crispus, was another person in Corinth whom Paul both baptized personally and called by name (1 Cor. 1.14).² Hence, it is natural to assume that he was not regarded by Paul as one of his opponents and might actually be one of Paul's friends when he wrote 1 Corinthians.³ This seems to be supported by the fact that he was Paul's host⁴ when Paul later visited Corinth (Rom. 16.23). But again one cannot say for sure if he was a strong supporter of Paul at the time when 1 Corinthians was written, even though one might like to think so. Since he was able to serve as a host to Paul and the whole congregation (Rom. 16.23) apparently his house was not small. Many scholars have therefore rightly regarded him as a man of some wealth and a patron to the church.⁵

Apart from the three mentioned above, Fortunatus and Achaicus are mentioned as part of a group of envoys sent by the church to see Paul (1 Cor. 16.17). The fact that Paul asks the church to recognize them has led Fee⁶ to regard them as belonging to 'Paul's people' in the church (1 Cor. 16.18). Not much is known, however, about their background. Both names are of servile origin.⁷ But it does not necessarily follow that they could not be independent or rich in Corinth, a

---

1. I am indebted to my fellow researcher, Dr Nicholas Taylor, for this insight.
2. It has sometimes been suggested that Gaius could be identified as Titius Justus (Acts 18.7) (F.F. Bruce, *The Pauline Circle* [Grand Rapids: Eerdmans, 1985], p. 95). However, there is not enough evidence to make a definite judgment. After all, if Gaius was to be identified as Titius Justus, the identification will not add much to what we already know from Paul's letters about Gaius. Since Justus is only mentioned in Acts, he will not be included in the analysis of the relational ties in the Corinthian church.
3. So Theissen, *Social Setting*, p. 55.
4. The meaning of ξένος (Rom. 16.23) is related to guest-friendship and hospitality (A.T. Robertson, *Word Pictures in the New Testament*, IV [Grand Rapids: Baker Book House, 1931], p. 430).
5. Judge, 'Early Christians', p. 130; Theissen, *Social Setting*, p. 89; Meeks, *First Urban Christians*, p. 57; Marshall, *Enmity*, p. 345.
6. Fee, *First Corinthians*, p. 832.
7. A. Robertson and A. Plummer, *A Critical and Exegetical Commentary on the First Epistle of St Paul to the Corinthians* (Edinburgh: T. & T. Clark, 1914), p. 296; cf. L.R. Taylor, 'Freedmen and Freeborn in the Epitaphs of Imperial Rome', *AJP* 82 (1961), p. 125.

2. The Church in Roman Corinth

Roman colony.[1] Some scholars do see them as independent freedmen.[2] But many scholars regard them as dependents, if not slaves, of Stephanas.[3] In either case, they could hardly be people of 'high social status'.[4] If they were slaves of Stephanas, they could hardly be seen as patrons in the church or patrons of Paul.[5]

Chloe's people are mentioned by Paul with reference to the church's divisions and strife (1 Cor. 1.11). Again, not much can be said with certainty about Chloe[6] or those people of Chloe. Recently Fiorenza,[7] on the basis of the observation that the grammatical form of τῶν Χλόης is the same as the expression which characterizes followers of Paul and of other leaders, argues that they were followers of Chloe and were likely to be official messengers from Corinth who brought oral information and written communication from the church to Paul. It is doubtful, however, that one grammatical point gives enough support to her thesis. The common view which sees Chloe's people as slaves or freedpersons[8] of the household of Chloe who informally brought to Paul's attention the divisions in the church, a picture not suggested in their letter to Paul, seems more acceptable.[9] Whether they were members of the Corinthian church or not,[10] they probably

---

1. Cf. Kent, *Inscriptions*, nos. 134, 224, 228.
2. Robertson and Plummer, *First Corinthians*, p. 396; Meeks, *First Urban Christians*, pp. 56-57.
3. So von Dobschütz, *Primitive Church*, p. 57; Moffatt, *First Corinthians*, p. 278; Fee, *First Corinthians*, p. 831.
4. Theissen, *Social Setting*, p. 95.
5. *Contra* Judge, 'Early Christians', p. 130; Marshall, *Enmity*, p. 345.
6. The identity of Chloe is difficult to tell. Meeks surmises that Chloe was a Christian and could even have been among the powerful few in the church (*First Urban Christians*, pp. 59, 217 n. 54; cf. Fiorenza, 'Rhetorical Situation', pp. 394-95). But others are more sceptical (Barrett, *First Epistle to the Corinthians*, p. 42; Conzelmann, *I Corinthians*, p. 32).
7. Fiorenza, 'Rhetorical Situation', p. 395.
8. Theissen, *Social Setting*, pp. 57, 92-94; Meeks, *First Urban Christians*, p. 59; Barrett, *First Corinthians*, p. 42. Chloe's people could also imply members of Chloe's family (J.B. Lightfoot, *Notes on Epistles of St Paul* [London: Macmillan, 1895], p. 152). But Theissen has shown that it is a less likely option (*Social Setting*, pp. 92-94).
9. Dahl, 'Church at Corinth', p. 323; Theissen, *Social Setting*, p. 57.
10. Some think that they were members of the Corinthian church (Theissen, *Social*

were known by the Corinthians. Thus, they could be seen as part of the Corinthian network. But if they were informal messengers to Paul, their action in bringing news about the church's strife to Paul may imply that they were on the side of Paul.[1] We cannot, however, be entirely certain about this.

It appears that most of the people we have looked at so far were not particularly distinguished socially. There were a few persons of independent means and one who could have served formerly in a significant position as a synagogue ruler. Presumably these people could be regarded as belonging to the patronal class. But it does not appear that they were rich enough[2] or prestigious enough to be considered as socially outstanding. The impression we get of these people therefore looks not unlike Meeks's depiction of the 'typical' Christian in the Pauline churches. He writes,

> It is hardly surprising that we meet no landed aristocrats, no senators, *equites*, nor (unless Erastus might qualify) decurions. But there is also no specific evidence of people who are of the poor, peasants, agricultural slaves, and hired agricultural day laborers... The 'typical' Christian... is a free artisan or small trader... Some of the wealthy provided housing, meeting places, and other services for individual Christians and for whole groups. In effect, they filled the roles of patrons.[3]

Significantly, the people we have looked at so far were potential supporters of Paul in the church. Of course, they do not represent the whole of the Corinthian church. I will now look at an interesting figure whose presence might alter significantly our perception of the social background of the Corinthian community. He is Erastus.

As Meeks seems to have implied, Erastus's role could have been quite unusual among the Corinthians. In Rom. 16.23, Erastus is mentioned with reference to his official role in the city as ὁ οἰκονόμος τῆς πόλεως. The exact meaning of the title, however, has been a matter of scholarly discussion for some time. H. Cadbury sees the Erastus of Rom. 16.23 as a public slave.[4] Since the discovery of an

---

Setting, p. 92; Meeks, *First Urban Christians*, p. 59). Others think that they were not (e.g. Fee, *First Corinthians*, p. 54).

1. See discussion in Fee, *First Corinthians*, p. 54.
2. When considering this matter, one should take into consideration the fact that Corinth at that time was a rich city.
3. Meeks, *First Urban Christians*, p. 73.
4. H.J. Cadbury, 'Erastus of Corinth', *JBL* 50 (1931), pp. 42-58.

inscription which tells of an Erastus who later became an *aedilis* and a benefactor in Corinth, many scholars[1] are persuaded that Erastus was an extremely rich and significant person in Corinth. But there is another important point which is especially noteworthy, namely, his links with the secular authorities. By virtue of his wealth and his public connections, he could well be ranked among the powerful few in the church (1 Cor. 1.26). As such, he would be able to wield more influence than most patrons in the church.[2]

The fact that the church could attract such powerful leaders as Erastus, assuming that he later became the *aedilis* of Corinth, is especially noteworthy. For it means that some of the people in the church were able to link up with the powerful people in town. In view of his connections, a leader like Erastus might be one with unusual influence in the Corinthian network. Consequently, it may also be surmised that such persons could be very powerful patrons in the church and, as such, could upset the power balance in the church seriously. However, it should perhaps be emphasized that Erastus is mentioned only in later correspondence, not in 1 Corinthians. So we do not know if he, and others of similar influence already made up part of the Corinthian network at the time when 1 Corinthians was being written. But if they were already in the church, why did Paul not mention their names? Does that suggest anything about Paul's perception of his relationship with them? This naturally leads us to examine further the situation behind 1 Corinthians.

Conflicts and Divisions?
What then was the relationship between Paul and the church at this

---

1. Theissen, *Social Setting*, pp. 75-83; Meeks, *First Urban Christians*, pp. 48, 58-59; Furnish, *II Corinthians*, p. 25.
2. Even if he was simply a public slave, it does not necessarily mean that he can be disregarded as a man without any influence. It has been shown that, because the imperial freedmen or slaves had direct access to the emperor, they were some upwardly mobile people who could often serve as powerful mediators (Meeks, *First Urban Christians*, pp. 21-22; P.R.C. Weaver, 'Social Mobility in the Early Roman Empire: The Evidence of the Imperial Freedmen and Slaves', *PP* 37 [1967], pp. 3-20; idem, *Familia Caesaris: A Social Study of the Emperor's Freedmen and Slaves* [Cambridge: Cambridge University Press, 1972]). By the same token, a public slave in Corinth who had access to municipal powers might also have been able to exert some influence in a church that was made up mostly of humble people.

stage? Could there have been tensions between them? How did the Corinthians relate to one another? Were they divided? To answer these questions, I will examine specifically some of the indicators in 1 Corinthians which reflect the orientation of the relational ties. Some of the indicators considered below include the report of Chloe's people, the sending of envoys to see Paul and Paul's responses in 1 Corinthians.

Divisions in the church. From Chloe's people Paul learns that there were contentions or quarrels (ἔριδες) in the church (1 Cor. 1.11). Paul then paints a picture of a divided church in which different groups of people rally round famous missionaries (1 Cor. 1.12). One cannot rely simply on Paul's words, as Fiorenza has reminded us,[1] and say that there were actual divisions in the church. Nevertheless, there may be some truth in Dahl's suggestion that there probably were troubles, even divisions, in the church.[2] As a matter of fact, from another source, if not also from Chloe's people, Paul is told that there were divisions (σχίσματα) at the Lord's table when those who had not were humiliated by those who had (1 Cor. 11.17-34). Not insignificantly, as Theissen has shown,[3] these two cases of divisions in the church were plausibly caused by the patrons in the church. While the conflict among followers of various apostles could have been a struggle for position of influence in the church, the divisions at the Lord's table quite clearly are in part a result of social distinctions. Hence, while the church apparently still met together as one group,[4] and did not break up, it was perhaps no longer a unified and harmonious community (cf. 1 Cor. 1.10). For more indications in this direction, we will have to enquire further. Before we do that, a feature in the report of Chloe's people is worth exploring.

The fact that Paul mentions in particular the report of Chloe's people on the quarrels and strife in the church at Corinth is interesting. According to Theissen it indicates that Paul is taking the side of the weak and the lowly against the strong and the powerful in the

1. Fiorenza, 'Rhetorical Situation', p. 396.
2. Dahl, 'Church at Corinth', p. 323.
3. Theissen, *Social Setting*, pp. 54-57, 145-74.
4. Barrett, *First Corinthians*, p. 261.

church.[1] I would like to add another point for consideration. The information provided by Chloe's people seems to imply a negative judgment on the squabbling Corinthians. It seems to suppose that members of a Christian community should live in unity and not in strife, an outlook not unlike that of Paul's teachings in 1 Thess. 4.9-10 and 1 Cor. 12.12-13.[2] In this sense, could we then infer that Chloe's people were among those who accepted Paul's point of view?

The sending of Stephanas and his companions to Paul. Whether Chloe's people were Paul's people or not, as suggested earlier, Stephanas is probably one of Paul's ardent supporters in Corinth. Dahl even makes the intriguing suggestion that Stephanas was probably the one responsible for encouraging the church to seek Paul's advice in the midst of controversy.[3] In any case, the fact that Stephanas, Fortunatus and Achaicus were sent to visit Paul at this time (1 Cor. 16.17-18), presumably with a letter from the church to seek his advice on some controversial issues raised by other people in the church,[4] is suggestive. Even though Hurd does not see Paul's authority being challenged by the Corinthians, he concludes, after a detailed study, that the questions raised in the Corinthians' letter could in fact be objections put before Paul.[5] If this was the case, it not only suggests that there were divisions in the church, but that those divisions could have been related directly to Paul.

That Paul was aware of the existence of some kind of opposition to himself in the church may also be suggested by his reaction to the coming of the envoys from Corinth. On the surface, Paul expresses his joy over the coming of Fortunatus and Achaicus, and suggests that their presence has made up for what the church failed to do for him[6]

---

1. Theissen, *Social Setting*, p. 57.
2. The danger of πορνεία is another Pauline concern (1 Cor. 5.9; 1 Thess. 4.3-6). As Paul probably learnt of the case of immorality from an oral source, it is sometimes suggested that Chloe's people were the ones who passed on the information to Paul (cf. Hurd, *I Corinthians*, p. 50). If so, it may be seen as another pointer which suggests that Chloe's people were supporters of the Pauline view.
3. Dahl, 'Church at Corinth', pp. 324-25.
4. Hurd, *I Corinthians*, pp. 48-50.
5. Hurd, *I Corinthians*, p. 207.
6. The meaning of τὸ ὑμέτερον ὑστέρημα οὗτοι ἀνεπλήρωσαν is ambiguous. It can mean either (1) 'these filled up my lack of you' or (2) 'these filled

and has refreshed his spirit (1 Cor. 16.17-18). But Paul's comment may just be a subtle reference to the fact that his own authority[1] was caught up in the problems of the church. For it may imply that there were people in the church who failed or refused to supply what Paul needed, and thus testified to real and continuing tensions between themselves and Paul.[2]

Paul's recommendation of Stephanas to the Corinthians. It is of interest to note that, before the envoys from Corinth are commended by Paul (1 Cor. 16.17-18), Stephanas and his household have been singled out by Paul for recommendation (1 Cor. 16.15-16).[3] Why did Paul have to do this? A plausible explanation is that Stephanas was not respected by some of the people in the church,[4] and that Paul wanted to support his loyal friend.[5] If so, it would confirm indirectly the picture projected by the oral reports that the church was not at peace and provides further details of the 'divisions' in the church. But Stephanas was probably one of the leaders or patrons in the church. So who would and could challenge Stephanas, a supporter of Paul? L.W. Countryman conjectures that a patron of a Christian community could be slighted because of the egalitarian nature of the Christian community.[6] This is not impossible. But under normal circumstances, it seems more likely that patrons in an organization or a club would be supported rather than despised by the ordinary members. Unlike Countryman, Meeks proposes to see those who looked down upon

up your lack of me' (Robertson, *Word Pictures*, IV, p. 203. Cf. Orr-Walther, *I Corinthians*, p. 364). While both meanings could be intended by Paul, Conzelmann prefers the idea that 'they have given me what you failed to give' (*I Corinthians*, p. 299).

1. Dahl, 'Church at Corinth', pp. 324-25.
2. Conzelmann, *I Corinthians*, p. 299 n. 12.
3. On 1 Cor. 16.15-16 and 16.17-18 as letters of recommendation, see C.H. Kim, *Form and Structure of the Familiar Greek Letter of Recommendation* (Missoula MT: Scholars Press, 1972), p. 120; S.K. Stowers, *Letter-Writing in Greco-Roman Antiquity* (Philadelphia: Westminster Press, 1986), p. 156.
4. Dahl, 'Church at Corinth', p. 324.
5. In addition to previous discussion, see also Marshall, *Enmity*, p. 150.
6. Countryman's view quoted by Meeks (see *First Urban Christians*, p. 78). Note that Fiorenza seems to see in Paul's recommendation of Stephanas an attempt to suppress the quest for freedom by the poor and the powerless ('Rhetorical Situation', p. 399).

2. *The Church in Roman Corinth*

Stephanas as the 'disruptive' *pneumatikoi* in the church.[1] In the light of the enthusiastic outlook of the Corinthians, the authority of Stephanas as a patron might be challenged by the enthusiasts who could gain influence because they possessed charismatic gifts, such as speaking in tongues (1 Cor. 12–14).[2] But perhaps more is involved. Theissen makes the suggestion that the problem of 'parties' should be seen as originating from competition among patrons in the church for a more influential position.[3] So perhaps the despisers of Stephanas should also be understood against such a background. In other words, we may surmise that they could be other patrons in the church.

Paul's recommendation in 1 Cor. 16.15-16 may give us some more hints concerning his relationship with some of the people in the church. In emphasizing that Stephanas and his household are his 'first fruits' in Corinth, Paul has identified himself closely with Stephanas. Significantly, Paul commends Stephanas and his household because they have devoted themselves to serving the church.[4] He then asks the Corinthians to subordinate themselves to Stephanas and others who join in and work hard (συνεργοῦντι καὶ κοπιῶντι). What Paul asks for is most probably a spontaneous submission[5] in response to the good work of people like Stephanas and his household, not to their respective social positions.[6] But Paul's mentioning of work and labour as the ground for the submission is interesting. The kind of work and labour Paul had in mind probably is work for the sake of the gospel

---

1. Meeks, *First Urban Christians*, pp. 58, 78, 120.
2. On the relationship between the *pneumatikoi* and other problems in the church, see further discussion in Chapter 3.
3. Theissen, *Social Setting*, pp. 54-57.
4. The line, εἰς διακονίαν τοῖς ἁγίοις ἔταξαν ἑαυτούς, finds a close parallel in Plato, *Republic* 371C. The picture behind the metaphor is that of tradesmen who saw the need of the public and set themselves to serve the people by retailing their produce. Two points may be noted. First, such tradesmen are regarded as the weak (physically) in the city. As there could have been some strong people in the church (1 Cor. 1.26; 4.11; 10.22), could Paul have regarded Stephanas as among the weak? Secondly, in contrast to the tradesmen who served the public, those who were served by Stephanas were the saints in the church.
5. Findlay, 'First Epistle to the Corinthians', p. 950; Conzelmann, *I Corinthians*, p. 298.
6. Fee, *First Corinthians*, pp. 830-31. Cf. 1 Thess. 5.12-13. Note that, when used in Rom. 13.1-6 (cf. Tit. 3.1), the verb ὑποτάσσω refers to the subjection or obedience due to the secular authorities.

or Christ.[1] But the idea of work and labour reminds us of the image Paul himself projects in the letter.[2] He ministers and suffers for the gospel (1 Cor. 3.8; 15.10; 2 Cor. 11.23-27), but at the same time plies a trade to support himself (1 Cor. 4.12). Paul apparently has to defend his style as a working apostle (1 Cor. 9.1-6). This seems to suggest that Paul was also challenged by some people in the church on the ground that he worked to support himself. If so, it may be inferred that those who despised Stephanas also despised Paul and that the despisers of Stephanas were people who did not appreciate the value of toil and labour. Should we then look for these people among the powerful patrons in the church?

Paul's sending and commending of Timothy to the Corinthians. If Paul's commendation of Stephanas is an implicit indication that Paul's people and even Paul himself might have been looked down upon by some people in the church, then Paul's sending and commendation of Timothy to the Corinthians may indicate further that a kind of negative attitude in the church was expected by Paul. Of course, the action of sending Timothy to Corinth in itself may not suggest that the church was in any way negative towards Timothy or towards Paul. For Timothy was also sent to the Thessalonians (1 Thess. 2.17–3.13) and to the Philippians (Phil. 2.19-24) who apparently were positive towards Paul and vice versa. Nevertheless, the announcement of the sending in 1 Cor. 4.14-21,[3] when compared with that of 1 Thess. 2.17–3.13, gives the impression that there may have been problems in the church. First of all, the warm language of Paul's desire to see the recipients which appears in 1 Thess. 2.17-18 is absent in 1 Cor. 4.14-21. Moreover, when Paul mentions his coming, he threatens to discipline some of the Corinthians.[4] Secondly, while the emphasis on Paul's

---

1. Barrett, *First Corinthians*, pp. 394-95; Fee, *First Corinthians*, p. 831.
2. Hock, *Social Context*, p. 60.
3. For a more detailed discussion of Paul's announcement of the sending of an emissary and his coming, see R.W. Funk, 'The Apostolic *PAROUSIA*: Form and Significance', in Farmer, Moule and Niebuhr (eds.), *Christian History and Interpretation*, pp. 249-68.
4. Paul did talk about his plan to visit Corinth in 1 Cor. 16.6-7. But the discussion there still lacks the warmth and earnest desire we see expressed in 1 Thess. 2.17-18. Instead, it is full of uncertainties. Words and phrases like ὅταν (1 Cor. 16.5), τυχόν (1 Cor. 16.6) and ἐὰν ὁ κύριος ἐπιτρέψῃ (1 Cor. 16.7) are used.

2. The Church in Roman Corinth

authority is not prominent in 1 Thess. 2.17–3.13, the authority of Paul as father to the Corinthians is underscored in 1 Cor. 4.14-16. Significantly, it should also be noted that Paul does not simply announce the coming of Timothy, but actually explains why Timothy is sent (1 Cor. 4.17).[1] Since the Corinthians seem to have forgotten them, they therefore had to be reminded of Paul's ways. This parting of the ways implies that the church was at odds with Paul.

But equally telling is Paul's undue concern for the reception of Timothy by the Corinthians. Paul later asks the Corinthians to make sure that Timothy has nothing to fear (1 Cor. 16.10) and especially is not despised (1 Cor. 16.11). Why did Paul appear to fear that Timothy might be despised by the church? Part of the reason may be that Timothy was still young.[2] But perhaps Paul already knew that there were people in the church who were against him, and therefore feared that such people might despise Timothy because of him.[3] In the light of such a situation, it is understandable that Paul has to put much emphasis on his authority in 1 Cor. 4.14-21, and that he has to back Timothy up with his own authority and identifies himself closely with Timothy by calling Timothy his beloved and faithful child (1 Cor. 4.17) who does the Lord's work as Paul himself does (1 Cor. 16.10).

Paul's announcement of his coming. Regarding Paul's relationship with the church, Paul's announcement of his coming is most suggestive. Since obvious supporters of Paul, like Stephanas and Timothy, may have been despised by some people in the church, I have already surmised that Paul probably would also be rejected by the same people in the church. That this could be the case seems to be hinted at when Paul announces that he will visit Corinth shortly (1 Cor. 4.18-21). In the announcement, Paul refers specifically to a group of arrogant Corinthians who do not expect him to return (1 Cor. 4.18) and

---

The reason behind this uncertainty can only be surmised. Could one of the reasons behind Paul's apparent uncertaintites be that he did not want to confront his opponents in the church immediately because they were powerful?

1. Findlay, 'First Epistle to the Corinthians', p. 805.
2. Barrett, *First Corinthians*, p. 391; H. Lietzmann, *An die Korinther I-II* (Tübingen: Mohr, 5th edn, 1969), p. 89. The connection between Timothy's lack of authority and his youth is not suggested by Paul's words in 1 Corinthians, but may be supplied by the Pastoral tradition. Cf. 1 Tim. 4.12.
3. Fee, *First Corinthians*, pp. 822-23.

threatens to discipline them if they so choose (1 Cor. 4.19-21). So a clear note of discord is sounded. Moreover, as Findlay and Dahl have pointed out,[1] the reference to a group of 'puffed-up' people is, in effect, an attempt by Paul to single out a group of people in the church who apparently were hostile to his ways. If this is true, it again seems likely that the church was divided and that some people in the church were against Paul.[2]

To sum up, when the relational indicators examined above are weighed individually, some appear to be ambiguous, but when considered as a whole, they seem to give an impression which supports what Dahl has suggested regarding the situation in Corinth, that is, that at the time when 1 Corinthians was written, the church was no longer a unity, and that some of the Corinthians were against Paul. One may argue against such a conclusion on the basis of the fact that Paul appears to address the church as a unity. But as Dahl has rightly pointed out,[3] the unity could be an image projected by Paul, plausibly to prevent the quarrellings in the church from developing into actual divisions.

Moreover, from the discussion above, there seems to be some indication that those who opposed Paul could be the powerful patrons in the church.[4] My reconstruction of the situation in the church at the

---

1. Note the use of contrastive δέ and τινές in 1 Cor. 4.18 (Findlay, 'First Epistle to the Corinthians', p. 805). See also Dahl, 'Church at Corinth', pp. 328-29.

2. Against this background, we will be able to appreciate better the self-image Paul projects in 1 Corinthians. Such an image is first seen in the opening of 1 Corinthians. While 1 Thessalonians, a letter written to a church which loves and remembers Paul (1 Thess. 3.6), begins in a straightforward way with the names of the senders, 1 Corinthians begins with special emphasis on Paul's role as a 'called apostle' (1 Cor. 1.1). In 1 Corinthians, the title 'apostle' is reserved for Paul, and for Paul alone. Sosthenes, the co-sender of 1 Corinthians, is designated simply as the brother. But in 1 Thess. 2.7, the title 'apostle' is used with reference to both Paul and the co-senders. Paul's projection of his image as an authority figure in 1 Corinthians is best seen as Paul's way to counteract some kind of opposition in Corinth (Fee, *First Corinthians,* p. 28). The image of an 'apostle' of Christ Jesus is seen again in 1 Cor. 9.1-3; 15.9. In addition, we see other images of authority projected in the letter. In 1 Cor. 3.10, Paul casts himself in the role of a skilled master-builder. In 1 Cor. 4.14-15, Paul appears as the father of the church.

3. Dahl, 'Church at Corinth', p. 328.

4. L.M. White, another scholar who is interested in network studies, has pondered the possibility that the change in the church's attitude toward Paul might be

time when 1 Corinthians was written is supported by the finding of M. Bünker via a different path. After a detailed study of the rhetorical arrangement in 1 Cor. 1.10–4.21, Bünker concludes that, while the whole church is addressed, in reality Paul is arguing only with the powerful few in the church.[1] If the opponents of Paul were the powerful few in the church, why should they oppose Paul? Next, I will examine other indications which may suggest a connection between the powerful patrons and some of the conflict-points in the church.

Patronal Relations in the Church

In Rom. 16.1-2 Paul refers to Phoebe as a διάκονος of the church of Cenchreae and a προστάτις of many, including Paul. Both of these titles have evoked much discussion.[2] It seems fair to say that Phoebe was an independent woman with some wealth and a leader in the church of Cenchreae.[3] But Paul's use of προστάτις with reference to Phoebe is most interesting. It seems to make the best sense to take προστάτις as an equivalent of 'patroness'.[4] In that case it clearly suggests that the convention of patronage in the early Empire was known to Paul, and that some of the early Christians made use of the benefits it provided.[5]

---

because some new and more prominent patrons than those attracted by Paul were added to the church (White, *'Domus Ecclesiae—Domus Dei'*, p. 564 n. 185). This, of course, cannot be proved, but it is an attractive suggestion.

1. M. Bünker, *Briefformular und rhetorische Disposition im 1. Korintherbrief* (Göttingen: Vandenhoeck & Ruprecht, 1984), p. 52.
2. See, e.g., Meeks, *First Urban Christians*, p. 60; J.D.G. Dunn, *Romans* (Dallas: Word Books, 1988), p. 889; E.S. Fiorenza, *In Memory of Her: A Feminist Theological Reconstruction of Christian Origins* (London: SCM Press, 1983), pp. 47-48.
3. Meeks, *First Urban Christian*, p. 60. Cf. C.E.B. Cranfield, *The Epistle to the Romans*, II (Edinburgh: T. & T. Clark, 1979), p. 783.
4. Judge, 'Cultural Conformity and Innovation', pp. 20-21; W. Sanday and A.C. Headlam, *The Epistle to the Romans* (Edinburgh: T. & T. Clark, 5th edn, 1902), p. 418.
5. Judge, 'Early Christians', pp. 128-29; *idem*, 'Cultural Conformity and Innovation', pp. 20-21. Regarding Paul's attitude toward patronage, Malherbe is of the opinion that Paul does not regard such patrons or patronesses as having authority simply because they were in that position (Malherbe, *Social Aspects*, p. 98). The

Patronage in the early Empire helped to provide many services or benefits to those who needed them. These services ranged from providing food and lodging (Rom. 16.23) to assuming legal responsibility (Acts 17.5-9; Rom. 16.1-2). Patron–client relations, however, involved obligations, and were undergirded by certain conventions. For example, the interest of the patronal class was often protected. One thing which a patron would treasure most is honour and praise. From the regulations of the burial society in Lanuvium we can see that a patron could expect to be honoured by his dependents for benefactions dispatched. Moreover, the honour of a patron would be expected to be protected. So during a banquet, those who dared to abuse the *quinquennalis* would be penalized. It is not immediately clear how patrons would treat those who were not under their patronage. Would they also support those who were not of their own? Or would they marginalize them?

Against such a background, I will explore further the relationship between patronage and the conflicts and tensions in the church at Corinth. There are two particular problems in 1 Corinthians which have been studied with profitable results in the light of the phenomenon of patronage. The first concerns the controversy over financial support for missionary workers, and the second, the conflicts at the Lord's table. Before I deal with these two issues, it may be helpful to digress so as to investigate the relationship between Apollos and the Corinthians. An understanding of their relationship may help us not only to understand the Corinthians' preference for Apollos, but also to see a plausible case of patronage in the church.

Apollos

If Paul appears to expect a negative response from the church towards him and those who stood on his side, such as Timothy, he gives the impression that the church was more positive towards Apollos. As mentioned before, it appears that some people in the church did not expect Paul to go back. Significantly, some apparently were expecting Apollos to visit them again. It may be assumed that these were the people who did not expect Paul to return to Corinth. In any case, Paul apparently was asked if and when Apollos would visit Corinth

---

problem is complicated. In Chapter 4, I will attempt to examine the implications of Paul's directives in 1 Corinthians for patronal ties in Corinth.

2. The Church in Roman Corinth

again.[1] Hence, in 1 Cor. 16.12, Paul gives his reply, indicating that even though for the moment Apollos would not go back to Corinth, he had urged Apollos strongly to do so. What does this indicate? Hurd suggests that, in clarifying his stance with regard to Apollos's next visit to Corinth, that is, in suggesting that he did not try to stop Apollos from visiting Corinth again, Paul gives the impression that he is trying to avoid unnecessary misunderstanding.[2] The problem does not appear to be between Apollos and Paul. For Paul at times names Apollos as his co-worker (1 Cor. 3.9) and his brother (1 Cor. 16.12). The problem again seems to be between Paul and some of the Corinthians. The different attitudes the Corinthians showed towards Apollos and Paul not only suggests that the church was indeed divided, but also that some preferred Apollos to Paul (1 Cor. 4.6).[3] One may then ask why the Corinthians responded so favourably toward Apollos and yet so negatively toward Paul. A probe into Apollos's background and style of ministry may provide some hints to an answer.

Apart from Paul, Apollos appears to be the only teacher who had visited the church prior to the writing of 1 Corinthians (1 Cor. 3.5-9; Acts 18.24–19.1).[4] According to Acts 18.24-28 Apollos was an

---

1. Hurd has shown that, in the church's letter to Paul, a request was probably made to inquire if Apollos would visit them again soon (*I Corinthians*, pp. 206-207).

2. Hurd, *I Corinthians*, pp. 206-207.

3. The prepositions ὑπέρ... κατά should be taken as 'for... against' (Robertson, *Word Pictures*, IV, p. 105; J.T. Fitzgerald, *Cracks in an Earthen Vessel: An Examination of the Catalogues of Hardships in the Corinthian Correspondence* [Atlanta: Scholars Press, 1988], p. 127 n. 27). It seems best to see Paul as referring to the Corinthians' preference of one teacher to another, namely, Apollos against Paul (Findlay, 'First Epistle to the Corinthians', p. 800; Barrett, *First Corinthians*, p. 107; Meeks, *First Urban Christians*, p. 117; Fee, *First Corinthians*, p. 169).

4. Some have suggested that Cephas himself also visited Corinth and that the influence of Cephas was behind the problems in the church at Corinth (e.g. Barrett, 'Cephas', in *Essays on Paul*, pp. 28-39; P. Vielhauer, 'Paulus und die Kephaspartei in Korinth', *NTS* 21 [1975], pp. 341-52; F. Young and D.F. Ford, *Meaning and Truth in 2 Corinthians* [London: SPCK, 1987], pp. 49-50). Others do not agree (Hurd, *I Corinthians*, pp. 54, 99-100, 214; Dahl, 'Church at Corinth', p. 323 n. 1; J. Murphy-O'Connor, *I Corinthians* [Dublin: Veritas Publications, 1979], p. 11). In any case, it is not necessary to assume that Cephas actually visited Corinth in order to account for the problems in 1 Corinthians.

Alexandrian Jew who was eloquent (λόγιος)[1] and well versed in the Scriptures. From this it has been inferred that Apollos, not unlike Philo, would probably be acquainted with Hellenistic Jewish philosophy and allegorical interpretation of the Scriptures,[2] and that he would also be a man with rhetorical abilities.[3]

Since this picture of Apollos is not derived directly from Paul, Munck rightly cautions against any hasty acceptance of its representation.[4] However, Paul is obviously reacting to matters related to rhetoric (1 Cor. 1.17; 2.1-5; 4.19-20) and wisdom (1 Cor. 2.6–3.3) in the early chapters of 1 Corinthians.[5] It may be inferred that these were the things which the Corinthians were interested in.[6] It is then possible to suggest that Apollos would have strengthened, if not introduced,[7] the development of such interests among the Corinthians. If Apollos and the Corinthians shared these common interests, it would also not be surprising to see a cordial relationship develop between Apollos and some of the Corinthians. As a corollary, since Paul, according to his own account, had no use of rhetorical skill in his preaching (1 Cor. 2.1-5; 2 Cor. 10.10), this would explain partly why

---

1. The word λόγιος can mean both 'eloquent' (RSV) or 'learned' (NIV). Munck is hesitant to choose between the two meanings (*Paul and the Salvation of Mankind*, p. 144). Bruce suggests that Apollos could be both eloquent and learned (*The Pauline Circle*, p. 52).
2. Bruce, *The Pauline Circle*, pp. 51-57; J. Stambaugh and D. Balch, *The Social World of the First Christians* (London: SPCK, 1986), p. 165.
3. Meeks, *First Urban Christians*, pp. 61, 117; Bruce, *The Pauline Circle*, p. 52.
4. Munck, *Paul and the Salvation of Mankind*, pp. 143-48.
5. For a discussion of the various shades of meaning of σοφία in the early chapters of 1 Corinthians, see Barrett, *Essays on Paul*, pp. 8-12; see also R.A. Horsley, 'Wisdom of Word and Words of Wisdom in Corinth', *CBQ* 39 (1977), pp. 224-39.
6. Meeks, *First Urban Christians*, pp. 61, 117-18.
7. R.A. Horsley asserts that Apollos was the one responsible for introducing the Corinthians to matters related to the heavenly Sophia ('"How Can Some of You Say that There is no Resurrection of the Dead?" Spiritual Elitism in Corinth', *NovT* 20 [1978], p. 229). R.M. Grant, however, suggests that 'it was Apollos who permitted the Corinthians to interpret their religion as a form of popular philosophy' ('The Wisdom of the Corinthians', in *The Joy of Study* [ed. S.E. Johnson; New York: Macmillan, 1951], p. 55). It is also possible that Apollos and the Corinthians who were interested in *sophia* and rhetoric simply reinforced one another (Fee, *First Corinthians*, pp. 56-57).

Paul was not favoured by some of the Corinthians.

But who could the people be who were interested in rhetoric? It is significant to note that the socially powerful[1] and the rich[2] in the early Empire had a special love for rhetoric. Not surprisingly, such people were those whom itinerant philosophers or teachers, such as the sophists, sought to befriend in order to gain political and material benefits.[3] Many of these sophists became rich through their charging of fees (μισθοί) for the instructions they provided.[4] Since some of the Corinthians, presumably the supporters of Apollos, apparently loved rhetoric, it would therefore be natural to suspect that they were the educated and the rich, that is, the patrons in the church.[5] If this was the case, it points again to the possibility that those who were against Paul could be powerful patrons in the church. If Apollos was a friend of the rich patrons in the church, may we then surmise, as P. Marshall does,[6] that Apollos was one who accepted financial assistance from the Corinthians, that is, a teacher who accepted the patronage of the rich and the powerful in the church?

The image of Apollos, in any case, looks not unlike that of an itinerant teacher.[7] He was a traveller and, as mentioned above, he came from Alexandria. Soon we see him in Ephesus (Acts 18.24), and

---

1. The importance the powerful people in the early Empire placed on rhetoric and the connection between rhetorical and oratorical ability and political pursuit in the early Empire seem to be reflected in some of the letters of Pliny the Younger. When Pliny recommends a candidate for a post, one of the qualities which he often mentions is the candidate's literary or oratorical ability (*Ep.* 2.9.4; 2.13.6-7; 3.2.3; 7.22.2). He actually claimed that he liked introducing promising young men with oratorical ability to the courts in order to set them on the way to fame (*Ep.* 6.23.2). As Corinth was a Roman colony, the ruling elites there might share a similar kind of mentality. See also Gelzer, *Roman Nobility*, pp. 80-86; Garnsey and Saller, *Roman Empire*, pp. 180-82.

2. Trimalchio, a rich freedman, who invited among others, Agamemnon, a teacher of rhetoric, to dinner might also have reflected a typical situation in the early Empire (Petronius, *Satyricon* 48).

3. Garnsey and Saller, *Roman Empire*, p. 182. For a detailed discussion, see Bowersock, *Greek Sophists*.

4. Hock, *Social Context*, pp. 52-53.

5. Theissen, *Social Setting*, pp. 97-98. Cf. Munck, *Paul and the Salvation of Mankind*, pp. 152-53, 162 n. 2.

6. Marshall, *Enmity*, p. 253.

7. Bruce, *The Pauline Circle*, p. 52.

then in Corinth (1 Cor. 3.6; Acts 19.1). Before long, he was possibly back to Ephesus again (1 Cor. 16.12). Meeks interprets Apollos's ability to travel independently as an indication that he was a man of some wealth.[1] Yet Tit. 3.13 gives the impression that Apollos was also dependent on others' support for his travel.[2] So Apollos's financial status remains ambiguous.

But it is significant to note that, in the undisputed letters of Paul the problem of μισθός is discussed predominantly in 1 Corinthians (1 Cor. 3.8, 14; 9.17, 18).[3] It is also noteworthy that the train of thought is somehow interrupted[4] by the raising of the issue of μισθός in 1 Cor. 3.8b with reference to the work of Paul and that of Apollos. Moreover, while in 1 Cor. 3.8a, Paul suggests that he and Apollos are equal, in 1 Cor. 3.8b, he seems to emphasize their difference in terms of their work and the pay each will receive for it.[5] Why does Paul raise the issue of reward or pay at this point? What purpose does it serve to emphasize the difference between Paul and Apollos in terms of work and pay?

Paul's reference is not immediately clear. The idea of μισθός may be introduced to echo the idea that Paul and Apollos are nothing before God and can only hope for a reward from God if the work of each is acceptable (1 Cor. 3.13-15).[6] Or it may serve to emphasize the idea that both Paul and Apollos work under another who determines their pay (1 Cor. 4.1-5).[7] What is less clear is the reason why Paul should want to emphasize their difference in terms of their work and

---

1. Meeks, *First Urban Christians*, p. 61.
2. The author of the letter asks the reader to send Apollos on the way and to see that he lacks nothing (Tit. 3.13) (Malherbe, 'Hospitality', p. 230 n. 11). Since this image of Apollos is preserved in the Pastoral tradition, it is therefore somewhat dubious. But what would give rise to such an image if Apollos did not actually receive support for his travel?
3. Apart from 1 Corinthians, the word μισθός is used only in Rom. 4.4. On the debate over financial support by the philosophers, see Hock, *Social Context*, ch. 4.
4. Conzelmann, *I Corinthians*, p. 74 n. 50.
5. Roberston and Plummer suggest that the repeated use of ἴδιον 'marks the separate responsibility' (*First Corinthians*, p. 58). Fee however sees the difference in terms of the pay each will receive (*First Corinthians*, p. 133). Perhaps both ideas could be included (Findlay, 'First Epistle to the Corinthians', p. 789).
6. Conzelmann, *I Corinthians*, p. 74; Fee, *First Corinthians*, p. 133.
7. Fee, *First Corinthians*, p. 133.

their pay. At this stage, Paul only mentions it in passing,[1] since, presumably, he does not want to dwell on the issue. Hence, we cannot be sure as to what Paul's point could be. But it is to be noted that the issue of μισθός is brought up again in 1 Cor. 9.1-18 where Paul clearly underlines the difference between his work and the μισθός which he receives and the work of the rival apostles and the μισθός which they receive. While the μισθός which the rival apostles receive for their services appears to be material benefits, such as financial aid (1 Cor. 9.6, 12a), the μισθός which Paul receives for his preaching of the gospel may be the boast that he preaches it free of charge (1 Cor. 9.17-18).[2] It is thus tempting to see Paul's emphasis on the distinction between Apollos and himself in 1 Cor. 3.8b as paralleled by the contrast presented in 1 Corinthians 9. For that matter, we could legitimately deduce that Apollos was one of those rival teachers who accepted payment for his teaching.[3]

If the above is the case, two points can be inferred. First, Apollos's acceptance of pay and Paul's refusal to accept financial support from the church may be another reason why Apollos was preferred to Paul. Secondly, if Apollos did receive financial aid from the church, he would resemble a friend or client of some of the rich patrons in the church. In that case, we have an example in Corinth which indicates that patronal relations were already at work in the church.

Paul and Financial Support

Whether or not Apollos was a client who received money from some rich patrons in the church, the problem of μισθός, as mentioned above, is discussed in 1 Corinthians 9 with reference to the apostleship of Paul (1 Cor. 9.1-3). This discussion in 1 Corinthians 9 is part of a larger unit which deals with the problem of food offered to idols (8.1–11.1). In 1 Cor. 8.13 Paul asks the Corinthians to forego their right to eat meat for the good of others. 1 Corinthians 9 follows naturally from this theme and highlights the apostle Paul as one who forsakes his right to claim material support. Hence, Paul's discussion in

---

1. Barrett, *First Corinthians*, p. 86.
2. Barrett, *First Corinthians*, p. 21. See also E. Käsemann, *New Testament Questions of Today* (London: SCM Press, 1969), pp. 217-35; Hock, *Social Context*, p. 62.
3. Marshall, *Enmity*, p. 253; Fee, *First Corinthians*, p. 409.

1 Corinthians 9 could serve a paradigmatic function.[1] But Paul's defence (ἀπολογία) could also serve an apologetic purpose.[2] One of the reasons why Paul has to defend himself is his foregoing of his right to claim financial support from the church (1 Cor. 9.12). It is this particular aspect of Paul's defence which concerns us here.

Why did Paul have to defend himself on the issue of financial support? What did such support represent? Who in the church would care about financial matters? If, as I have suggested, Paul could have been challenged by some of the rich patrons in the church, could Paul's defence of his refusal to accept financial support from the church be directed to these people?

Since Paul's policy of not accepting financial support from the Corinthian church is explained in Paul's defence of his apostleship (1 Cor. 9.1-18), it may suggest that Paul's action might have led the church to doubt if Paul could be a real apostle (cf. 2 Cor. 11.7-15; 12.11-13).[3] Paul's discussion thus implies that certain norms regarding financial support which were accepted by the Corinthians may have been violated. The nature of such norms may be understood in various ways. Theissen suggests that Paul's working to support himself and his refusal to accept financial support from the church could have been seen as a violation of the norm of the early Christians, that is, the requirement of charismatic poverty and a trust in God's grace, which is reflected in the Synoptic tradition (cf. Lk. 10.3-8).[4] Generally speaking, Theissen's suggestion is not impossible. It is, however, doubtful if the ideal of 'poverty' reflected in the Synoptic tradition, would be treasured by the opponents of Paul in the Hellenistic city of Corinth who, as Theissen has also suggested, could be the powerful patrons in the church.[5] It is also likely that Theissen's typology, that is, the itinerant charismatics versus the community

---

1. W. Willis, 'An Apostolic Apologia: The Form and Function of I Corinthians 9', *JSNT* 24 (1985), pp. 33-48; C.H. Talbert, *Reading Corinthians: A Literary and Theological Commentary on 1 and 2 Corinthians* (New York: Crossroad, 1987), p. 61; E.S. Fiorenza, 'I Corinthians', *HBC*, p. 1180.

2. Barrett, *First Corinthians*, pp. 199-202; Hock, *Social Context*, pp. 60-61; Fee, *First Corinthians*, pp. 392-94.

3. Theissen, *Social Setting*, p. 41.

4. Theissen, *Social Setting*, p. 43.

5. Theissen, *Social Setting*, p. 57.

organizers, is an oversimplified one. In this respect, Hock's study seems the more helpful.

Hock has shown that the means of support which a philosopher should adopt was an issue often debated by philosophers in Paul's day who upheld different ideals. Hock has been able to identify four possible means of support. They are charging fees, entering the household of the rich and the powerful, begging, and working.[1] Against this background Hock goes on to argue that the Corinthian situation basically involved two of these options, namely, 'Paul *working* to support himself, and his opponents *entering the households of well-to-do Corinthians*'.[2] Hock's study is illuminating and would fit the Hellenistic context of Corinth well.[3] If Hock is right, then patronage could have been an important factor in the Corinthian situation addressed by Paul.

That a teacher or a missionary worker should have accepted financial support from the rich and the powerful might even have been the norm accepted by the Corinthians, especially the richer ones. If that was the case, Paul appears to have distanced himself from it. In his conclusion Hock suggests that the Corinthians expected Paul to accept their support. Since Paul decided to work to support himself, he may have prompted resistance and criticism.[4] The possibility that the conflict between Paul and some of the Corinthians could be precipitated by Paul's refusal to accept financial support from the rich Corinthians is noted by Judge, and is further developed by Marshall in the light of the convention of friendship. According to this convention, 'status (was) conferred by the greater to the lesser', and 'full conformity with the wishes of the initiator' was expected.[5] Marshall argues that the rich and powerful Corinthians may have offered to give Paul money as a symbol of friendship, not as pay.[6] Paul's refusal to accept the money therefore amounted to a rejection of friendship. Consequently the patrons may have felt that they were dishonoured and enmity between Paul and these patrons could have been

1. Hock, *Social Context*, pp. 52-59.
2. Hock, *Social Context*, p. 65.
3. Hock's reconstruction is accepted by Fee, *First Corinthians*, pp. 399-400.
4. Hock, *Social Context*, p. 65.
5. Judge, 'Cultural Conformity and Innovation', p. 15. For a full discussion of the convention of friendship and enmity, see Marshall, *Enmity*, pp. 1-129.
6. Marshall, *Enmity*, pp. 218-33.

generated.[1] Marshall's study partly explains the hostility between Paul and the rich and powerful Corinthians. Perhaps we may add that what Judge and Marshall call 'friendship' is, in effect, patronage. If Judge and Marshall are right, then those who opposed Paul in the church would have been the rich and powerful patrons who sought to extend their patronage to Paul. In which case, it is clear that Paul's opponents probably should be looked for among the rich and powerful patrons in the church, and also that patronage does help us understand some of the problems in the Corinthian church.

The Rich and the Poor

In Chapter 1 we saw how patronage might have provided a way for integrating unequal relationships in a household and a club. Since members of the Christian community in Corinth obviously met and worshipped in the houses of the richer members (Rom. 16.23), it might have looked somewhat like a club which met in a house. It may also be inferred that, through letting the church meet in his house, a householder functioned as a patron to that church.[2] Hence, Judge is able to paint the following picture of a house church:

> Far from being a socially depressed group, then, if the Corinthians are at all typical, the Christians were dominated by a socially pretentious section of the population of the big cities. Beyond that they seem to have drawn on a broad constituency, probably representing the household dependents of the leading members. . . Certainly the phenomenon led to constant differences among the Christians themselves, and helps to explain the persistent stress on not using membership in an association of equals to justify breaking down the conventional hierarchy of the household. . . The interest of the owner and patron class is obvious in this. It was they who sponsored Christianity to their dependents.[3]

It is important to note, as Judge has observed, that the hierarchical difference in a house would have been preserved in a house church. Against this background, we may briefly examine the problem of divisions in the church when it met to eat the Lord's supper (1 Cor. 11.17-34).

What could have given rise to the problem of divisions at the Lord's

---

1. Marshall, *Enmity*, pp. 257-58.
2. Judge, *Christian Groups*, pp. 49-61; Meeks, *First Urban Christians*, p. 78; Malherbe, *Social Aspects*, pp. 97-98.
3. Judge, *Christian Groups*, p. 60.

2. The Church in Roman Corinth

table? It is significant to note, as Meeks does,[1] that the problem does not appear to have involved 'the jealousy between followers of Apollos and partisans of Paul or the "realized eschatology" of the *pneumatikoi*'. On the other hand, Paul's treatment strongly suggests, as Theissen and others have noted,[2] that the divisions were related to social distinctions, that is, between the rich and the poor. For those who have nothing, Paul says, are humiliated by those who have houses (1 Cor. 11.22). Our concern here is the relationship between this aspect of the problem and patronage.

What relationship could patronage have with the humiliation of the poor at the Lord's table? When the Corinthians gathered to observe the Lord's supper, it is conceivable that each member of the community would bring his own portion of food to the meal[3] and that the rich would have brought more.[4] But it is not impossible that the richer patrons could have provided all that was needed for the celebration of the Lord's supper.[5] Moreover, it is also conceivable that, in accordance with the usual practice in clubs or private feasts, more food, even better food, could have been apportioned to the patron or his social equals and less to the poor or the ordinary members.[6] This might have been what Paul had in mind when he suggests that some of the Corinthians eat their own suppers, and that while one goes hungry, another gets drunk (1 Cor. 11.21). While the arrangement of seats for the meal would probably be limited by the physical environment,[7] it is not impossible that the poor could also have been humiliated when seats in the triclinium were reserved for the rich and powerful patrons while they were left to find their places in the atrium.

If this was the situation behind the conflict at the Lord's table, we

---

1. Meeks, *First Urban Christians*, p. 67.
2. Theissen's study on this problem is especially noteworthy (*Social Setting*, pp. 145-74). See also Meeks, *First Urban Christians*, p. 68; Barrett, *First Corinthians*, p. 261; Fee, *First Corinthians*, p. 531).
3. So von Dobschütz, *Primitive Church*, pp. 60-61.
4. Barrett, *First Corinthians*, p. 263.
5. Theissen, *Social Setting*, p. 148.
6. Theissen, *Social Setting*, pp. 153-59; Meeks, *First Urban Christians*, p. 68.
7. The triclinium could only accommodate about 9 to 12 guests at table. On the problem of accommodating the whole church in one place, see especially J. Murphy-O'Connor, *St Paul's Corinth* (Wilmington, DE: Michael Glazier, 1983), pp. 153-61.

would have another example which strongly suggests that patronage does help to explain some of the problems in the church at Corinth. In short, the poor could have been humiliated by the rich and honourable patrons when the conventions of patron–client relationship were followed and different classes of people were treated differently.

Conclusion

As mentioned at the beginning of this chapter, I do not presume that I can supply more accurate information concerning the situation at Corinth. I can only utilize various hints to 'supply' the missing information, to glean the 'social data'[1] of the situation in Corinth confronted by Paul in 1 Corinthians. If my investigation into the social situation in the Corinthian church is acceptable, then it allows me to make two remarks. First, it seems plausible to suggest that, when Paul wrote 1 Corinthians, he had been challenged by some rich and powerful patrons in the church partly on the grounds that he did not look like an apostle since he worked to support himself and refused to accept financial support from the church, that is, from them. Secondly, it is plausible that patron–client ties made up an important part of the relational ties in the church, and that light could be shed on some of the problems inside the church, such as divisions at the Lord's table, when they are understood against the background of patronage. Can we glean any further social data from 1 Corinthians?

---

1. Fiorenza, 'Rhetorical Situation', p. 390.

Chapter 3

THE POWER OF THE PATRONS

Some time after he left Corinth Paul wrote his first letter to the church at Corinth (1 Cor. 5.9). Not much is known about the content of Paul's 'previous' letter to the church.[1] It is even more difficult to assess Paul's purpose in writing the letter. We only know that, in his 'previous' letter to the Corinthians, Paul advised them not to associate with immoral people (1 Cor. 5.9). Since Paul had to clarify the meaning of his earlier instruction in 1 Corinthians (1 Cor. 5.10), obviously his instruction was either misunderstood or misinterpreted by the Corinthians. According to Hurd, it is likely that the Corinthians deliberately misrepresented Paul's earlier instruction in order to make him look ridiculous and to object to his directions to them.[2] If this was the case, it would lend further support to my contention in Chapter 2 that Paul's authority was not respected by some of the people in the church.[3]

At this point it is more important to note the instruction in the 'previous' letter which Paul had to clarify. Since Paul denied that it was his intention to ask the Corinthians to withdraw totally from the world (1 Cor. 5.10),[4] this implies that the relationship between the Corinthians and the pagan world was a point at issue. If, as Hurd has suggested, the Corinthians were arguing with Paul on this issue, it suggests that some people in the church were quite keen to maintain contacts with their pagan neighbours. As a matter of fact, several of

1. For a detailed discussion of Paul's previous letter to the Corinthians, see Hurd, *I Corinthians*, pp. 214-70.
2. Hurd, *I Corinthians*, pp. 149-54.
3. Fee, *First Corinthians*, p. 221.
4. The use of οὐπάντως suggests that the separation from the immoral men in the world is not to be understood as total or absolute (Barrett, *First Corinthians*, p. 130).

the problems which Paul discusses in 1 Corinthians are problems which arose out of contacts with the pagan world. We see a man associating with his stepmother who probably was not a member of the church (1 Cor. 5.1).[1] We find another member of the community bringing a suit against a Christian brother before the pagan judge (1 Cor. 6.1).[2] Others took part in idolatrous pagan feasts (1 Cor. 8.10; 10.1-22). Hence, it is natural to ask who these people were and why they wanted to maintain their ties with the pagans. Should we also look for them from among the rich and powerful patrons in the church?

Opponents in 1 Corinthians

Some of the problems mentioned above, such as eating at table in an idol's temple and the cohabiting of a man with his father's wife, have often been studied in terms of their relationship with the theology or religiosity of the Corinthians. It is necessary to review briefly some of the representative studies on the religiosity of the Corinthians so as to highlight the approach followed in this chapter and to suggest how we may build upon and move beyond these studies.

Generally speaking, one may classify studies on the theological context of the Corinthian opponents[3] into three main categories. Some hold that the influence behind 1 Corinthians is best explained in the light of Gnosticism.[4] Many, however, believe that such opponents can be better characterized as enthusiastic Hellenists or upholders of a

---

1. Since Paul did not pass judgment on the wife, a stepmother, many commentators suggest that she probably was not a member of the church (e.g. Robertson and Plummer, *First Corinthians*, p. 96; Barrett, *First Corinthians*, p. 121).
2. Paul actually uses the word ἄπιστοι in 1 Cor. 6.6. See also Barrett, *First Corinthians*, p. 135; Orr and Walther, *I Corinthians*, pp. 193-94.
3. By 'opponents', I mean those in the Christian community at Corinth who opposed Paul at the time of the writing of 1 Corinthians. It does not appear that false teachers from outside were already in the church at this stage (so D. Georgi, *The Opponents of Paul in Second Corinthians* [Philadelphia: Fortress Press, 1986], p. 317; E.E. Ellis, 'Paul and His Opponents', in *Christianity, Judaism and Other Greco-Roman Cults*, I [ed. J. Neusner; Leiden: Brill, 1975], p. 286).
4. So, e.g., Schmithals, *Gnosticism*.

3. *The Power of the Patrons*

kind of realized eschatology.[1] There are others who regard these opponents as reflecting a Hellenistic-Jewish theological outlook.[2]

Gnosticism

It has been quite common to designate Paul's opponents in Corinth, even those behind 1 Corinthians, as Gnostics.[3] The major proponent of this view in the past few decades is Schmithals who sees the opponents in Corinth as Jewish Gnostics.[4] The problem of the origin, nature and history of Gnosticism is too big a problem to be discussed adequately here. It seems fair to say with R.McL. Wilson that, while 'Gnostic' ideas which subsequently built up the Gnostic system can be found in 1 Corinthians, it does not follow that 1 Corinthians can be interpreted in the light of 'Gnosticism' without resulting in distortion.[5] Schmithals's definition of the Corinthian opponents as Gnostics clearly suffers from this basic weakness.[6] In addition, some of the prominent ideas in 1 Corinthians, like the *pneumatikos–psychikos*

---

1. See, e.g., Käsemann, *New Testament Questions of Today*, pp. 108-37; A.C. Thiselton, 'Realized Eschatology at Corinth', *NTS* 24 (1978), pp. 510-26.
2. See, e.g., R.A. Horsley, 'Pneumatikos vs. Psychikos: Distinctions of Spiritual Status among the Corinthians', *HTR* 69 (1976), pp. 169-288; 'Wisdom of Word', pp. 224-39; 'The Background of the Confessional Formula in 1 Kor. 8.6', *ZNW* 69 (1978), pp. 130-35; ' "How Can Some of You Say?" ', pp. 203-31; 'Consciousness and Freedom among the Corinthians: 1 Corinthians 8–10', *CBQ* 40 (1978), pp. 574-89; 'Spiritual Marriage with Sophia', *VC* 33 (1979), pp. 30-54; 'Gnosis in Corinth: 1 Corinthians 8.1-6', *NTS* 27 (1980), pp. 32-51.
3. See also Georgi, *Opponents*, p. 317; Theissen, *Social Setting*, pp. 132-36; U. Wilckens, *Weisheit und Torheit: Eine exegetisch-religionsgeschichtliche Untersuchung zu 1 Kor 1 und 2* (Tübingen: Mohr, 1959); J.D.G. Dunn, *Unity and Diversity in the New Testament* (London: SCM Press, 1977), pp. 277-79.
4. Schmithals, *Gnosticism*, pp. 289-93.
5. On the problem in seeing Gnosticism as a system in first-century texts, such as 1 Corinthians, R.McL. Wilson writes, 'To speak of Gnosis in Corinth, and then to interpret the teaching of Paul's opponents by a wholesale introduction of ideas from the second-century systems, is to run the risk of seriously distorting the whole picture' (*Gnosis and the New Testament* [Philadelphia: Fortress Press, 1968], p. 52. See also R.McL. Wilson, 'How Gnostic were the Corinthians?' *NTS* 19 [1972], pp. 65-74).
6. Conzelmann, *1 Corinthians*, p. 15; Fee, *First Corinthians*, p. 11. See also G.W. MacRae's review of *Gnosticism in Corinth*, *Int* 26 (1972), pp. 490-91.

language, has not been discussed adequately by Schmithals.[1] In any case, even if the opponents in Corinth can be called 'Gnostics or proto-Gnostics', this identification has not been able to provide, in particular, an adequate explanation for the problems Paul dealt with in 1 Cor. 5.1–6.11 which are of interest to us.[2] Schmithals himself actually admits that the litigation before the pagan court is an odd piece of evidence which bears no direct relationship with his Gnostic scheme.[3] In view of these problems, many scholars are justified in holding the view that, if a contemporary parallel can be found, it is not necessary to resort to Gnosticism for light on problems in 1 Corinthians.[4] We have to look elsewhere for a way to unravel the significance of the problems behind 1 Cor. 5.1–6.11.

Hellenistic Enthusiasm

First-century Corinth was basically a city with a Hellenistic past. It is only natural to look to its Hellenistic religio-philosophical heritage for ideological parallels to the theology of the Corinthians. Hence, some scholars see the problems in the church at Corinth as originating from interaction with 'its pagan past and its environment'.[5] In this respect, Käsemann's view may be quoted as an example. It is Käsemann's contention that the Corinthians were Hellenists, and that the problems in Corinth were manifestations of a Hellenized form of Christianity. He draws the following picture of the Corinthians:

1. It has been pointed out by B.A. Pearson that the anthropological contrast which Schmithals works with is one between *pneumatikos–sarkikos*, and not one between *pneumatikos–psychikos* (*The Pneumatikos-Psychikos Terminology in 1 Corinthians: A Study in the Theology of the Corinthian Opponents of Paul and its Relation to Gnosticism* [Missoula, MT: Scholars Press, 1973], p. 87 n. 10).
2. H. Koester identifies the 'strong people' in Corinth as 'gnostics or protognostics', but fails to see a connection between these people and the problems dealt with in 1 Cor. 5.1–6.11 (*Introduction to the New Testament*, II [New York: de Gruyter, 1982], pp. 121, 122).
3. Schmithals, *Gnosticism*, pp. 286-87.
4. Thiselton, 'Realized Eschatology', pp. 525-26; W.A. Meeks (ed.), *The Writings of St Paul* (New York: Norton, 1972), p. 24. But J. Murphy-O'Connor simply rejected the view that the Corinthians were influenced by Gnosticism ('The First Letter to the Corinthians', *NJBC*, p. 801).
5. Bornkamm, *Paul*, p. 72.

3. *The Power of the Patrons*   117

Today we may take it for granted that the dominant group in Corinth believed themselves to have reached the goal of salvation already—in the shape of baptism—and Christian experience here on earth meant for them solely the temporal representation of heavenly being. For that the resurrection of the dead has already happened was not only the slogan of the heretical teachers of II Tim. 2.18; it was the basic assumption of that Christianity which, moving in circles where the writ of Hellenism ran, understood the Christian religion as a mystery religion.[1]

Käsemann's position is defended further by Thiselton who describes the Corinthian position as 'an over-realized eschatology' which 'leads to an "enthusiastic" view of the Spirit'.[2] In accordance with this view, the Corinthians who adopted such a position believed that they were free and above moral obligation. The cohabiting of a man with his father's wife and the eating of food offered to idols are seen as manifestations of the newly found freedom.[3] The effort to characterize the Corinthian position as reflecting a kind of 'realized eschatology' has not gone unchallenged.[4] Such a characterization of the Corinthian outlook may need to be refined at different points.[5] Nevertheless, it may perhaps be granted that it is a 'sufficient' explanation, as has been argued,[6] for the theological outlook of the opponents at Corinth.[7] Having said that, it should be pointed out that ideas, even libertarian ideas, do not come to expression in a vacuum. It is therefore necessary to look also into the social situation in which such ideas were expressed in Corinth.

Hellenistic-Jewish Philosophy
Regarding the situation in Corinth, we should not overlook the fact that some members of the Christian community there were Jews.

1. Käsemann, *New Testament Questions of Today*, p. 125.
2. Thiselton, 'Realized Eschatology', p. 512.
3. 'Realized Eschatology', pp. 515-16, 520. Cf. also Dahl, 'Church at Corinth', pp. 332-33.
4. E.E. Ellis, 'Christ Crucified', in *Reconciliation and Hope: New Testament Essays in Atonement and Eschatology Presented to L.L. Morris* (ed. R. Banks; Exeter: Paternoster Press, 1974), pp. 69-75.
5. For a critique of the idea of a realized resurrection, see Horsley, '"How Can Some of You Say?"', pp. 203-204.
6. Thiselton, 'Realized Eschatology', p. 512.
7. Cf. A.J.M. Wedderburn, 'The Problem of the Denial of the Resurrection in I Corinthians XV', *NovT* 23 (1981), pp. 233-34.

Moreover, Apollos, a Jew from Egypt, was able to gather together a group of followers in the church. Following this lead, some scholars believe that Hellenistic-Jewish traditions may provide as good, if not better, a context for explaining the religiosity of the Corinthians.[1]

On parallels between Hellenistic-Jewish traditions and the religiosity of Paul's opponents in 1 Corinthians, works by R.A. Horsley cover most, though not all, of the problems in Corinth, and deserve special mention.[2] According to Horsley[3] the Corinthians probably were caught up in an enthusiastic devotion to heavenly Sophia who was not necessarily identical with Christ whom they regarded only as 'a teacher of divine Sophia, a great mystagogue, perhaps similar to Moses in Philo's writings'.[4] Because they possessed this heavenly Sophia the Corinthians believed that they had reached the highest spiritual status and were spiritual people. The empirical manifestation of their transcendental spiritual status was their eloquent expression and 'the individual experience of ecstatic prophecy, including glossolalia'.[5] Since they had achieved such a status, they believed that they were no longer attached to earthly and bodily matters. So they denied the resurrection of the dead (the body), and were not interested in the cross of Christ. Moreover, they were able to claim a higher status over those who were not 'spiritual' people.

Horsley's attempt to draw a parallel between the theological outlook of the Corinthians and the Hellenistic-Jewish traditions is intriguing, to say the least. He has succeeded in giving a possible explanation for the elitist attitude of the Corinthians. Since 1 Cor. 8.4 seems to indicate that the Corinthians accepted the Jewish idea of monotheism, it renders Horsley's thesis even more attractive. However, it should also be pointed out that it is perhaps not Horsley's intent to put forward

---

1. It is the contention of Pearson that the *pneumatikos–psychikos* terminology should be understood in terms of a Hellenistic-Jewish context (*Pneumatikos–Psychikos Terminology*, p. 82). But see Horsley's critique of Pearson's position, 'Pneumatikos vs. Psychikos', pp. 270-73.
2. In addition, see J.A. Davis, *Wisdom and Spirit: An Investigation of 1 Corinthians: 1.18–3.20 against the Background of Jewish Sapiential Traditions in the Greco-Roman Period* (Lanham, MD: University Press of America, 1984).
3. See especially Horsley, '"How Can Some of You Say?"'.
4. ' "How Can Some of You Say?"', p. 230.
5. ' "How Can Some of You Say?"', p. 230. See also Horsley, 'Wisdom of Word', p. 231.

3. *The Power of the Patrons* 119

some Philonic parallels as the only source for the religiosity of the Corinthians. In fact, Horsley himself admits that the uniquely Corinthian terminology, like the *pneumatikos–psychikos* contrast, is not found in Philo,[1] and that it can be paralleled in various sources.[2] In any case, Horsley has not dealt with some of the problems in Corinth which are of interest to us, notably the attempt to settle disputes in court (1 Cor. 6.1-11) and the rite of baptism for the dead (1 Cor. 15.29). It is therefore necessary to look further for an explanation to these problems.

Summary
I may now conclude this brief review of studies on the theological nature of the opposition behind 1 Corinthians. What lessons can we draw from this review? First, it may be said that our understanding of the context with which to explain the religiosity of the Corinthians has been enhanced greatly. Nonetheless, it appears that none of the interpretations discussed above has been able to account for every detail of the theological outlook of the Corinthians. Generally speaking, the theological outlook of the Corinthians can be understood, without resorting to Gnosticism, in the light of the syncretistic milieu of Hellenism with special reference to Hellenistic-Jewish traditions. In any case, the following comment by Conzelmann still serves as a good reminder. He writes,

> We must not seek to define this material too precisely. Ideas of Jewish and Greek origin (popular philosophy), such as could be picked up on the streets, traditional views of Greek religion, products of the mysteries (initiations, ecstasies)—all these are present and cannot be neatly separated.[3]

Secondly, the above-mentioned studies into the religiosity of the Corinthians focus mainly on the self-understanding of the Corinthians. They have been able to explain how the Corinthians could have justified their actions in the name of freedom as provided by their theology. The social reality behind such actions, especially those which arose from contacts with the pagan world, and the implications of such actions for power relationships in the church, have not been

1. Horsley, 'Pneumatikos vs. Psychikos', p. 280.
2. Horsley, '"How Can Some of You Say?"', p. 207.
3. Conzelmann, *I Corinthians*, p. 15.

explored fully by them. As seen in the discussion in Chapter 2, Theissen and others have carried out some work in this direction with interesting results.[1] Still, some of the problems in the church are worth further examination in the light of the social context in first-century Corinth. In particular, were actions such as presenting their case before the pagan court aimed only at expressing their newly found freedom? Was such freedom available to all? Would every Corinthian seek redress for damages before the pagan court? It has been argued that the Corinthians apparently were very enthusiastic about heavenly things. If so, how could they behave in so secular a fashion as to settle disputes before the pagan judges? Likewise, how could a man, in breach of Roman and Jewish laws, be able to unite with his stepmother without being prosecuted? So too, we might ask, what significance did the participation in idols' feasts have on the power relationships in the church? Who were the people who underwent baptism on behalf of the dead? What did the rite signify?

The Corinthians and the Pagans

In this chapter, I propose to examine, from a socio-historical perspective, the nature and the significance of those actions of the Corinthians which arose out of contacts with pagans. Such actions include the attempt to settle disputes before the pagan magistrate, the union of a man with his father's (pagan) wife, the participation in pagan feasts and the reception of the baptismal rite on behalf of the dead. They have only received partial illumination from the hypotheses just discussed, or no illumination at all. I hope that through an examination of the sociopolitical context especially the patronal linkages in first-century Corinth, our understanding of the identity of the opponents may be enlarged and further light may be shed on the nature of the problems under study.

At this point, I must qualify further the scope of my study in this chapter. First, it is basically an attempt to understand the social background of such problems and not another study of the theology of the Corinthians. Since it is by nature a different kind of study, it is not necessary to choose between a theological explanation and the social

---

1. See the review in the Introduction and discussion in Chapter 2 and the rest of this chapter.

3. *The Power of the Patrons*

explanation proposed below. The relationship between the two may best be seen as complementary. A sociological explanation need not constitute a denial of more explicitly theological or ideological factors, and may contribute to a more fully rounded picture of the historical reality. Secondly, it should be emphasized that our understanding of the actions taken by the Corinthians is extremely limited and can easily be misguided by Paul's rhetoric. Hence the explanation proposed below for some of the actions taken by the Corinthians is unavoidably tentative. However, if my explanation makes good sense of the limited data in 1 Corinthians it should be given consideration as throwing further light on other aspects of the complex situation confronting Paul at Corinth.

Why then have I singled out the above problems for study? It may already have been noted that the main feature of the Corinthians' actions to which I have drawn particular attention is their apparent connection with pagans. In one sense, such actions may be seen as external networks or relational ties which link up two different groups of people, namely the Christians and the pagans. What significance can we attach to these ties or external networks? Boissevain,[1] on the basis of his study of the changing patterns of personal ties in Malta, has shown that ties are important channels through which resources, such as power, favours and honours, are exchanged. Thus, in the first half of this century, personal ties in the villages used to focus on parish priests, for they could influence the dispatching of benefits such as licenses and scholarships. But such powers were later transferred to government committees and boards which included foreign experts and unknown people. Consequently, people turned to other mediators, such as local members of parliament, for help. It follows that the establishment and the maintenance of certain ties most probably implies that such ties are important and of value to those who are involved. However, not all ties are of the same strength. Wellmann draws our attention to the fact that ties which connect a person in a group or community with the outside world may carry important consequences for the person's position in a local community. Thus, cosmopolitans or people who are connected to larger networks and have direct access to outside resources tend to have more

---

1. Boissevain, 'When the Saints Go Marching Out', pp. 81-96.

influence in a local network such as a community.[1]

I have already made use of the above principles in the study of the networks in Roman Corinth. The network of ties maintained by Julius Spartiaticus, an extremely important and influential figure in first-century Corinth, is typical.[2] On the one hand, he seems to have made an effort to cultivate his relationship with the Roman authorities which may be seen as a kind of trans-local tie or external network. This is seen in his involvement in activities which honoured the imperial house as a high priest of the house of Augustus in perpetuity and an *agonothetes* of the Caesarean games. On the other hand, by serving as a patron to the tribe of Calpurnia and apparently a benefactor of the colony, he would have won strong local support at Corinth. With these connections and support, it is not surprising that he was able to occupy some key influential positions in the imperial system, as procurator of Caesar and Augusta Agrippina and the first man of the Achaeans.[3] By the same token, it appears that the way ties were maintained by Spartiaticus is an indicator of the power he enjoyed in Roman Corinth.

In addition, perhaps not insignificantly, the importance of ties for the acquisition and furtherance of personal power may also be seen as being reflected in a philosophical type, namely the unjust yet honourable and powerful man, found in Plato's *Republic*:

> With his (*the unjust*) reputation for virtue (or *justice*), he will hold offices of state, ally himself by marriage to any family he may choose, become a partner in any business, and, having no scruples about being dishonest, turn all these advantages to profit. If he is involved in a lawsuit, public or private, he will get the better of his opponents, grow rich on the proceeds, and be able to help his friends and harm his enemies. Finally, he can make sacrifices to the gods and dedicate offerings with due magnificence, and, being in a much better position than the just man to serve the gods as well as his chosen friends, he may reasonably hope to stand higher in the favour of heaven. So much better, they say, Socrates, is the life prepared for the unjust by gods and men.[4]

1. Wellmann, 'Network Analysis', p. 176.
2. See discussion in Chapter 1.
3. It should be noted that Spartiaticus is but one of the many examples in first-century Corinth. Many of the local notables in Corinth also involved themselves in activities which would bring honour to Rome. See discussion in Chapter 1.
4. Plato, *Republic* 362B-C. The translation is quoted from F.M. Cornford, *The Republic of Plato* (Oxford: Clarendon Press, 1941), p. 46.

3. The Power of the Patrons

It may appear to be rash to make the above connection between networks and the passage from Plato without further documentation. It is not my intention to do so. However, it is interesting to note that Plato mentions marriage arrangements, lawsuits and sacrifices as being among the means by which the unjust who appear to be just and honourable advance and maintain their social position and power. This suggests some interesting parallels with conduct in Corinth criticized by Paul in 1 Corinthians.

In the light of the principles of networks and the examples we have seen in first-century Corinth, I would like therefore to offer the hypothesis that the Corinthians who kept their contacts with pagans, namely the immoral man, the litigants and the idolaters, may have been people who by their social status within Corinth were able to exercise influence in the church. In the following section, I will investigate the data and see if that could be the case.

The Powerful Patron

I will begin the discussion with the problem of a certain lawsuit among the Corinthians. From 1 Cor. 6.1 we know that there was at least one case of legal dispute[1] which was brought before the pagan magistrate. We also know that Paul would like to see no dispute in the church (1 Cor. 6.7-8). However, if they could not avoid having disputes among themselves, the parties involved should try to settle their disputes in the church (1 Cor. 6.2-6).[2] Even though Paul's advice is relatively clear, the reality behind 1 Cor. 6.1-11 is not easy to grasp.[3]

The Corinthians' action in bringing their grievances before the pagan court can in itself be revealing. Unfortunately, while scholars' attention has for a long time been devoted to theological questions in Corinth, important studies on Corinth by Käsemann, Thiselton and

---

1. Hurd, *I Corinthians*, p. 86; Fee, *First Corinthians*, p. 231. Robertson also thinks that Paul had a specific case in mind (*Word Pictures*, IV, p. 117). For a different opinion, see Robertson and Plummer, *First Corinthians*, p. 110.
2. Meeks, *First Urban Christians*, pp. 104, 129; M. Delcor, 'The Courts of the Church of Corinth and the Courts of Qumran', in *Paul and Qumran: Studies in New Testament Exegesis* (ed. J. Murphy-O'Connor; London: Chapman, 1969), p. 69.
3. Fiorenza, 'I Corinthians', p. 1175; P.S. Minear, 'Christ and the Congregation: 1 Corinthians 5–6', *RevExp* 80 (1983), p. 341.

Horsley apparently have not spent much time, if any, unravelling the significance of litigation among the Corinthians. Schmithals, too, has failed to see a direct relationship between the legal case and his Gnostic scheme.[1] Small wonder that Koester suspects that in 1 Cor. 5.1–6.11 Paul is not necessarily dealing with the behaviour of the strong people in the church.[2] Koester's doubt is understandable, but not necessary. As Talbert has shown, the Corinthians' attempt to seek justice before the pagan magistrate can be understood in light of their freedom from moral law (1 Cor. 6.12; 10.23) and their indifference to fleshly matters (1 Cor. 6.13; 8.8-9).[3] Hence, the litigants were probably among the 'spiritual people' in the church. Having said that, we must not conclude that the significance of the legal case has been exhausted by investigations into the theological background of the Corinthians.

Whatever the Corinthians' view of spiritual matters or heavenly things, it should be recognized, as the litigants' attempt to achieve their objectives through the pagan court strongly implies, that they were also interested in earthly or secular matters. For that matter, other questions belonging to the realm of secular society should be posed and examined. Who, in the church, for example, would resort to legal action for settling disputes? Why did the Corinthian believers go to court against each other? What was involved in the case? I will next look at the last question.

The Case

What was the litigation about? J.H. Bernard is one of the few who has sought to probe the reality behind 1 Cor. 6.1-11.[4] He postulates a situation in which the immoral son who cohabited with his stepmother (1 Cor. 5.1) was prosecuted by the father. Although such a lawsuit

---

1. Schmithals, *Gnosticism*, pp. 286-87.
2. Koester, *Introduction*, II, p. 122.
3. Talbert, *Reading Corinthians*, pp. 26-27. Cf. E. Dinkler's view quoted by Schmithals (*Gnosticism*, p. 287 n. 2).
4. J.H. Bernard, 'The Connexion between the Fifth and Sixth Chapters of 1 Corinthians', *Expositor* 7.3 (1907), pp. 433-43. Bernard's thesis has recently been revived by P. Richardson ('Judgment in Sexual Matters in 1 Corinthians 6.1-11', *NovT* 25 [1983], pp. 37-58). For a critique of such a position, see Fee, *First Corinthians*, p. 228 n. 2.

could have been linked to the case alluded to in 1 Cor. 5.1,[1] Bernard's thesis, as it stands, is less likely. For the language Paul uses with reference to the dispute, for example, the term βιωτικά which is not discussed at all by Bernard,[2] is best understood as referring to a case concerning financial or mercantile matters[3] rather than one concerning sexual infidelity and adultery. Hence, some commentators prefer to assume that the case involved fraud in business matters.[4] Most recently, Fiorenza sees an indirect connection to financial matters, but proposes a different cause for the litigation. She suggests that, if we read 1 Cor. 6.1-11 in the light of 6.20–7.40, the legal problem might be related to institutional marriage which could pertain to 'questions of dowry, divorce settlements, or inheritance'.[5] Fiorenza's conjecture is worth further consideration.

I would like to support further Fiorenza's insight in the light of the circumstantial factor and the language Paul uses in 1 Cor. 6.1-11 and to suggest that the case might feasibly be related to the problem of inheritance. Based on the fact that the Roman law of succession, especially the law of legacies, received disproportionately detailed attention in the Roman Empire, it has been suggested by an expert in the field of Roman laws that cases related to inheritance and legacy must have been brought frequently to the court.[6] More importantly, the feasibility of my conjecture that the case might be one which involved inheritance seems to be hinted at by the language Paul uses in this passage. As mentioned above, Paul's use of the word βιωτικά strongly implies that the case was about material possessions or property. But the idea of the deprivation of inheritance rights[7] may be highlighted

1. Barrett, *First Corinthians*, p. 139.
2. Βιωτικά basically means things related to this life (so Robertson and Plummer, *First Corinthians*, p. 113; Barrett, *First Corinthians*, pp. 136-37), and seems to involve money and property (R.H. Fuller, 'First Corinthians 6.1-11: An Exegetical Paper', *Ex Auditu* 2 [1988], pp. 99-100). It follows that ἀποστερεῖσθαι and πλεονεξία should be understood as related to financial matters and not, as Bernard suggests, to sexual immorality.
3. So, e.g., Theissen, *Social Setting*, p. 97; Meeks, *First Urban Christians*, p. 66; Fee, *First Corinthians*, p. 228.
4. Fee, *First Corinthians*, p. 241.
5. Fiorenza, 'I Corinthians', p. 1175.
6. F. Schulz's view quoted in de Ste. Croix, *Class Struggle*, pp. 329-30; cf. also Garnsey, *Social Status*, p. 181 n. 1.
7. While the verb ἀδικεῖσθαι may be a general reference to all kinds of

especially by the use of the verb ἀποστερεῖσθαι which has the effect of sharpening the focus of the case.¹ Then there is the apparently abrupt suggestion that the unrighteous will not be able to *inherit* the kingdom of God (1 Cor. 6.9-10).² I suggest that Paul's warning here can best be seen as an attempt to guide the plaintiff from fixing his eyes on inheritance in this life to the inheritance in God's kingdom. Whether the case involved problems related to inheritance or not, it is best seen as involving things of this life or material possessions. Moreover, for whatever reason the case was brought before the pagan magistrate, Paul was against the action (1 Cor. 6.1, 7).

Why did the plaintiff bring a case against the brother before the pagan judge? What did the plaintiff seek to achieve? From Paul's rhetoric in 1 Cor. 6.7-8 it seems obvious, to some commentators, that the plaintiff was the offended one who sought to redress the damage done to him by the defendant.³ It was a logical thing to do. Assuming that this was the case, G. Shaw submits that Paul's attempt to discourage the plaintiff from starting a lawsuit is unreasonable, and that it is an indicator of Paul's desire to control the church.⁴ If the plaintiff's objective was to seek justice, then Shaw's concern about Paul's integrity is not unreasonable. The problem, of course, is whether legal action was necessarily started with the aim of achieving justice. It certainly could be, but not necessarily so in every case. For the litigants could also be the offenders in the sense that by bringing a case to the magistrate they sought to gain from it.

wrongdoing (BAGD, p. 17) including wrongdoing in matters related to property (Lysias 32.17), ἀποστερεῖσθαι is often used in cases related to disputes over property or inheritance (Isaeus 6.4; 8.3; Lysias 32.10, 22; Demosthenes 21.80, 157; cf. Plutarch, *Ages* 4.2).

1. Fee, *First Corinthians*, p. 241.
2. The expression is certainly conventional and not particularly Pauline (Conzelmann, *I Corinthians*, p. 106). But it should be noted that the idea of inheritance is not frequent in Paul (1 Cor. 6.9, 10; 15.50; Gal. 3.18; 4.30; 5.21). Its introduction here might be because of the Corinthians' keen interest in things of this life.
3. According to Fee, Paul shames the plaintiff for bringing his case to the pagan court (1 Cor. 6.7b) but warns the defendant for doing wrong (1 Cor. 6.8) (*First Corinthians*, pp. 228-29, 239-42). Cf. F.F. Bruce, *I and II Corinthians* (Grand Rapids: Eerdmans, 1971), pp. 60-61.
4. G. Shaw, *The Cost of Authority: Manipulation and Freedom in the New Testament* (Philadelphia: Fortress Press, 1982), p. 72.

3. *The Power of the Patrons*

Could such a situation have arisen in Corinth? Such cases are certainly not inconceivable in the early Empire. In fact, it was not uncommon for the strong to use the court to damage people for personal gain.[1] There are even cases which tell of how a powerful plaintiff sought to lay claims to a weak defendant's patrimony.[2] Moreover, it was also sanctioned by Roman law that a patron had the right to sue the freedman's heirs if he was defrauded of his due share in the freedman's legacy. If this was the case, one would be in a better position to understand Paul's apparent unreasonableness in arguing against the starting of a lawsuit (1 Cor. 6.1) and asking the plaintiff to suffer wrong rather than to do wrong (1 Cor. 6.7b-8).

Which of the two options above is more likely? It is difficult to tell from this distance. In any case, Paul might have in mind the litigants when he refers to the πλεονέκται in 1 Cor. 6.10.[3] This suggests that the litigants could be regarded as people who were eager to enrich themselves in material terms, whether through lawsuits or fraud.

The Litigants

What more do we know about the litigants? Assuming that the case involved financial matters, Theissen surmises that the litigants were people with property.[4] From this, he deduces that the litigants were 'members of the upper classes' in the church.[5] Meeks, however, is less

1. For some examples, see discussion in Chapter 1 above.
2. Pliny, *Ep.* 6.33.6.
3. It has been argued that, because Paul makes use of traditional materials in the listing of vices (1 Cor. 6.9-10), we are not supposed to see the list as related in any way to the situation in Corinth (Conzelmann, *I Corinthians*, p. 106; Fiorenza, 'I Corinthians', p. 1175). But the possibility that individual items in the list are specific should not be dismissed out of hand. For even though the form of the list of vices is conventional, the major items listed, such as immorality, idolatry and greed, were real problems in the church (D. Aune, *The New Testament in Its Literary Environment* [Philadelphia: Westminster Press, 1987], p. 195; Moffatt, *First Corinthians*, p. 60; P. Zaas, 'Catalogues and Context: 1 Corinthians 5 and 6', *NTS* 34 [1988], pp. 622-29). Fuller may be right in suggesting that Paul could have quoted the list in 1 Cor. 6.9-10 just for the sake of the vice of πλεονεξία ('First Corinthians 6.1-11', p. 102).
4. Theissen, *Social Setting*, p. 97.
5. *Social Setting*, p. 97. Cf. von Dobschütz, *Life*, p. 14; G.H. Ewald, *Die Sendschreiben des Apostels Paulus übersetzt und erklärt* (Göttingen: Verlag der Dieterichschen Buchhandlung, 1857), p. 154.

willing to speculate on the level of affluence of the parties involved.[1] However, in offering an ironical suggestion that the Corinthians should be wise enough to settle the disputes among themselves (1 Cor. 6.5), Paul seems to hint that the litigants and the 'wise' in the church were one and the same group of people.[2] Since such 'wise' people have already featured in Paul's earlier discussion (1 Cor. 1.26-27; 3.18-19) and since they could well be the socially powerful in the church,[3] this seems to fit in with my conjecture that the litigants were among the powerful people in the church. In the following section, I seek to provide further support for such a view in the light of the legal system in the early Empire.

With regard to the structure of the legal system in the early Empire, it has been successfully shown that it tended to serve the interest of the governing elite.[4] A person of a higher status was often protected from being prosecuted. For example, a freedman was barred from taking any harmful action against a patron without the permission of the *praetor*; on the other hand, a patron could take action against his client without seeking such permission. This inequality clearly existed in the legal procedure involving civil cases. The plight of the humble is ably described by Garnsey. He writes,

> The possibility of suits brought by men of comparatively humble origin and position against men of rank cannot be ruled out; but they are unlikely to have been a frequent occurrence... if it is conceivable that a powerful defendant was ready to go to law because he was confident of his prospects, it is much more likely that a man of low rank who had suffered at his hands would be discouraged from seeking redress by litigation, because he knew, or suspected (from his own previous experiences or from those of acquaintances), that a court would decide against him. Another factor which might discourage him was the threat of retaliation from the potential defendant, who might, in extreme cases, do him physical harm, and, in any event, was likely to be in a position to damage his interests. In addition, he was unlikely to make any showing in front of a court without legal assistance and representation. We should like to know how easy it was for men of low rank to find jurisconsults, or jurisconsults of any quality, who were prepared to take on their cases... Nor should

1. Meeks, *First Urban Christians*, p. 66.
2. Theissen, *Social Setting*, p. 97.
3. Theissen, *Social Setting*, pp. 70-73.
4. On the built-in inequality of the Roman legal procedure, see especially Garnsey, *Social Status*.

the possibility be overlooked that ignorance of the law might hold back a man of low status from consulting jurisprudents, or, for that matter, from attempting to sue at all. Doubtless there were some patrons who were ready to provide their clients with most of what they lacked, contacts, money, and knowledge. But it may be conjectured that, in general, patrons were most faithful to those of their clients who were well placed to offer worthwhile reciprocal services, and that meant clients whose social and economic station was not far below their own. Finally, if a would-be plaintiff did try to initiate legal proceedings, it was quite possible that the praetor would reject his application for a suit, especially if the particular action requested put a defendant's status in jeopardy.[1]

Since inequality was built into the legal system and improper influence could also be exercised on the administration of justice in the early Empire under normal circumstances, it is less likely that the court would be used by the weak and the powerless to redress the damages done to them by the socially powerful. On the other hand, a person or an official who had close connections with the city authorities, including the magistrates, and judicial power to judge some financial cases, for example, an *aedile*, would be more prone to settle disputes through litigation.[2] Significantly, such kinds of people could well be in the church.

Based on our understanding of the way justice was apportioned in the early Empire, it is quite reasonable to conclude that the litigants, or the plaintiff at least, were among the relatively powerful people in the church, even though we cannot be entirely certain about their level of affluence. Since the litigants, as Paul seems to imply (1 Cor. 6.5) and as Talbert and Theissen have suggested, were among the wise and the strong in the church, it is natural to assume that they were people who could have been interested both in material things and in speculative wisdom. Significantly, Philo the philosopher and politician appears to have been one who was interested in heavenly wisdom and also involved in judicial matters.[3] Philo therefore provides a good paradigm for understanding the behaviour of the enlightened Corinthians. Actually if what Horsley is correct in arguing that the Corinthians were under the influence of Philonic traditions, the

1. Garnsey, *Social Status*, pp. 217-18.
2. Theissen, *Social Setting*, p. 97; Malherbe, *Social Aspects*, p. 76. Cf. P. Veyne, *A History of Private Life*, I (Cambridge: Belknap Press, 1987), p. 167.
3. Georgi, *Opponents*, p. 405.

supporters of such traditions might well have been people who were prominent and sophisticated, not unlike Philo. Again, if people like Erastus were already in the church, they certainly would be regarded as prominent people by the church.

If the taking of legal action was a manifestation of the Corinthians' freedom from earthly matters, it should again be pointed out that this freedom was not necessarily available to all. The lowly and the inferior would probably not avail themselves of it. On the contrary, the Corinthian theology with its emphasis on freedom (1 Cor. 6.12; 10.23) would probably serve the strong's interests better. If the litigants, people who were powerful and keen on acquiring material goods, were identical with the 'wise', people who were engrossed in speculative wisdom, then it would be reasonable to surmise that the legal case was not an isolated incident. That is to say, other problems in the church which involved relationships with the pagans and which could be legitimized in the name of freedom may be related as well to some kind of interest in material matters or secular affairs.

The Rich Patron

In 1 Cor. 5.1-13 a case of gross immorality which Paul heard of is disclosed. A man, a member in the church, cohabited with his stepmother[1] who apparently is not a member of the church (1 Cor. 5.1). In the eyes of Paul such a relationship is not acceptable even in a pagan world,[2] and certainly not to himself. Paul is therefore of the opinion that the community should exclude the man from their midst (1 Cor. 5.3-5, 7, 13). However, it seems to have surprised Paul that the church not only accepted the man, but appears to be proud of the man (1 Cor. 5.2, 6).

That there was such a case of immorality in the church and that it was approved by the church certainly arouses interest. Could this case of immorality, like the case of litigation, be concerned with material benefits? What do we know about the man? Could he be one of the 'strong' people? How could the church be proud of the man if it was

---

1. On γυνὴ πατρός as a reference to stepmother, see Lev. 18.8 (LXX).
2. Talbert has marshalled some helpful parallel materials from Jewish and Graeco-Roman sources showing the unacceptability of this kind of relationship (*Reading Corinthians*, pp. 12-14).

so clear-cut to Paul that the man should be excluded from the community? The answer to the last question lies partly in the self-understanding of the Corinthians. They probably believed that the man's action was a valid expression of their newly found freedom in the Spirit.[1] To Schmithals, it is Gnostic *eleutheria*.[2] But Thiselton sees in this case a testimony to the over-realized eschatological outlook of the spiritual people at Corinth.[3] Horsley has not spent any time on this episode. While the nature of such freedom has been explained in different terms, its inner logic is probably coherent. The Corinthians might have believed that no physical action has any moral significance (1 Cor. 6.13, 18b).[4] Because they had wisdom and knowledge (1 Cor. 1.5; 3.18; 8.1-3) they were therefore free from moral law (1 Cor. 6.12).[5] They might also have believed that they were protected by the baptism they had received (1 Cor. 1.13-17).[6] Consequently they were proud (1 Cor. 5.2; 4.6, 18) and boastful (1 Cor. 5.6; 1.29; 3.21; 4.7). They were like kings (1 Cor. 4.8) and could be judged by no one else (1 Cor. 2.15-16a). Since the man was only exercising his freedom, the church not only could not judge him, but should actually have reasons to be proud of the man's courage.

The man's action could certainly be justified theologically in the name of freedom in the Spirit. But a theological explanation does not answer all the questions concerning the social reality of the man's relationship with his stepmother. From our study of the problem of litigation we have seen that freedom to seek justice before the pagan magistrate might in reality have been exercised by only a few powerful Corinthians and not necessarily by all, and that their freedom might also have been exercised for material gain. It leads one to wonder if a similar kind of situation lies behind this case of immorality. To enlarge our understanding of the situation some questions have to be examined. For example, could any person who experienced the freedom in the Spirit act in such a way, even though it meant a

---

1. E.g. Moffatt, *First Corinthians*, p. 54; Barrett, *First Corinthians*, pp. 121-22.
2. Schmithals, *Gnosticism*, pp. 236-37.
3. Thiselton, 'Realized Eschatology', p. 516.
4. Murphy-O'Connor, 'First Letter to the Corinthians', p. 803.
5. Talbert, *Reading Corinthians*, p. 15.
6. Keck, *Paul and his Letters*, pp. 106-107.

132   *Patronage and Power*

violation of both Jewish[1] and Roman law?[2] What kind of a son would the man be who sought apparently to maintain a kind of incestuous relationship with his stepmother? Why would the man choose to live with the stepmother? What was the nature of that relationship?

The Relationship
Regarding the relationship between the son and the stepmother, it would be safe to assume that it was a long-term one.[3] Beyond this, scholars differ in their assessment concerning the nature of their relationship. Conzelmann and Fiorenza[4] prefer to see it as cohabiting rather than marriage. Their judgment is based mainly on the assumption that a son is forbidden to marry a stepmother by both Jewish and Roman law. But Barrett, who builds his argument on Paul's use of ἔχειν, suggests that the relationship could have been one of either marriage or concubinage.[5]

As to the nature of the relationship, it should first be pointed out that it would be difficult to draw a clear line between marriage and living together in those days.[6] For the deciding factor lies basically with the intention of the couple, that is, whether they intended to live together as husband and wife.[7] Unfortunately, intention is something

1. Lev. 18.8; Deut. 22.30; 27.20; *Jub.* 33.10-13.
2. Gaius 1.63: 'I may not marry one who once was my stepmother. We say, who once was, since if the marriage producing that alliance were still continuing, I should be precluded from marrying her on another ground' (D. Daube, 'Pauline Contributions to Pluralistic Culture: Re-creation and Beyond', in *Jesus and Man's Hope* [ed. D.G. Miller and D.Y. Hadidian: Pittsburgh: Pittsburgh Theological Seminary, 1971], p. 241 n. 3). Cf. also Sandars, *Institutes*, pp. 35-36.
3. The long-term nature of the relationship is suggested by Paul's use of ἔχειν (e.g. Robertson and Plummer, *First Corinthians*, p. 96; Barrett, *First Corinthians*, p. 122; Fee, *First Corinthians*, p. 220).
4. Conzelmann, *I Corinthians*, p. 96; Fiorenza, 'I Corinthians', p. 1174.
5. Barrett, *First Corinthians*, p. 122. According to Robertson and Plummer, Origen also sees the relationship as a marriage (*First Corinthians*, p. 96). Cf. 1 Cor. 7.2.
6. Robertson and Plummer, *First Corinthians*, p. 96.
7. Sandars, *Institutes*, pp. 31-32; Crook, *Law and Life*, p. 101. For further discussion on marriage in the Roman world, see P.E. Corbett, *The Roman Law of Marriage* (Oxford: Clarendon Press, 1930), pp. 47-51; J.F. Gardner, *Women in Roman Law and Society* (London: Croom Helm, 1986), pp. 31-80; Garnsey and Saller, *Roman Empire*, pp. 130-36.

3. The Power of the Patrons

which is very difficult to assess from this distance in time. Having said that, on balance it still appears that the relationship is best seen as marriage or concubinage.[1]

In response to those, such as Fiorenza, who do not regard the relationship as marriage or concubinage because of legal prohibitions, two points can be made. First, as far as Jewish law is concerned, it should be noted (although not all rabbis would agree[2]) that it was possible for the man to argue that, because he was a proselyte, his former social relations were dissolved and that he could marry his stepmother.[3] It is, of course, questionable if the status as a proselyte could render the requirement of the Roman law ineffective. But then we should not forget the fact that Roman law, as seen from our previous discussion, could be manipulated by the strong and the powerful for their own ends. Secondly, whether the relationship was marriage or not, it is important to underscore the long-term nature of the relationship. In actual effect, a long-term cohabiting would perhaps be regarded as a marriage by a contemporary.

Furthermore, as Fiorenza has observed, Paul's discussion in 1 Corinthians 7 on marital problems could have been occasioned by Paul's earlier discussion of the relationship between the insiders and the outsiders in 1 Corinthians 5 and 6.[4] So if 1 Cor. 5.1 is read in the light of 1 Corinthians 7, it can be inferred that the problem which involved the immoral man might be one related to the institution of marriage. Fiorenza seems to accept also the view that a fragment of Paul's previous letter to the Corinthians (1 Cor. 5.9) might have been preserved in 2 Cor. 6.14–7.1 where the problem of intermarriage with unbelievers is probably discussed. This connection is not assumed in our discussion. But if the above view is right, then we would have a perfect match between the situation in 1 Cor. 5.1 and part of the situation presupposed in Paul's previous letter to the church.

---

1. So von Dobschütz draws the following conclusion: 'There is tolerable agreement among exegetes as to the nature of the case of incest concerned; it was marriage (not only an immoral relationship) with the stepmother (probably not belonging to the Church) after the father's death' (*Life*, p. 387).
2. Conzelmann, *I Corinthians*, p. 96 n. 29.
3. H.W.A. Meyer, *Critical and Exegetical Handbook to the Epistles to the Corinthians*, I (Edinburgh: T. & T. Clark, 5th edn, 1883), p. 140; Daube, 'Recreation and Beyond', pp. 223-24; Fiorenza, 'I Corinthians', p. 1174.
4. Fiorenza, 'I Corinthians', p. 1174. She sees 1 Cor. 5–7 as a unity.

To sum up, the relationship between the man and the woman is best seen as one of marriage or concubinage. This being so, can we know why the man took his stepmother and not another woman? Why especially did the man choose an outsider to the church rather than an insider? Would an insider be more understandable and natural? Granted that to associate with a stepmother could be a good way to express the freedom one enjoyed, the action itself is still difficult to understand. For there may be truth in the suggestion that, in most cases, there were tensions rather than affection between children of the former wife and the stepmother even in the Roman Empire.[1] Why then did the man marry the stepmother?

Could it be because she was still young and attractive? Could it be for sexual pleasure?[2] Because girls in the Roman Empire tended to marry early,[3] it is quite possible that the stepmother was still a young woman. We have no way of knowing if she was especially attractive. But if tensions in the relationship between a son and a stepmother were as common as suggested, that would speak against these two otherwise reasonable guesses. More importantly, it should be pointed out that to see sex as the main reason for a long-term relationship is to overestimate the role of sex in ancient marriage arrangements. For the idea that the aim of marriage is to enjoy sexual pleasure does not appear to have been a prevalent one in the early Empire. Philosophers such as Musonius Rufus taught that the aim of having sex in marriage was to have children, not pleasure.[4] The satirist also emphasized the

1. Plutarch, *Cato the Elder* 24.4; *Comparison of Aristides and Cato* 6.1. B. Rawson points also to 'the sinister nature of the stepmother's role in Tacitus's treatment of Livia and Agrippina junior' (*The Family in Ancient Rome* [London: Croom Helm, 1986], pp. 36, 55 n. 112).

2. This is suggested especially by Moffatt, *First Corinthians*, pp. 53-54; Murphy-O'Connor, *I Corinthians*, p. 43.

3. Recent studies have shown that, on average, girls in the Roman Empire married between nine to twelve (e.g. Crook, *Law and Life*, p. 100), and usually to older men (Garnsey and Saller, *Roman Empire*, p. 131). Thus, it would be difficult for young widows to remain single for the rest of their life. It was common for women in the Roman Empire to marry for a second time.

4. Musonius Rufus: 'Men who are not wantons or immoral are bound to consider sexual intercourse justified only when it occurs in marriage and is indulged in for the purpose of begetting children, since that is lawful, but unjust and unlawful when it is mere pleasure-seeking, even in marriage' (Lutz, 'Musonius Rufus', p. 87).

3. The Power of the Patrons

non-affective relationship between husband and wife.¹ Furthermore, marriage as an institution among the well-to-do in Rome who could enjoy sex in other ways might not have been popular at all. Indeed some laws may have been passed by Augustus to encourage marriage and the procreation of children.² Actually, it was claimed by some of the Corinthians, probably those who were overtaken by enthusiasm,³ that it was good for a man/a husband not to touch (or to have sexual relationship with) a woman/a wife (1 Cor. 7.1).⁴ Since the man could be one of those who were devoted to enthusiasm,⁵ it is not impossible that he would hold such a view. Of course, it does not necessarily follow that the man could not have sexual relationships with other women (1 Cor. 6.12-20). But it is reasonable to argue that sex might not be a very important factor in the relationship between the son and the stepmother.

If the son did not live with the stepmother because of physical attraction, what could be the reason behind his action? Again, Fiorenza's observation may provide us with a clue. As mentioned before, she suggests that the legal case in 1 Cor. 6.1 could be about one of those problems related to marriage, like dowry, inheritance and so on.⁶ In which case, just as the litigants were interested in material possessions, the man's association with the stepmother could also be related to material concerns.

This close relationship between marriage and wealth management in first-century Corinth is spotlighted in the marriage arrangement of two important personages known to the people in the colony. The first one concerned Lollia Paulina, a lady with immense wealth.⁷ She was

---

1. Juvenal, *Satires* 6. The study of J.P. Hallett has shown that women, especially elite women, in Roman society clung closer to their fathers and kins than to their husbands (*Fathers and Daughters in Roman Society: Women and the Elite Family* [Princeton: Princeton University Press, 1984], pp. 219-43).
2. Tacitus, *Ann.* 3.25. See also R.I. Frank, 'Augustus' Legislation on Marriage and Children', *CSCA* 8 (1975), pp. 41-52.
3. Thiselton, 'Realized Eschatology', p. 518; Talbert, *Reading Corinthians*, p. 38.
4. See, e.g., Orr and Walther, *I Corinthians*, pp. 206, 207-208; Barrett, *First Corinthians*, p. 154.
5. Thiselton, 'Realized Eschatology', p. 516.
6. Fiorenza, 'I Corinthians', p. 1175.
7. According to Pliny the Elder, she owed her wealth to her grandfather and was

first the nominal wife of Memmius Regulus, the popular governor of Achaia from AD 35-44, but later became the bride of Caligula.[1] Part of the reason why Lollia Paulina was chosen by Caligula as his bride could have been because she was wealthy.[2] Another case involved a freedman and a woman from a rich family.[3] As a result of this marriage, the name of the freedman, Cleogenes, was included on an inscription of the Augustan age made to the family of Quintus Cornelius Secundus who probably built a meatmarket and a fishmarket at Corinth. Whether Cleogenes was accepted because he was wealthy or became rich through the marriage is not clear, but that material benefits might have been involved in the union of a man and woman should not be difficult to see. Small wonder that, in his correspondence, Pliny states clearly that, when arranging for a marriage, for the sake of the children, he would consider seriously the financial factor.[4]

Could a man gain from the taking of a wife and if so, how? A dowry,[5] of course, was what the husband could immediately gain from a marriage. There were, however, other material benefits to be gained from a marital relationship at that time. According to the Augustan marriage laws[6] unmarried men and women would be

able to wear 40 million sesterces worth of jewellery at a party (*Natural History* 9.117-18). Cf. Tacitus, *Ann.* 12.22.

1. Suetonius, *Caligula* 25; Dio Cassius 59.12.
2. On wealth and the choice of an emperor's consort, see Tacitus, *Ann.* 12.1; cf. Oliver, 'Lollia Paulina, Memmius Regulus and Caligula', pp. 150-53.
3. West, *Latin Inscriptions*, nos. 124, 125; Kent, *Inscriptions*, no. 321.
4. Pliny, *Ep.* 1.14.9.
5. For a good discussion of dowry in the early Empire, see R.P. Saller, 'Roman Dowry and the Devolution of Property in the Principate', *CQ* 34 (1984), pp. 195-205; Gardner, *Women*, pp. 97-116. According to Saller, in Greek marriage the size of the dowry could be very substantial because it was related to the daughter's share of the family's inheritance. It could amount to a quarter of the whole estate ('Dowry', p. 195). In comparison, the size of the dowry in Roman marriage at the time of the early Empire was smaller, but not too small. It varied from tens of thousands among the local aristocracy to millions among the wealthiest in the empire ('Dowry', pp. 200-202). It may be worth noting that the capital of a town councillor at Comun was assessed to be 100,000 sesterces (Pliny, *Ep.* 1.19.2).
6. For detailed discussions of the Augustan marriage laws, see P. Csillag, *The Augustan Laws on Family Relations* (Budapest: Akademiai Kiado, 1976). Cf. also P.A. Brunt, 'The Augustan Marriage Laws', in *Italian Manpower: 225 BC-AD 14*

3. The Power of the Patrons 137

penalized by heavier taxes;[1] bachelors were forbidden to receive inheritances or legacies; the childless married could only take half of any bequest.[2] Besides, there was also the likelihood that a man could have access in an informal way to the wife's inheritance and material possessions of the wife's relatives.[3] If a man married a widow, his chance of gaining direct access to the wife's inheritance was even higher, since it would be likely that her father was already dead by then.[4] Apart from making material gains, one could also marry for the preservation of family wealth. The following comment by J.F. Gardner serves to sum up the phenomenon well:

> In the senatorial class, the political aspects of such marriage alliances are too well attested to need comment; and both there and at lower levels of society a degree of endogamy could be a strategy, to restrict the dispersal of family property.[5]

From this discussion we may conclude that, in Paul's day, material interests, which might include money and power, rather than sex and affection seem to have a bigger role to play in the establishment of a marital relationship. Indeed, for the sake of keeping wealth, men in those days could do some strange things. The satirists tell us that there were husbands who were willing to condone their wives' acts of

---

(Oxford: Clarendon Press, 1971), pp. 558-66; A. Wallace-Hadrill, 'Family and Inheritance in the Augustan Marriage Laws', *PCPhS* 27 (1981), pp. 58-80; J.A. Crook, 'Women in Roman Succession', in Rawson (ed.), *Family in Ancient Rome*, pp. 58-82.

1. Tacitus, *Ann.* 3.25; Dio Cassius 54.16.1.
2. Gaius 2.286. See Sandars, *Institutes*, pp. 228-29; Wallace-Hadrill, 'Family and Inheritance', p. 62; Brunt, 'Augustan Marriage Laws', p. 564.
3. This possibility is reflected in an epitaph of the Augustan age (Ehrenberg and Jones, *Documents*, no. 357 = Braund, *Augustus to Nero*, no. 520). In this eulogy of the wife, her courage to fight for the right to keep her father's possessions and her willingness to share it with the husband is praised highly by the latter. While such total sharing might not be common in those days (Gardner, *Women*, p. 72), different degrees of sharing can perhaps be assumed with confidence. Even Pliny claims that the property of the mother of his former wife is at his free disposal (*Ep.* 3.19; 1.4).
4. According to Saller's estimation, roughly one third of the brides would have lost their fathers when they got married, and three out of four married girls would outlive their father ('Dowry', p. 197 n. 14).
5. Gardner, *Women*, p. 35.

adultery in return for the control of their dowries.¹ If we measure the immoral man's action against these husbands, his behaviour would appear less shocking and more understandable.

To see in the man's action, whatever his theological views, a way to preserve or to increase family wealth may well provide a better explanation of why the son chose to associate with the stepmother against all the odds. For on the one hand, through marriage, he would not have to pay higher taxes. On the other hand, he would immediately be able to have total control over his share of the inheritance from the father who probably was dead at that time.² Better still, through marrying his stepmother he might have been able to preserve in his house his stepmother's dowry to his father and might even have access to the possessions of his wife's family.

Although the above reconstruction of the situation behind 1 Cor. 5.1 depends quite heavily on the assumption that the relationship involved was one of marriage, it nevertheless makes good sense and fits in well with the general context of 1 Corinthians 5–7. First, the material interests which might involve the immoral man could well

---

1. Juvenal, *Satires* 6.135-141; cf. Andocides 4.13. This may be one of the reasons why Augustus made the husband's condoning the wife's adulterous act a crime (Crook, *Law and Life*, p. 106). At this point, it is worth explaining briefly the marriage custom in the Principate and its relationship to the management of the dowry. The more common form of marriage at this time is the so-called 'free marriage' which allowed the wife to have independent control over the property she inherited from her father's family. Dowry was under the control of the husband until the marital relationship was dissolved by divorce or death (Saller, 'Dowry', pp. 196-97; Corbett, *Law of Marriage*, pp. 154-55, 181-82).

2. Although it is not immediately clear whether the association of the man with his father's wife took place while the father was still alive or after he was dead (Barrett, *First Corinthians*, p. 121), it looks more likely that the latter is the case. Bernard's attempt to sustain the thesis that the lawsuit in 1 Cor. 6.1 was started by the father by assuming that the father was still alive is not necessary and not required by the text ('Connexion', pp. 437-38). On the contrary, given the fact that the father was given enormous power over the son in those days (Lacey, '*Patria Potestas*', *Family in Ancient Rome*, pp. 121-44; Garnsey and Saller, *Roman Empire*, pp. 136-37), it is difficult to conceive that the son could have his way if the father was still alive. Moreover, recent studies have shown that, because of the late marriage age of men in the Roman Empire, usually in their late twenties, the average age difference between father and child was about 40 years. Hence, few fathers lived to see their sons' marriages (Garnsey and Saller, *Roman Empire*, pp. 136-37).

3. *The Power of the Patrons* 139

have led to the kind of litigation in 1 Cor. 6.1-11, as suggested by Fiorenza and further developed previously. Secondly, Paul's asking of the church not to associate with a person who bears the name of a brother, but is in fact a πόρνος and a πλεονέκτης, could have been a reference to the immoral man (1 Cor. 5.11). In associating with his stepmother, he is certainly a πόρνος. If he did so for material reasons he could also be seen as a πλεονέκτης, a person who is eager to have more,[1] more money and even more power.[2]

The Immoral Man
In 1 Cor. 5.2, the community is accused by Paul of being 'puffed-up' because it did not cast the immoral man from its midst. The 'puffed-up' people appear to be Paul's opponents in the church (1 Cor. 4.18).[3] In 1 Corinthians 1–4 they are behind the divisions in the church (1 Cor. 4.6). In 1 Cor. 8.1 and 13.4 they are people who have knowledge but no love. Hence it is very likely that, in 1 Corinthians 5 Paul is still responding to the opponents in 1 Corinthians 1–4 and those in 1 Corinthians 8–10.[4] It is therefore natural to identify the immoral man as one of those who were puffed up and did not expect Paul to return (1 Cor. 4.18). As seen from our previous discussion,[5] it looks likely that the opponents of Paul were the powerful people in the church. This again points to the conclusion that the immoral man was one of the powerful patrons in the church.

In the light of the above discussion, it may be inferred that the case of immorality basically concerns a man with material possessions. In that case, the problem in 1 Cor. 5.1 was not a problem of the have-nots or of the slaves, but one of a rich man who was rich enough to have concerns about preserving or increasing wealth. If so, more was involved in the case of immorality than simply religious freedom. The

1. BAGD, p. 667. See G. Delling, 'πλεονέκτης', *TDNT*, VI, pp. 266-74; F. Selter, 'πλεονεξία', *NIDNTT*, I, pp. 137-39.
2. πλεονεξία is also used to represent the immoral lust for power or ambitions on the part of the politically powerful. See Ezek. 22.27; Jer. 22.17; 2 Macc. 4.50 (LXX); Dio Chrysostom, *Or.* 17.
3. G. Forkman, *The Limits of the Religious Community: Expulsion from the Religious Community within the Qumran Sect, within Rabbinic Judaism, and within Primitive Christianity* (Lund: Gleerup, 1972), p. 139.
4. Dahl, 'Church at Corinth', p. 331.
5. See discussion in Chapter 2.

immoral man, not unlike the litigants, while devoted to the pursuit of freedom in the Spirit, was probably greatly interested in material matters. It may be further surmised that the man might be one of the patrons in the church. We have seen how the Corinthians could have approved the man's action by reference to their theology of freedom. If the spiritual and immoral man was also a rich patron in the church, he would certainly have a better chance of being approved by the church. For who would want to dishonour a powerful patron who could provide protection and benefaction to the church? On the contrary, as faithful clients, members in the Christian church should perhaps support and honour such a patron. The church's boasting in the immoral man's action can, to a certain extent, also be seen against this background.

We may now look briefly at another problem. If it was illegal for a son to marry a stepmother, how did the man manage to survive without being prosecuted? In his attempt to understand why the church failed to take action against the immoral man, Moffatt surmises that the man could have been 'too important or wealthy' for the church to raise any objection.[1] I have shown that the man could have been a wealthy man. But it is difficult to tell if the man was in fact an important person. However it looks probable that the church had some important persons in its midst. We have seen previously how the Roman law served the interests of the powerful and could be manipulated by the powerful for their own ends. If the immoral man was a man of influence and power, it is doubtful that any one would dare to challenge his action. This, I submit, would help partly to explain how the man could associate with the stepmother without being prosecuted.

So the immoral man may have been a rich and powerful man. But Paul is insisting that the church should exclude the man from the Christian community (1 Cor. 5.2-5, 13). While encouraging the church to discipline the immoral man, Paul also asks the church not to eat with any member in the church who bears the name of brother but is in fact a πόρνος and a πλεονέκτης (1 Cor. 5.11).[2] In the light of the reports of sexual immorality and litigation in the church, such an appeal is understandable. But it is also of interest to note that an unworthy brother is depicted not only as a πόρνος and a

---

1. Moffatt, *First Corinthians*, p. 53.
2. Moffatt sees the problems listed as definite offences (*First Corinthians*, p. 60).

3. The Power of the Patrons

πλεονέκτης, but also an εἰδωλολάτρης. Does this imply that there were people who participated in the worship of idols and who were powerful people, not unlike the immoral man and the litigants?

The Political Patron

The problem of εἰδωλολατρία is highlighted in a case put forward by Paul in which a man who has knowledge is seen eating in an idol's temple (1 Cor. 8.10) This problem of εἰδωλολατρία is discussed, especially in 1 Cor. 10.1-22, as part of a larger discussion concerning εἰδωλόθυτα or food offered to idols.[1] Paul's advice for the Corinthians gives the impression that he has shifted his position from prohibition in 1 Cor. 10.1-22 to acceptance in 1 Cor. 10.23–11.1. But some scholars believe that it makes the best sense to see Paul's apparent ambivalent attitude as his response to two different issues, that is, the eating of food offered to idols (1 Cor. 10.23–11.1) and the eating at table in an idol's temple (1 Cor. 8.8-12; 10.16-22).[2] He accepts the eating of meat offered to idols, but forbids any action which implies actual participation in another cult.[3] The problem of εἰδωλόθυτα is more complex than can be treated fully here.[4] For our purposes, I will limit our study to understanding the social significance of the eating of meals in an idol's temple against the background of the imperial cult in Corinth.

The general problem of eating food or meat offered to idols has been the focus of many significant studies on Corinth, notably those by Hurd, Thiselton, Horsley and Theissen.[5] Fee seeks to show that the

---

1. The unity of 1 Cor. 8–10 has been questioned by Schmithals (*Gnosticism*, pp. 92-93). But many more scholars prefer to see it as a unity (e.g. Conzelmann, *I Corinthians*, p. 137; Barrett, *First Corinthians*, pp. 16-17; Meeks, *First Urban Christians*, pp. 98-99).
2. Talbert, *Reading Corinthians*, p. 56; Keck, *Paul and his Letters*, pp. 88-90.
3. Meeks, *First Urban Christians*, pp. 98-102.
4. For a detailed exegetical study of 1 Cor. 8–10, apart from major commentaries, see especially Willis, *Idol Meat*. Cf. H. von Soden, 'Sacrament and Ethics in Paul', in Meeks (ed.), *The Writings of St Paul*, pp. 257-68; C.K. Barrett, 'Things Sacrificed to Idols', in *Essays on Paul*, pp. 40-59.
5. Hurd, *I Corinthians*, pp. 115-49; Theissen, *Social Setting*, pp. 121-43; Thiselton, 'Realized Eschatology', pp. 519-20; Horsley, 'Consciousness and Freedom'; *idem*, 'Gnosis in Corinth'.

problem of εἰδωλολατρία, that is, the eating of food offered to idols at a cultic setting in a pagan temple, is in fact the main problem which Paul addresses in 1 Cor. 8.1–10.22.[1] Willis holds a similar view. He assumes that in their letter to Paul the Corinthians had asked if it was permissible to eat in an idol's temple.[2] While we may not want to emphasize as much as Fee does the central role of the problem of eating cultic meals in a pagan temple in Paul's discussion, neither should we regard it as a hypothetical situation put forward by Paul for rhetorical purposes.[3] The eating of cultic meals was simply too common a practice to be avoided.[4] Since it is specified in 1 Cor. 8.10 and is implied in 1 Cor. 10.7-8,[5] it seems more likely that the problem of eating at table in an idol's temple was more real than not. If so, this is another Corinthian problem which would involve contacts with pagans.

What then is the significance of these occasions which involved eating with pagans? Why would some of the Corinthians want to take part in the worship of idols, as Paul seems to imply? What could be the occasions behind 1 Cor. 8.10 and Paul's appeal to flee from εἰδωλολατρία in 1 Cor. 10.14? Who could these idolaters have been?

It is commonly assumed that the problem of the eating of food offered to idols and the problem of participation in the worship of the idols were created by the behaviour of the 'strong' people in the

---

1. Fee, *First Corinthians*, p. 359. But it should be noted that Fee also admits that the problem of marketplace food is also discussed in 1 Cor. 10.23–11.1 (*First Corinthians*, p. 363).
2. Willis, *Idol Meat*, p. 267.
3. There are a few scholars, like Hurd, who argue that the situation portrayed in 1 Cor. 8.10, that is, the eating in an idol's temple, is only hypothetical, and is produced by Paul to strengthen his argument (*I Corinthians*, p. 143). Cf. Fiorenza, 'I Corinthians', pp. 1189-82. Hurd's argument is partly based on the claim that the 'weak' nowhere appears to be a distinct group of people. Nevertheless, most interpreters still hold to the idea that the presence of the 'weak' was real and seek to define them in different ways (Willis, *Idol Meat*, pp. 92-94, 104). For further critique of Hurd, see especially Fee, *First Corinthians*, pp. 359-61.
4. Murphy-O'Connor, *St Paul's Corinth*, pp. 161-65; Willis, *Idol Meat*, pp. 13-15.
5. Fee, *First Corinthians*, p. 360; Willis, *Idol Meat*, pp. 265-66; Moffatt, *First Corinthians*, pp. 140-41. Schmithals also sees in 1 Cor. 10.14-22 a general situation where the Corinthians took part in 'cultic ceremonies in the service of pagan gods' (*Gnosticism*, pp. 225-27).

church.¹ As with other problems in the church, the problems related to food offered to idols, including the eating at table in an idol's temple, have been seen as manifestations of the theology of the Corinthians.² The 'strong' in the church very probably claimed that they had knowledge (1 Cor. 8.1). They might have believed that there is only one God in this world and no idols (1 Cor. 8.4), and that food is morally neutral (1 Cor. 8.8).³ It therefore mattered little whether they ate food offered to idols or not. According to Schmithals⁴ the presence of such a viewpoint suggests that Gnostic influence was at work in Corinth. But, as pointed out by Horsley, it is not necessary to see the Corinthians as Gnostics.⁵ Instead, a Philonic type of religious enlightenment can explain more than adequately the gnosis of the Corinthians of one God and of the nothingness of the idols.⁶ Horsley further suggests that the Corinthians' freedom to eat food offered to idols might also be based on their belief that their relationship with God was secure because they possessed Sophia.⁷ Horsley's explanation is helpful. His attempt to define more precisely the Corinthian position should also be appreciated. Nevertheless, he has not clarified all the issues relating to 1 Corinthians 8–10. The gnosis of the Corinthians would allow them to eat idol-meat, yet it is doubtful if a Hellenistic-Jewish viewpoint would allow the Corinthians to take part in other cults, a problem Paul addresses in 1 Cor. 8.10 and 10.1-22.⁸ Moreover, in asserting that the idea of the magical influence of a

1. Koester, *Introduction*, II, p. 124.
2. Some of the ideas held by the Corinthians could actually have been contained in Paul's response (e.g. 1 Cor. 8.1, 4). For a convenient summary of the opinions of different scholars on this matter, see Hurd, *I Corinthians*, pp. 67-68.
3. J. Murphy-O'Connor, 'Food and Spiritual Gifts in 1 Cor. 8.8', *CBQ* 41 (1979), pp. 292-98.
4. Schmithals, *Gnosticism*, pp. 141-55, 218-29.
5. Horsley, 'Gnosis in Corinth', pp. 49-50.
6. Horsley, 'Gnosis in Corinth', pp. 36, 48.
7. Horsley, 'Consciousness and Freedom', pp. 577-78; *idem*, 'Gnosis in Corinth', pp. 47-48.
8. On the security of those who have the Sophia, Horsley refers his reader to Wis. 15.2-3; 14.27 ('Gnosis in Corinth', p. 47). But in the light of their context, the two passages, especially Wis. 14.27, seems to condemn rather than to allow the sin of idolatry (E.G. Clarke, *The Wisdom of Solomon* [Cambridge: Cambridge University Press, 1973], pp. 87-102). Interestingly, idolatry is probably a problem Paul seeks to address in 1 Cor. 8.10 and 10.16-22.

cultic meal originated with Paul, Horsley seems to have disregarded the possibility that the Corinthians themselves could also have believed in the power of religious ritual.[1] The Corinthians' seeming reliance on the power of ritual is first implied, as Käsemann suggests,[2] in Paul's warning in 1 Cor. 10.1-22. But one should note especially the fact that some of the Corinthians practised a kind of vicarious baptism for the dead which is best understood as reflecting a trust in the efficacy of the rite (1 Cor. 15.29).[3] This trust may be compared to the Romans' trust in the efficacy of religious rites.[4] In any case, although it would appear to be paradoxical, the Corinthians do seem to hold on to a trust in religious rites and at the same time a sceptical outlook towards idols.[5]

Although the Corinthians' sceptical view of idols and their eating behaviour could be the result of their being enlightened by the teachings of Paul[6] or of Apollos,[7] this may not be a total explanation for the presence of such an attitude. For if the enlightened Paul still found participation in pagan cults dangerous, and if the weak in the church might be offended by others' eating in pagan temples,[8] then enlight-

  1. Horsley seems to recognize the possibility that the Corinthians were practising some sort of 'sacrament', but simply wants to spiritualize it ('Gnosis in Corinth', p. 48).
  2. E. Käsemann, *Essays on New Testament Themes* (London: SCM Press, 1964), pp. 116-17.
  3. R. Bultmann, *Theology of the New Testament*, I (London: SCM Press, 1952), pp. 135-36; G. Wagner, *Pauline Baptism and the Pagan Mysteries* (trans. J.P. Smith; Edinburgh: Oliver & Boyd, 1967), pp. 271-72.
  4. According to Ogilvie, the Romans believed that the gods could be controlled through properly executed rites. He writes, 'There were prescribed methods of treating with the gods which had been proved efficacious by experience, but, provided that you followed them scrupulously, it did not matter whether you were yourself good or bad or whether your prayers were for worthy ends' (*Romans and their Gods*, p. 19).
  5. Cf. also von Soden, 'Sacrament and Ethics in Paul', p. 259; Talbert, *Reading Corinthians*, pp. 62-64; Fee, *First Corinthians*, p. 362.
  6. E.g. Robertson and Plummer, *First Corinthians*, p. 163.
  7. Horsley, '"How Can Some of You Say?"', p. 229.
  8. That there were some 'strong' people in the church should need no further explanation. As mentioned before, the presence of the weak is also assumed in most commentaries. There were two groups of people who might be regarded as the weak. First, because of their customs, many Jewish Christians very likely would abhor the eating of the meat offered to idols, not to mention participating in pagan cults

enment may not be enough to account for the behaviour of the Corinthians. In this respect, Theissen's observation regarding the problem of eating meat in Corinth may provide a helpful supplementary explanation. He has made an important contribution in highlighting the social significance of the conflicting attitudes in the church towards the eating of food offered to idols.[1] He has shown that the strong who insisted on their 'right' (1 Cor. 8.9; 10.23) and 'freedom' (1 Cor. 10.29) to eat as they pleased, were probably the rich and the socially powerful in the church (1 Cor. 1.26), because they were likely to be people who could afford to eat meat.[2] In that case, the enlightened ideas they accepted and the eating habits of the strong could reinforce one another. Against this background, if there were idolaters in the church, it is easy to assume that the rich and the powerful were among them.

Why then would these powerful people want to take part in meals at a cultic setting? This is an especially interesting question. For, according to some scholars, the Corinthians' participation in cultic meals should not be seen as accidental, but probably deliberate and in accordance with their convictions.[3] The motive for the strong's action is not stated by Paul. Several answers have been proposed. It could be that, through their eating, the Corinthians wanted to demonstrate their newly found freedom.[4] Or they might even think that, by their example, they could edify the weak.[5] These two answers are certainly possible. In the light of Theissen's study of the problem of eating meat and my study of the problems of litigation and immorality, there are grounds to suspect that more than theological interests were involved in the Corinthians' action. Based on the sociopolitical function of eating, it has been suggested that the Corinthians ate with pagan friends because they wanted to have fun and did not want to give up

(*4 Macc.* 5.1-38; *2 Macc.* 5.27) (Barrett, *First Corinthians*, p. 188; Dunn, *Romans*, p. 801). Secondly, some of the Gentile converts, who participated in pagan cults before turning to the new faith, might have regarded the eating of the sacrificial meat as offensive and incompatible with their new faith (1 Cor. 8.7) (Orr and Walther, *I Corinthians*, p. 234; Conzelmann, *I Corinthians*, pp. 146-47).

1. Theissen, *Social Setting*, pp. 121-43.
2. Theissen, *Social Setting*, pp. 125-29.
3. So Conzelmann, *I Corinthians*, p. 137; Willis, *Idol Meat*, pp. 110-11.
4. Robertson and Plummer, *First Corinthians*, p. 171.
5. Willis, *Idol Meat*, p. 104; Moffatt, *First Corinthians*, pp. 110-11.

on their former friends.[1] This is probably right. But Theissen's observation is more intriguing. He sees a connection between πλεονεξία and the Corinthians' eating of meat.[2] If the rich and the powerful Corinthians, Theissen suggests, wanted to increase their wealth or to strengthen their official position, they would have to cultivate relationships with pagans. One way to do it would be to eat with the pagans. We have already seen how litigation and the son's association with the stepmother could have been related to πλεονεξία. It may therefore be surmised that the strong might also want to gain from their eating in different settings. After all, they had strong theological reasons to justify their actions before the church. Since Theissen deals basically with the problem of eating idol-meat, I would like to follow his lead and investigate further to see if the socially strong's eating in an idol's temple could be related to the problem of πλεονεξία.

The Context
In first-century Corinth the occasions which might involve idolatry or temple feasting were many.[3] Therefore it is very difficult, if not impossible, to be certain about the *exact* celebration which the Corinthians took part in and which to Paul carried implications of εἰδωλολατρία. It is, however, common to see such occasions as harmless social occasions, such as marriages or funerals, which involved meals, either at home or in a pagan temple.[4] But it could just as well be an occasion of formal worship of a pagan god.[5] A few scholars, taking note of Paul's reference in 1 Cor. 8.5 to κύριοι in heaven or on earth, have argued that Paul might have in mind deified men or Roman emperors.[6] Moffatt, commenting on 1 Cor. 10.14-22,

1. Willis, *Idol Meat*, p. 103; Moffatt, *First Corinthians*, p. 142; Barrett, *First Corinthians*, p. 196.
2. Theissen, *Social Setting*, pp. 130-31.
3. For a catalogue of the cults in Corinth, see R. Lisle, 'Cults of Corinth' (PhD dissertation, Johns Hopkins University, 1955), pp. 99-125. For a discussion of various possible occasions for the taking of pagan meals, see Willis, *Idol Meat*, pp. 13-15; Conzelmann, *I Corinthians*, p. 147 and nn. 9, 10 and 11.
4. Murphy-O'Connor, *I Corinthians*, p. 81.
5. Willis, *Idol Meat*, p. 265.
6. W. Foerster, 'κύριος', *TDNT*, III, p. 1091; J. Weiss, *Der erste Korintherbrief* (Göttingen: Vandenhoeck & Ruprecht, 9th edn, 1910), p. 222; Deissmann, *Light from the Ancient East*, p. 355. Such an understanding, however,

3. *The Power of the Patrons* 147

also makes the suggestion that, among other feasting occasions, the Corinthians could have attended one of the 'civic religious ceremonies at which municipal officials' were present.[1] In Chapter 1 we saw how the imperial cult was organized and promoted in Corinth, especially in the first half of the first century, by the socially powerful, namely the government officials and local leaders, possibly with an eye to acquiring or remaining in power. Against this background I would like to investigate further and see if this has any bearing on the problem of idolatry and the eating of sacrificial meat in Corinth. It should, of course, be noted that I merely see the case of imperial cult as illustrative, and by no means the only context through which the significance of the Corinthians' participation in meals at an idol's temple can be appreciated.

To understand how the imperial cult might bear on the problem of food offered to idols in the church in general and the problem of eating in an idol's temple in particular, it is necessary to take a closer look at the details of its celebration. So what made up the imperial cult in the early Empire? In a broad sense it was made up of those actions which sought to honour the Roman emperors and/or members of the imperial family. The expressions of such honouring might vary slightly from one place to another,[2] but they usually included the building of altars[3] or imperial temples,[4] the setting up of imperial statues,[5] the holding of games or festivals,[6] the staging of processions,[7] and the

---

has been denied by Conzelmann (*I Corinthians*, p. 143) and Bruce (*I and II Corinthians*, p. 80).

1. Moffatt, *First Corinthians*, p. 141. See also pp. xvii-xix.
2. This study is concerned mainly with the public honouring of the emperors.
3. Narbo, AD 12–13 (Ehrenberg and Jones, *Documents*, no. 100 = Braund, *Augustus to Nero*, no. 125).
4. Eresus, later years of the Augustan age and early years of Tiberius's reign (Price, *Rituals and Powers*, p. 3). Cf. the Alexandrians' proposal to Claudius, AD 41 (Smallwood, *Documents*, no. 370 = Braund, *Augustus to Nero*, no. 571).
5. Forum Clodii, AD 18 (Ehrenberg and Jones, *Documents*, no. 101 = Braund, *Augustus to Nero*, no. 126); Olympia, Nemea, Delphia and Isthmus, AD 37 (Smallwood, *Documents*, no. 361 = Braund, *Augustus to Nero*, no. 564).
6. Gytheum, AD 15 (Ehrenberg and Jones, *Documents*, no. 102a = Braund, *Augustus to Nero*, no. 127).
7. Gytheum, AD 15 (Ehrenberg and Jones, *Documents*, no. 102a = Braund, *Augustus to Nero*, no. 127); Alexandria, AD 41 (Smallwood, *Documents*, no. 370 = Braund, *Augustus to Nero*, no. 571).

offering of sacrifices[1] in honour of the imperial house.

In Corinth, a Roman colony, there are more than enough indications that activities which honoured the imperial house, such as those mentioned above, were present and alive. First of all, there is the discovery of dedications to the emperor and his house.[2] Secondly, there is the presence of personnel devoted to the cult. They include *flamen*,[3] *pontifex*[4] and *augustalis*.[5] Thirdly, there is the building of structures for cultic purposes. An altar was constructed in the forum, probably in the Augustan age.[6] Temple E, the Roman temple located at the west end of the forum, was probably first built in the reign of Claudius. Fourthly, there is the holding of the imperial games. In fact, the development of such games in the period immediately before and probably during Paul's visit to Corinth suggests that the imperial cult not only existed but was also actively participated in and well

---

1. Sardis, 5–2 BC (Ehrenberg and Jones, *Documents*, no. 99 = Braund, *Augustus to Nero*, no. 124); Narbo, AD 12–13 (Ehrenberg and Jones, *Documents*, no. 100 = Braund, *Augustus to Nero*, no. 125); Gytheum, AD 15 (Ehrenberg and Jones, *Documents*, no. 102a = Braund, *Augustus to Nero*, no. 127); Forum Clodii, AD 18 (Ehrenberg and Jones, *Documents*, no. 101 = Braund, *Augustus to Nero*, no. 126); Achaea and Boeotia, AD 37 (Smallwood, *Documents*, no. 361 = Braund, *Augustus to Nero*, no. 564).

2. To the deified rulers, see Kent, *Inscriptions*, no. 50 (Julius Caesar), nos. 51-53 (Augustus); cf. Kent, *Inscriptions*, no. 55 (Augusta). For the safety of Tiberius, see West, *Latin Inscriptions*, no. 15 = Ehrenberg and Jones, *Documents*, no. 130 = Braund, *Augustus to Nero*, no. 159; West, *Latin Inscriptions*, no. 110 = Ehrenberg and Jones, *Documents*, no. 113 = Braund, *Augustus to Nero*, no. 140. For the victories of Claudius, West, *Latin Inscriptions*, nos. 86-90; Kent, *Inscriptions*, nos. 158-63.

3. West, *Latin Inscriptions*, no. 67 = Smallwood, *Documents*, no. 263 = Braund, *Augustus to Nero*, no. 468; West, *Latin Inscriptions*, no. 68 = Smallwood, *Documents*, no. 264 = Braund, *Augustus to Nero*, no. 469.

4. West, *Latin Inscriptions*, no. 68 = Smallwood, *Documents*, no. 264 = Braund, *Augustus to Nero*, no. 469; West, *Latin Inscriptions*, no. 132.

5. West, *Latin Inscriptions*, no. 77; Kent, *Inscriptions*, nos. 52, 53, 59. It is noteworthy that these Roman priesthoods and associations devoted to the imperial cult were more common in the west than in the east (A.D. Nock, '*Severi and Augustales*', in *Essays on Religion and the Ancient World* [ed. Z. Stewart; Oxford: Clarendon Press, 1972], p. 349; Price, *Rituals and Power*, p. 88). Their presence serves to remind us of the strength of the Roman tradition in Corinth.

6. See discussion in Chapter 1.

3. The Power of the Patrons

supported too.¹ For by AD 50, two more programmes were added, alongside the traditional Isthmian games: the Caesarea for honouring Augustus, the deified one, and his house, and the 'imperial contests' for honouring the reigning emperor. In fact c. AD 35 the Caesarea was for the first time celebrated before the Isthmian Games.² It is almost self-evident that the imperial cult was an important event in Corinth.

Concerning the worshipping aspect of the cult in Corinth, no direct information is available. But since competition among cities in the early Empire was not rare, it is reasonable to expect that activities which were practised elsewhere would also have been practised in Corinth.³ Let us then take a look at a comparable case. In AD 18 the people in Forum Clodii, a town in Etruria, proposed the following programme for the celebration of the birthdays of the emperors:

> For the birthday of Augustus, 24th September, two victims, which were usually sacrificed in perpetuity at the *altar dedicated to Augustan divinity*, should be sacrificed on 23rd and 24th September; likewise, on the birthday of Tiberius Caesar the decurions and people, to do so in perpetuity, should dine—an expense which Quintus Cascellius Labeo promises to pay in perpetuity, so that he should be thanked for his munificence—and that on that birthday a *calf* should be sacrificed each year. And that on the birthdays of Augustus and Tiberius Caesar, before the decurions go to eat, their *geniuses* should be invited to feast with *incense* and *wine* at the *altar of Augustan divinity*. We have had an altar built for Augustan divinity at our own expense; we have had *games* presented over six days from 13th August at our own expense. On the birthday of Augusta we gave honey-wine and a cakelet to the women of the community for Bona Dea at our own expense. Likewise, at the dedication of the *statues* of the Caesars and of Augusta we gave to the decurions and people honey-wine and cakelets at our own expense and we swore that we would give them in perpetuity on the day of that dedication; and so that that day may be more celebrated each year we shall keep it on 10th March, on which day Tiberius Caesar was most felicitously made pontifex maximus.⁴

1. Note the imagery of games behind 1 Cor. 9.24-27 (O. Broneer, 'The Apostle Paul and the Isthmian Games', *BA* 25 [1962], pp. 2-31).
2. West, *Latin Inscriptions*, no. 81 = Braund, *Augustus to Nero*, no. 664.
3. On this spirit of competition, see, e.g., Dio Chrysostom's attempt to enhance the pride and dignity of Prusa by erecting new buildings, holding festivals and obtaining the right to hold court (*Or.* 40.10-11; 43.1; 45.12-13). Dio Chrysostom also mentions the comparison between Athens and the island of Rhodes (*Or.* 31.121). See also Price, *Rituals and Power*, pp. 126-32.
4. Ehrenberg and Jones, *Documents*, no. 101 = Braund, *Augustus to Nero*,

150   *Patronage and Power*

From this account it seems clear that, among other things, sacrifices and feasts were especially important activities in the celebrations of the imperial cult at Forum Clodii. Some of the features concerning the worshipping aspect deserve to be mentioned. First, although the celebrations were held in the name of the emperor, the exact role of the emperor in the worship is ambiguous. Taylor argues that in effect the emperor was worshipped and writes,

> He [Augustus] had the worship that was accorded to his Genius and his Lares as official gods of the state. The cult of his Genius was really a worship of himself.[1]

But sacrifices were made at the altar dedicated to the Augustan divinity. The geniuses of the emperors are also said to be involved in the celebration. Secondly, the exact mechanics of the sacrificial act are assumed and not explained.[2] We only know that the victim offered was a calf. After the sacrifice, it appears that the *decuriones* or members of the city council would eat as a separate group in a setting near the altar. The beginning of the feast was marked by the use of wine and incense at the altar to invite the geniuses of the emperors to partake in the feast. Thirdly, in addition to sacrifices and feasts, games were also staged and statues dedicated. Fourthly, the celebrations appear to have involved not only the *decuriones*, but also the populace, both male and female. The rich paid for the expenses of the feasts, presumably including the games and any other needed items. The populace were thus able to enjoy the food and the games.

As seen in the above discussion, sacrifices and feasting made up an important part of the imperial cult. However, the exact details of the sacrificial act are far from clear. Based on the description found on inscriptions,[3] the sacrificial scenes projected by reliefs[4] and the town

---

no. 126. The original is in Latin. The translation is Braund's. Italics are added for emphasis. For a programme of the celebrations in the Greek east, see the inscription from Gytheum, a town in Laconia (Ehrenberg and Jones, *Documents*, no. 102a = Braund, *Augustus to Nero*, no. 127).

   1. Taylor, *Divinity*, p. 245.
   2. The exact mechanics of the sacrificial act are less clear. For a general discussion of the procedure in sacrifice, see Ogilvie, *Romans and their Gods*, pp. 43-51.
   3. Forum Clodii (Ehrenberg and Jones, *Documents*, no. 101 = Braund, *Augustus to Nero*, no. 126); Gytheum (Ehrenberg and Jones, *Documents*, no. 102a = Braund, *Augustus to Nero*, no. 127).
   4. See especially Ryberg, *Rites of the State Religion in Roman Art*.

3. The Power of the Patrons

plan of Corinth,[1] a rough sketch of the sacrificial ceremony in Corinth may be given as follows.[2] A procession led by the city magistrates would first enter the forum, coming perhaps from the Asclepion(?). Then the victim would be offered by the priests or magistrates, presumably on the altar in the forum facing Temple E in which idols of the gods or of the emperors were placed. After the sacrifices a feast would probably follow, though in a relatively large city like Corinth,[3] probably not everyone would be able to take part in it.[4] But the officiating priests, the *decuriones* and other prominent people would possibly share a meal within the precincts of the temple, even under the watchful eyes of the statues of the emperors and other gods. As to the populace, shares of the sacrificial meat might have been given to them[5] and would have been available for sale on the market.[6] In any case, the imperial cult could be one of the occasions in which most, if not all, of the people in Corinth would take part.[7] The poor probably would not want to miss the entertainment and the sacrificial meat.[8] As to the rich and the public officials, they probably would like to use the occasions to honour themselves[9] and to strengthen

1. See discussion in Chapter 1.
2. Cf. Price, *Rituals and Power*, pp. 108-109.
3. According to one estimation, the population of Corinth in Paul's days was around 90,000 (Gill, 'Roman Corinth', p. 17).
4. We have one inscription which tells of the giving of a public banquet to all the inhabitants of Corinth by the first Corinthian *agonothetes* of the Isthmian and the Caesarean games, probably to celebrate the completion of the buildings of the Caesarea and the return of the control of the Isthmian games to the Corinthians (Kent, *Inscriptions*, no. 153).
5. Price, *Rituals and Power*, p. 113.
6. Pliny, *Ep.* 10.96.10.
7. In Gytheum, different classes of people, male and female, young and old, were asked to take part in the procession. Moreover, the programme was presented in the form of 'sacred law'. See Ehrenberg and Jones, *Documents*, no. 102a, ll. 25-28, 38.
8. That the poor seldom ate meat has been documented by Theissen (*Social Setting*, p. 128). See also A.D. Nock, *St Paul* (London: Oxford University Press, 1946), p. 180.
9. The leaders could honour themselves in different ways. By putting on special costumes when officiating at ceremonies, they showed themselves to be different, if not superior. Taking a seat on the first bench among other prominent people when watching the games is another sign of distinction. On such honours and privileges,

their ties with the powerful people in town.[1]

Under such circumstances it would also be logical to assume that most, if not all, of the Gentile Christians in Corinth might have eaten such sacrificial meat or even taken part in the cult before they turned to the new faith. Moreover, they might have found it difficult to avoid participation even after their turning to the new faith, whether they wanted to or not. In other words, the problem over the eating of sacrificial meat was almost bound to arise. Of course, some of the Corinthians, plausibly the powerful people in church, for reasons of personal honour or ambition, might not want to avoid the imperial cult. In that case, the problem of eating at table in idols' temples could arise. So the imperial cult could account for the problems involved in 1 Corinthians 8–10. But there is another aspect of the imperial cult which is worth mentioning. It concerns the attitude of the people at that time towards the imperial cult.

To understand how the imperial cult could have been viewed at that time, it is helpful to point to the fact that Corinth was both a Roman colony and a city with a Hellenistic past in a Hellenistic world. Out of such a context, there appear to have developed, alongside one another, two sets of traditions—the official Roman tradition and the local Greek tradition. This is reflected in the language used in Corinth. The official language was of course Latin, but the common language was Greek. Not surprisingly, while the title *flamen* was found,[2] another Greek term *hieromnemon* might also be used as a reference to a Roman priest.[3] Parallel to these two traditions, it is significant to recognize that there were two different perceptions of the Roman emperor in relation to the gods. According to the official position, that is, the Roman tradition, an emperor, in theory at least, was not a god while he was alive.[4] Hence, divine honours were usually refused by the emperors. An emperor was only deified after his death and then only if he was worthy.[5] If an emperor was worthy he would then

see, e.g., Ehrenberg and Jones, *Documents*, no. 105 = Braund, *Augustus to Nero*, no. 130 (Narbo).

1. See discussion in Chapter 1. Cf. Theissen, *Social Setting*, p. 131.
2. West, *Latin Inscriptions*, nos. 67, 68.
3. West, *Latin Inscriptions*, no. 81 and Price's comment in *Rituals and Power*, p. 76 n. 92.
4. Taylor, *Divinity*, p. 240.
5. Taylor, *Divinity*, p. 241; Price, *Rituals and Power*, p. 75.

3. The Power of the Patrons 153

be made a *divus* or a 'man made into god'.[1] But it should be noted that even a *divus* was not equivalent to a *deus* or a god.[2] In the actual development of the cult in Corinth, however, parallel to the official position, we see the rise of the local tradition which seems to give a strong impression that the emperor or members of the imperial house were scarcely distinguishable from the gods, if not actually gods. So the empress Livia was deified while she was still alive, possibly in AD 23, that is, before her death in AD 29 and her formal deification in AD 42.[3] Some of the imperial portraits in the first century AD also suggest a tendency to divinize members of the imperial household.[4] Although it is difficult to assess the influence of language on such development, perhaps the possibility should not be overlooked that the difference between *divus* and *deus* in Latin would be lost when θεός, a word which makes no such distinction, was used to describe the emperor.[5] To an ordinary Greek the line between a deified man and the divine or, in this case, between the emperor and a god, was often not clear.[6]

So, the two positions probably co-existed in Corinth, the one being elitist and sceptical, the other, popular and naive.[7] As a result, two slightly different pictures of the divine emperor were current. In the one, the emperor was man, deified perhaps, but still not exactly a god. In the other, the emperor was not easily distinguishable from a god. It may seem risky and misleading, as has been pointed out, to generalize and assign the two views above respectively to two distinct groups of people, namely, the governing elites and the masses. Moreover, to say that the elitist view is sceptical does not necessarily mean that its holders are not interested in religious matters at all.[8] Nonetheless, it

1. Taylor, *Divinity*, p. 241.
2. Price, *Rituals and Power*, p. 220.
3. Kent, *Inscriptions*, no. 153 and commentary.
4. Ridgway, 'Sculpture from Corinth', p. 433.
5. Cf. Meritt, *Greek Inscriptions*, no. 19. See Price, 'Gods and Emperors: The Greek Language of the Roman Imperial Cult', *JHS* 104 (1984), pp. 79-95.
6. Nock, 'Religious Development', p. 481; Price, *Rituals and Power*, pp. 54-56.
7. So K. Scott, 'Humour at the Expense of the Imperial Cult', *CP* 27 (1932), pp. 317-28; Bowersock, 'Greek Intellectuals and the Imperial Cult in the Second Century AD', pp. 179-206.
8. It has been recently shown that Seneca who made a joke of the imperial apotheosis might support the deification of emperors with suitable qualities (M. Altman, 'Ruler Cult in Seneca', *CP* 33 [1938], pp. 198-204) and that jokes are

still seems reasonable, as MacMullen argues,[1] to expect the former view to be supported by the sophisticated and the latter by the common folk. Such a two-tier classification is accepted even by Price who explains the different orientation of the two groups as follows:

> The local elites who organised the cults had access to complex philosophical ideas about the gods which were not available to the masses, and one might argue... that the ceremonial therefore could not be understood in the same fashion by the two groups.[2]

It is not my intention here to suggest a source for the Corinthians' attitudes regarding the whole problem of food offered to idols, especially the problem of idolatry. Nevertheless the two views regarding the imperial cult described above provide an interesting and possibly illuminating comparison with the two conflicting attitudes in the church, namely those of the strong and those of the weak. Just as the phenomenon of the imperial cult can help partly to explain how the problem of food offered to idols could arise, the two kinds of attitude towards the cult may also provide a context for understanding the conflicting attitudes of the Corinthians towards the problem of food offered to idols, including the problem of eating in pagan temples.

The Idolaters

For our purposes, it is more important to mark the outlook of the elite. The elite apparently were powerful and sophisticated people. But they probably were also people who were sceptical about the imperial cult. Building on Theissen's insight I have surmised that the idolaters, whatever the source of their scepticism regarding the existence of the idols might be, should be located among the strong or the socially powerful in the church. Significantly, Paul refers to those who ate at table in an idol's temple and destroyed the weak as people who had knowledge (1 Cor. 8.10-11). But Paul warns earlier that 'knowledge puffs up' (1 Cor. 8.1-3). This immediately reminds us of the rich and powerful opponents of Paul in the church (1 Cor. 5.2; 4.18). In the light of this connection and the similarity in the general outlook between the strong and the sophisticated local elite, there seems to be

---

made about things which matter most (Price, *Rituals and Power*, pp. 114-15).

1. R. MacMullen, *Paganism in the Roman Empire* (New Haven: Yale University Press, 1981), pp. 8-9.
2. Price, *Rituals and Power*, p. 116.

3. The Power of the Patrons 155

more ground for accepting my conjecture. Indeed it seems probable that some members of the church, perhaps because of personal honour or for other political reasons, might have taken part in the celebration of the imperial cult.

It is noteworthy that the official who was responsible for the imperial cult in Gytheum was the *agoranomos*, the equivalent of an *aedile*, and that local officials, namely the *ephori*, were expected to sacrifice a bull on behalf of the emperors.[1] Interestingly enough, if and when Erastus, an οἰκονόμος τῆς πόλεως (Rom. 16.23), later became an *aedilis* in Corinth, he would probably have been responsible for organizing such sacrificial activities. In any case, as a public official, he probably would have had the opportunity to eat together with other public officials in the precincts of an idol's temple after sacrifices were offered on behalf of the emperor. He might even have had to take part in the sacrificial ceremony. If such were the case, he certainly could have been one of those who claimed that they had the ἐξουσία, the 'duty' or the 'right' (1 Cor. 8.9) to eat in an idol's temple (1 Cor. 8.10), just as Paul as an apostle had the right to claim financial support from the church (1 Cor. 9.3-6).[2] Apart from public officials, in other towns some citizens, possibly rich men, could also

---

1. Ehrenberg and Jones, *Documents*, no. 102a = Braund, *Augustus to Nero*, no. 127.
2. The term ἐξουσία can mean 'liberty' (Robertson and Plummer, *First Corinthians*, p. 171), 'authority' (Barrett, *First Corinthians*, p. 195) or 'right' (Moffatt, *First Corinthians*, p. 110). Since it is possible that the term originated with the Corinthians (Barrett, *First Corinthians*, p. 195; Horsley, 'Consciousness and Freedom', pp. 579-80), its significance for the Corinthians has been studied in the light of various religious and philosophical contexts, including Gnosticism (e.g. Schmithals, *Gnosticism*, pp. 224-29), Stoicism (e.g. Conzelmann, *I Corinthians*, p. 108) and Judaism (e.g. Horsley, 'Consciousness and Freedom', pp. 575-77). Against the syncretistic background of Hellenism, Willis finds it difficult to specify more precisely the meaning of the term for the Corinthians, apart from the idea of the authority to eat as they pleased (*Idol Meat*, p. 103). Such authority or right is certainly related to the Gnosis of the Corinthians. Nevertheless, in the light of Paul's discussion in 1 Cor. 9, especially 9.4-6, where Paul's foregoing of his rights is put forward as an example, one wonders if ἐξουσία could also refer, of course very subtly, to the idea of a kind of 'right' which comes as a result of one's role. If a person has the duty to take part in official ceremonies, like the imperial cult, could he argue that he has the right to do so?

be chosen to offer sacrifices in honour of the emperors.[1] It is therefore feasible that some of the richer members in the church might be chosen to hold such posts. These people too would find it difficult to turn down the invitation. After all, to justify their participation, they could have argued that the emperors were not God, since there was no God, but One.

If my interpretation of the problem of idolatry against the background of the imperial cult is convincing, not only will it support Theissen's contention that the socially powerful or the patrons in the church were behind the problem of food offered to idols, but it will also establish the probability that they were those who ate in pagan temples. Furthermore, they possibly were not just ordinary patrons, but really powerful people since they probably were able to link themselves up with the prominent people in Corinth, even the secular authorities in the city. Such connections would not only give them an edge over other leaders in the church, but might also place them among the more powerful people in the colony.

In the previous discussion I referred to Theissen's observation that there may be a connection between πλεονεξία and the eating of idol meat. Here I can explain how a similar connection could have existed between πλεονεξία and the eating at table in pagan temples. In the discussion in Chapter 1 we saw how the local elites sought to cultivate significant relationships with the powerful if they wanted to gain recognition and power or to stay in power under the patronage system of the Roman Empire. In Corinth, a Roman colony, it would seem especially important to express one's loyalty to the Roman masters by organizing or participating in activities such as the imperial cult. To put it another way, for these ambitious people, the eating in imperial feasts certainly would not commend them to God, but it would commend them to the powerful elites in Corinth.[2] For to get ahead of other competitors in the struggle for more power and honour, the ability to eat with powerful people in town would probably make a difference and would not be a matter of indifference. In any case, a

---

1. In Narbo, three Roman *equites* and three freedmen, presumably rich men, were chosen every year each to sacrifice a victim at the altar in the forum on 23rd September (AD 12–13 [Ehrenberg and Jones, *Documents*, no. 100 = Braund, *Augustus to Nero*, no. 125]).

2. Cf. 1 Cor. 8.8.

person like Erastus would hardly be able to achieve such a status without feasting with other prominent people in honour of the Roman emperors. In this sense an εἰδωλολάτρης might just as well be a πλεονέκτης, one who desires to have more political power.[1]

With reference to the Corinthians, the various attempts to understand their gnosis and freedom in terms of *one* particular religious or philosophical context, be it Gnosticism, Judaism, Stoicism or the like, suggests that many scholars would assume that there was only *one* group of opponents in the church. Our study of the problems of immorality, of litigation and of idolatry, has revealed that it is possible to see only one group of people behind them, namely the socially powerful. Moreover, it may be said that while their actions could be expressions of their freedom, this freedom perhaps was not available to the weak and the lowly. Furthermore their actions could also be manifestations of their πλεονεξία. Against this background we can perhaps explain further the relationship between the behaviour of such people and their theology, whatever its source may be. I would suggest that the Corinthian ideas of knowledge, freedom and authority could easily be used to legitimize the actions of the strong. In effect the status quo would be reinforced rather than challenged.

The Priestly Patron

In our previous discussion we saw that some people in the church, probably some powerful patrons, were keen on keeping contacts with those outside the church. Hence there arose in the church problems such as litigation before the pagan court, union with a pagan wife and eating in idol's temples. In 1 Cor. 15.29 Paul mentions in passing a little-known practice in the church at Corinth, namely, a kind of baptismal rite for the dead. It has been suggested that the dead persons for whom the rite was undergone were unbelievers.[2] If so, one may say that this is another problem in the church which involved the outsiders. Again one wonders if the powerful patrons in the church could

---

1. In so doing, they could of course claim that their action was good and for the edification of the church (1 Cor. 8.10). For it could be argued that it was the church's honour to have such people in its midst to provide protection and benefaction. But to Paul, such would not be the case. For the weak could thereby be destroyed.
2. Murphy-O'Connor, 'First Letter to the Corinthians', p. 813.

somehow be involved in it. But first we should perhaps ask if there was such a practice in the church.

Paul's reference to this little-known practice has puzzled many scholars.[1] Perhaps because the rite is obscure, it is not discussed by some of the scholars whose works on other problems in Corinth are significant.[2] Others doubt that Paul could be referring to a rite for the dead without disapproval.[3] Hence, there have been recurrent attempts to explain the rite away by emending the punctuation[4] or understanding it metaphorically. Godet, for example, in the light of 1 Cor. 15.30-32a, sees baptism in 1 Cor. 15.29 as meaning martyrdom or baptism of blood.[5] Talbert, on the other hand, understands 'the dead' as 'corpses', that is, the baptized themselves.[6] Many intelligent explanations have been put forward to avoid the 'normal' exposition.[7] The 'normal' exposition that some of the Corinthians are being baptized on behalf of[8] people who have already died[9] still seems to be commonly

---

1. According to K.C. Thompson, up to 200 explanations have been offered ('I Cor. 15,29 and Baptism for the Dead', *Studia Evangelica*, II [TU, 87; ed. F.L. Cross; Berlin: Akademie-Verlag, 1964], pp. 647-59). For a helpful summary of various hypotheses, see B.M. Foschini, '"Those Who are Baptised for the Dead", I Cor. 15.29', *CBQ* 12 (1950), pp. 260-76, 379-88; 13 (1951), pp. 46-78, 172-98, 276-83; M. Rissi, *Die Taufe für die Toten* (Zürich: Zwingli Verlag, 1962); A.J.M. Wedderburn, *Baptism and Resurrection: Studies in Pauline Theology against its Graeco-Roman Background* (Tübingen: Mohr, 1987), pp. 6-37.

2. So Theissen, Thiselton and apparently Horsley. Meeks only mentions the presence of the rite without much discussion (*First Urban Christians*, p. 162).

3. Murphy O'Connor, 'First Letter to the Corinthians', p. 813. But this is not a weighty objection. For Paul apparently was utilizing an *argumentum ad hominem* here (Barrett, *First Corinthians*, p. 363; G.R. Beasley-Murray, *Baptism in the New Testament* [London: Macmillan, 1962], p. 191). It is therefore understandable that he neither approves nor disapproves of it.

4. E.g. Thompson, 'I Cor. 15,29 and Baptism for the Dead', pp. 647-59.

5. F. Godet, *Commentary on First Corinthians* (Grand Rapids: Kregel, 1977), p. 817. Cf. J. Murphy-O'Connor, '"Baptized for the Dead" (I Cor. XV, 29) A Corinthian Slogan?' *RB* 88 (1981), pp. 532-43.

6. Talbert, *Reading Corinthians*, p. 99; J.C. O'Neill, 'I Corinthians 15.29', *ExpTim* 91 (1980), pp. 310-11.

7. Conzelmann, *I Corinthians*, p. 275.

8. The preposition ὑπέρ is usually taken to mean 'on behalf of' (e.g. Barrett, *First Corinthians*, p. 363). M. Raeder wants to take ὑπέρ as meaning 'for the sake of' ('Vikariatstaufe in I Cor. 15.29?', *ZNW* 46 [1955], pp. 258-60). But such a rendering is rare.

3. The Power of the Patrons

accepted as the more probable meaning of 1 Cor. 15.29.[1]
If there was a baptismal rite for the dead in Corinth, how are we to understand it? If there were Corinthians who underwent baptism on behalf of dead people, it naturally implies that a kind of vicarious baptism was being practised in the Church.[2] It may also be that the practice was rare in the early church, if not a uniquely Corinthian phenomenon[3] for, as Schnackenburg has rightly observed,[4] there is simply no clear evidence that such a rite could have been practised in the first century. It has few, if any, exact contemporary parallels.[5] In the whole of the New Testament, 1 Cor. 15.29 is the only place where such a rite is mentioned. References to a similar rite only appeared at a later date in the second century.[6]

The lack of exact parallels certainly poses a real problem. But Barrett has pointed out that it is not impossible that the rite could have been practised by the Corinthians.[7] Reitzenstein actually suggests that this practice of baptism for the dead was a rite adapted from the mystery cults.[8] This view is accepted by Schmithals who, however,

---

9. Barrett, *First Corinthians*, p. 363.
1. E.g. Moffatt, *First Corinthians*, pp. 252-53; Weiss, *Der erste Korintherbrief*, p. 363; R. Parry, *I Corinthians* (Cambridge: Cambridge University Press, 2nd edn, 1926), p. 228; Raeder, 'Vikariatstaufe', pp. 258-60; Beasley-Murray, *Baptism*, pp. 185-92; Hurd, *I Corinthians*, pp. 136-37; Rissi, *Die Taufe für die Toten*, p. 85; Barrett, *First Corinthians*, p. 363; Orr and Walther, *I Corinthians*, p. 337; Fee, *I Corinthians*, pp. 763-64. This is recognized even by those who do not see it that way (e.g. Murphy O'Connor, 'First Letter to the Corinthians', p. 813).
2. For a survey of the different views which regard the rite as vicarious baptism, see Foschini, '"Baptised for the Dead"', *CBQ* 13 (1951), pp. 46-61.
3. Barrett, *First Corinthians*, p. 363; Beasley-Murray, *Baptism*, p. 190; Orr and Walther, *I Corinthians*, p. 337; Fee, *First Corinthians*, p. 764.
4. R. Schnackenburg, *Baptism in the Thought of St Paul* (Oxford: Basil Blackwell, 1964), pp. 100-101.
5. The often quoted parallels are Plato, *Republic* 364E-365A; *Orphica Fragment* no. 232. See Conzelmann, *I Corinthians*, p. 275 n. 116; A. Oepke, 'βάπτω κτλ.', *TDNT*, I, p. 542; A. Schweitzer, *The Mysticism of Paul the Apostle* (London: A. & C. Black, 2nd edn, 1953), pp. 283-84.
6. So John Chrysostom's reference to Marcionites (Conzelmann, *I Corinthians*, p. 276 n. 117).
7. Barrett, *First Corinthians*, p. 363.
8. R. Reitzenstein writes: 'I cannot regard the so-called proxy-baptism, which appears in the Corinthian community in the apostolic age... as a new Christian

160 *Patronage and Power*

compares those who practised it to Gnostics.[1] It is not necessary to see those who practised the rite as Gnostics. While mystery cults may perhaps provide a partial context for understanding the rite, the syncretistic religious context of the Graeco-Roman world with its quasi-magical overtones, as Wedderburn seems to imply,[2] should be adequate for understanding the rise of such a rite. In any case, what I seek to do below is of a different nature. I would like to investigate in order to see how the social context in the early Empire may help us understand such an enigmatic rite.

The Context
Foschini, who denies that such a rite existed, asserts that the idea of vicarious baptism could hardly have been borrowed from the cultural environment of Paul's day.[3] If we wanted to look for an exact antecedent, we probably would have to agree with Foschini's assertion. However, if we broaden our scope to see the rite in the light of patronal relations in the first-century world, we may be able to appreciate, though in a different way, the nature of such a cult. As mentioned above, the baptismal rite is probably vicarious in nature. In other words, it is an action taken by one party (the living) on behalf of another party (the dead) with the aim of achieving certain results. If we look for parallels in this direction we may be able to see that such kinds of 'vicarious action' were certainly not lacking in the first-century world, even in Corinth.

As far as the relationship between the baptized and the deceased in the baptismal rite is concerned, it is not unlike the relationship between the head of a Roman household and the dead of the household in a rite observed at *Lemuria*[4] or the day of Ghosts. At *Lemuria* the dead of the household, such as those who died young and who suppos-

---

creation, but only as an adaptation of a pagan mystery-usage to Christian conceptions and prescriptions' (*Hellenistic Mystery-Religions: Their Basic Ideas and Significance* [Pittsburgh: Pickwick Press, 1978], p. 287).

1. Schmithals, *Gnosticism*, pp. 256-59.
2. Wedderburn, *Baptism*, p. 290.
3. Foschini, '"Baptised for the Dead"', *CBQ* 13 (1951), p. 65.
4. Originally the *Lemuria* was both a public and a private cult. But only the ritual of the private cult is known (Ovid, *Fasti* 5.419-444; Ogilvie, *Romans and their Gods*, pp. 85-87; H.H. Scullard, *Festivals and Ceremonies of the Roman Republic* [London: Thames & Hudson, 1981], pp. 118-19).

3. The Power of the Patrons 161

edly would haunt the house, would be appeased by the head of the household for the well-being of the living members.[1] A similar kind of relationship is also seen in public cults. In an inscription from Cumae, a *prytanis*, a magistrate with police powers, was praised for fulfilling his duties. Some of the official's duties are recorded as follows:

> The people approve of the prytanis Kleanax and praise him for his continuous preservation of good will toward the people; all his duties at present as prytanis he has performed, on the one hand, on the New Year's Day, with sacrifices to the gods in the ancestral manner. . . and has made the sacrifices for the prosperity in the ancestral manner. . . and, on the other hand, he has made the sacrifices for the dead on the customary day in the ancestral manner. . .[2]

From the above inscription it seems clear that the *prytanis*, a public official, also had a priestly role to play. But it is especially significant to note that some of the sacrifices were offered for the dead by this public official, presumably to appease the dead and to secure the well-being of the local community. It is also noteworthy that a kind of 'vicarious action' is also seen in the celebration of the imperial cult. As mentioned before, the officials at Gytheum were asked to offer sacrifices on behalf of the emperors, past or present, for the safety of the rulers and the continuance of the imperial rule.[3] These actions are

---

1. The cult was celebrated every year on 9, 11 and 13 May. The ritual is summarized by Ogilvie as follows:

> After rising at midnight and washing his hands, he (the householder) walked barefoot through the house spitting nine black beans from his mouth. As he spat each bean, he looked away and intoned the magic spell 'with these I ransom me and mine'. The ghosts crept up and ate the beans, while his back turned he washed his hands again and beat a loud gong. Then intoning another spell nine times ('ancestral ghosts, depart'), he looked round and the ghosts vanished (*Romans and their Gods*, p. 85).

2. The translation is Sherk, *Roman Empire*, no. 7.2E. The inscription is dated c. 2 BC–AD 2.
3. Ehrenberg and Jones, *Documents*, no. 102a = Sherk, *Roman Empire*, no. 32, ll. 28-29: 'And when the procession comes to the Caesareion (temple of Caesar), the ephors shall sacrifice a bull on behalf of (ὑπέρ or 'for' [Braund, *Augustus to Nero*, no. 127]) the safety of our rulers and gods ('deified ones' [Lewis and Reinhold, *Roman Civilization*, II, p. 561]) and the eternal continuance of their rule'. According to Price, θεοί should be seen as referring to the emperors (*Rituals and Power*, p. 210 n. 19). Two other kinds of rites practised for the emperors may be mentioned here. (1) Pliny talks of praying on the behalf of Trajan for his safety (*Ep.*

understandable against the background of a patronage society in which favour or protection from danger is secured by the help of patrons or mediators. The people in Corinth, especially the powerful men who often served at the same time as imperial priests, would not be unfamiliar with this part of their culture.

In the light of such 'vicarious actions' it can perhaps be said that, although exact parallels in form to the rite of baptism for the dead might not be available, the ethos which could give rise to such a rite was there. It cannot be proved. But it is credible, as some suggest,[1] that the rite of baptism for the dead was an indigenous form of 'Christian' baptism undergone by the Corinthians. If this was the case, questions will naturally be raised concerning the agent through which such a rite was adapted. For our purposes, however, the more important questions which await further examination are, who would want to undergo such a rite, and for what purpose?

The Priest

Who would want to undergo such a rite? From Paul's discussion, it appears that the baptized ones bear the following characteristics. First, Paul refers to them as οἱ βαπτιζόμενοι which suggests that they belonged to a particular group of people in the community, and that the rite was not practised by the whole church.[2] Secondly, since the whole point of referring to such a custom in the church is to expose the apparently inconsistent position held by those Corinthians who denied the resurrection of the dead (1 Cor. 15.12), it is therefore best, as Wedderburn suggests, to identify the baptized ones as people not

---

10.13, 14; cf. 10.35, 100). (2) There were also people who practised the rite of *taurobolium* or baptism in bull's blood for the welfare of the emperor (Nock, 'Early Gentile Christianity', in *Essays*, pp. 102-103; MacMullen, *Paganism*, pp. 103, 105). On *taurobolium*, see S. Angus, *The Mystery-Religions: A Study in the Religious Background of Early Christianity* (New York: Dover, 1975), pp. 94-95; J. Ferguson, *The Religions of the Roman Empire* (London: Thames & Hudson, 1970), pp. 29-31, 104-106. On the possibility that *taurobolium* may have been related to the situation in Corinth, see G. Hollmann, *Urchristentum in Korinth* (Leipzig: Hinrichs, 1903), pp. 22-23.

1. Reitzenstein, *Hellenistic Mystery-Religions*, p. 287; Beasley-Murray, *Baptism*, p. 190.
2. Barrett, *First Corinthians*, p. 362; Fee, *First Corinthians*, p. 763 n. 15.

3. *The Power of the Patrons* 163

unlike those who deny the resurrection.¹ Thirdly, the importance attached to the practice of the rite also suggests that they were people who put their trust in the power of sacraments or religious rites.²

All these signs point to an outlook which we have seen earlier in our discussion. The trust in the power of religious ritual reminds us of the idolaters who claimed to have knowledge (1 Cor. 8.1, 4) and who seem to have put their trust in the power of 'sacraments' (1 Cor. 10.1-22). Indeed, Paul's reference to ἀγνωσία θεοῦ in 1 Cor. 15.34 could have been a subtle comment on people such as the idolaters who claimed to have knowledge.³ The denial of the resurrection, whatever it may mean specifically to the Corinthians, reflects basically an interest in the here and now.⁴ Such an outlook is not unlike that of the litigants who were interested in things of this world rather than the next (1 Cor. 6.1-11). The use of τινες with reference to those who have no knowledge of God (1 Cor. 15.34) seems to suggest that Paul has in mind a special group in the church.⁵ As the same word is used in connection to those who deny the resurrection (1 Cor. 15.12), and its singular form with the immoral man (1 Cor. 5.1) and the plaintiff (1 Cor. 6.1), this may imply that these different categories of people, including the baptized ones, belonged to one and the same group. As argued in our previous discussion, the immoral man, the plaintiff and the idolaters were plausibly the powerful people in the church. If so, there are reasons to believe that those who were among the deniers of the resurrection and who underwent baptism, presumably to secure benefits for the dead, could possibly be the powerful few in the church (1 Cor. 1.26).⁶

1. Wedderburn, 'The Denial of the Resurrection', p. 230. See also Weiss, *Der erste Korintherbrief*, p. 363; Schmithals, *Gnosticism*, p. 257; Conzelmann, *I Corinthians*, p. 276.
2. Bultmann, *Theology*, I, pp. 135-36; Nock, 'Early Gentile Christianity', in *Essays*, p. 117; Hurd, *I Corinthians*, p. 286.
3. Wedderburn, 'The Denial of the Resurrection', p. 233.
4. Thiselton, 'Realized Eschatology', p. 524.
5. Barrett, *First Corinthians*, p. 368.
6. It seems to make good sense to see this emphasis on here and now as an outlook more readily accepted by people who could enjoy special privileges in this life (cf. 1 Cor. 15.19) than by those who could not. A comparable model may be found in the outlook of the Sadducees who, as people in control of both political and religious powers, had no need of a resurrection theology (A.C. Sundberg, 'Sadducees', *IDB*, IV, pp. 160-63; Koester, *Introduction*, I, pp. 229-30, 404-405).

If those who underwent baptism for the dead were the powerful few in the church, they would not be unlike the local officials or the powerful people in Corinth and other places. As seen in the example quoted above, the *prytanis* not only served as a public official but also as a priest. This dual role of politician and of priest also appears to be an image projected by the powerful public figures in Corinth. Augustus, for instance, is sometimes presented as a priestly figure. One statue represents him as a priest or a magistrate pouring a sacrificial libation and wearing a toga over his head to form a sacrificial veil.[1] It is therefore small wonder that the government officials, and rich local notables often acted as some kind of priests. Patrons or leaders in associations and the head of a Roman household also assumed the role of priests. Those who already had power might have wanted to serve in a priestly role to win honour. For example, the *prytanis* mentioned above got his munificent deeds recorded on an inscription as his reward. The image of priest and magistrate projected by the imperial statue and symbolizing his power to secure both material and spiritual benefits might be another reward treasured by the rich and the powerful.

So the priest might at the same time be an authority figure. The authority of these powerful leaders was sometimes exercised in a very religious way. For example, there was a local leader in Corinth who founded a cult in honour of the emperor Claudius. It is also interesting to note that the father of the *prytanis* mentioned above, apparently also a *prytanis*, is said to have taken the initiative himself to assume the role of a priest and a benefactor in supporting the organization of the mysteries in the city.[2] In the light of these cases, assuming that baptism for the dead, as suggested by some, was an indigenous phenomenon, it may be surmised that the powerful people in the church would be in a strong position to encourage, if not to introduce, the practice of such a rite. Whether this was the case or not, if those who were being baptized for the dead were those who did not believe in the resurrection of the dead, why then did they undergo such a rite for the dead?

Paul's reference to the Corinthian practice of baptism for the dead

---

1. Johnson, *Sculpture*, no. 134; Swift, 'Imperial Portraits', *AJA* 25 (1921), p. 145.
2. Sherk, *Roman Empire*, no. 7.2E.

3. *The Power of the Patrons*   165

in his argument against the Corinthians' denial of the resurrection gives the impression that the Corinthians were being inconsistent in their practice and their belief, that is, a rejection of a life after death (cf. 1 Cor. 15.19, 32). Yet those who were baptized might not have seen it that way. The fact that the Corinthians practised such a rite seems to suggest that they believed in some kind of existence after death.[1] This has led some scholars to suspect that Paul might have misunderstood or misrepresented the Corinthians' position.[2] If these scholars are right, it would mean that the Corinthians' understanding of the baptismal rite for the dead was different from Paul's. Since what we can learn about the situation comes basically through Paul, any attempt to suggest the reason why some of the Corinthians practised a baptismal rite for the dead is bound to be tentative. Nevertheless, if the powerful patrons were indeed among those who were baptized, it makes sense to try to understand the rite in the light of their outlook as we see it attested elsewhere in the letter.

The practice of a rite for the dead naturally implies that it was received in order to impart some kind of benefit to those who had died unbaptized.[3] The nature of the benefit to be imparted of course escapes us. It is nevertheless conceivable that the rite might have been intended to make provisions for the dead, just as a patron in a house would look after the living in the house. Whether it was meant to appease the dead or to purify their sins is not clear.[4] However, if as argued before, the powerful patrons in the church were not uninterested in the present, it is feasible that the rite of baptism for the dead was undertaken with an interest in the blessings of the here and now. As to how it accommodated such an interest, one can only surmise. As mentioned before, the reward which the *prytanis* in Cumae and presumably the powerful leaders in Corinth received for their religious service was honour and a powerful image. We have also seen how it is plausible that some of the powerful patrons would be people who wanted to have more money and more power. If those who got baptized were also the powerful few, could part of the reason why they

---

1. Foschini, '"Baptised for the Dead"', *CBQ* 12 (1950), p. 263.
2. Wedderburn, 'The Denial of the Resurrection'; Bultmann, *Theology*, I, p. 169. Note also Hurd's discussion (*I Corinthians*, pp. 196-98).
3. Beasley-Murray, *Baptism*, p. 187.
4. Plato, *Republic* 364E-365A; *Orphica Fragment* no. 232.

practised the rite have been to gain rewards in terms of honour and recognition? Given the brevity and obscurity of the reference, we can do no more than raise the possibility and indicate a degree of plausibility.

Conclusion

In his comprehensive study on 1 Corinthians Hurd regards 'the case of incest, the case of litigation' as 'smaller issues'.[1] As seen from the above analysis, they can hardly be insignificant issues. On the contrary, they serve to enlighten other aspects of the opponents in Corinth. Here two concluding remarks can be made. First, it looks very likely that some relatively powerful patrons were behind the problems in the church discussed above, whatever the theological views they actually espoused. In other words, more support is given to the conclusion reached in Chapter 2, which is that at the time of the writing of 1 Corinthians, the church was possibly already dominated by some powerful people. Moreover, if such people were indeed involved in the problems discussed above, it is possible to postulate that they owed their influence not only to their wealth, but also to their connections with other powerful people in the colony. Secondly, if the various arguments presented above are correct, it would appear that there was a group of people in the church who, through lawsuits, marriage or social fellowship with the powerful leaders in the colony, constantly sought to gain more, including possessions, power and honour. If they were people of power, they would have fewer problems in claiming that they could do all things (1 Cor. 6.12; 10.23). If such were the people behind many of the problems in the church, how would Paul respond to their challenge? This question will be examined in the next chapter.

---

1. Hurd, *I Corinthians*, p. 107.

Chapter 4

THE RESPONSE OF PAUL

According to Dahl[1] one of the reasons why Paul wrote 1 Corinthians was to re-establish his authority as apostle and spiritual father of the church at Corinth. While Fiorenza agrees with Dahl that 1 Corinthians aims at establishing Paul's authority, she contends that 1 Corinthians does not seek to re-establish but to establish Paul as the unique authority in the church, namely the *sole* founder of the church at Corinth.[2] If Paul did seek to assert his authority in the church through the writing of 1 Corinthians, it would be interesting to know how the issue of authority was perceived by Paul and how his authority was applied to the situation in Corinth.

Fiorenza is of the opinion that Paul's authority could have been used in an oppressive way. She writes,

> In I Corinthians Paul introduces the vertical line of patriarchal subordination not only into the social relationships of the *ekklesia*, but into its symbolic universe as well by arrogating the authority of God, the 'father', for himself. He does so in order to claim for his interpretation of divine power the authority of the singular father and founder of the community. He thereby seeks to change the understanding of persuasive-consensual authority based on pneumatic competence accessible to all into that of compulsory authority based on the symbolization of ultimate patri-archal power. It is Paul who introduces into the early Christian special missionary movement 'Christian patriarchalism which receives its coloration from the warmth of the ideal of love'.[3]

In his own way G. Shaw also regards Paul as a person who exercised his authority with the aim of manipulating and dominating the

---

1. Dahl, 'Church at Corinth', p. 321.
2. Fiorenza, 'Rhetorical Situation', pp. 396-97.
3. Fiorenza, 'Rhetorical Situation', p. 397.

church.[1] Theissen steers a middle course. While he sees Paul preaching a kind of love-patriarchalism which 'takes social differences for granted but ameliorates them through an obligation of respect and love',[2] he seems to regard it positively as Paul's way to integrate people from various strata of society into the Christian community. Judge, however, is able to appreciate the 'revolutionary' implication of Paul's teaching. Judge accepts that Paul was probably involved in the patronage system of his day.[3] In the light of Paul's conflict with the Corinthians Judge goes on to argue that Paul repudiated 'the status convention which permitted people to exploit the system to private advantage'.[4] So was Paul a crafty apostle who manipulated the church to his own ends? Or was Paul at heart 'a radical critic' who was not afraid to confront the powerful patrons in the church?

In Chapter 2, I attempted to show that Paul was probably confronted by some of the rich and powerful patrons in the community. In Chapter 3, I sought to show that those problems which I examined were problems caused by the rich and powerful patrons in the church who had no scruples in exercising their power or right to pursue their own ambitions. If the various arguments are correct, it is plausible that such powerful patrons were the people who were able to exert influence in the church at the time of the writing of 1 Corinthians. How then did Paul respond to the situation in Corinth? What implications do Paul's instructions in 1 Corinthians have on the patronal ties in the church?

We can only hope to find an answer to the above questions, if an answer is possible, by examining what Paul has written in 1 Corinthians. It is therefore my intention in this chapter to examine Paul's response to the situation in Corinth, paying special attention to those actions which Paul encourages the church to take and their implications for the patron–client ties in the church.

At this point it will be helpful to remind ourselves of some of the important features regarding patron–client relation. The crucial element which makes a person a patron is the ability to monopolize the access to resources so that others who want to have access to such

1. Shaw, *Cost of Authority*.
2. Theissen, *Social Setting*, p. 107.
3. Judge, 'Paul as a Radical Critic', p. 196.
4. Judge, 'Cultural Conformity and Innovation', p. 12.

4. The Response of Paul

resources can do nothing but to depend on that person for help and favour. Often this dependent relation involves interpersonal obligations which can be expressed in terms of reciprocity and loyalty. A client, for instance, has an obligation to honour and to be loyal to the patron. Because the client has to depend on the patron, a vertical or hierarchical relationship is generated. The impact of patronage on interpersonal relationships is well expressed by Eisenstadt and Roniger as follows:

> These relations [patron–client relations] are undertaken between individuals or networks of individuals in a vertical fashion (the simplest manifestation of which is a strong dyadic one) rather than between organised corporate groups; and they seem to undermine the horizontal group organization and solidarity of clients and patrons alike—but especially of the clients.[1]

In the light of the above features of patron–client relations, it is conceivable that patrons in the church at Corinth could expect their dependents to be loyal to them, and that they themselves, in turn, might have to fulfil their obligations to some more powerful patrons outside the church. In the discussion in Chapter 3 I suggested that such a custom may partly explain the Corinthians' approval of the immoral man's association with his stepmother and their participation in idolatrous feasts. Here I will look more closely at Paul's response in 1 Corinthians.

Paul's Exhortations

The opening and closing of 1 Corinthians are worth our attention. As mentioned before, Paul begins 1 Corinthians by highlighting his role as an apostle of Christ Jesus (1 Cor. 1.1). This gives the impression that Paul wants to assert his authority in the church. But it should be noted that Paul apparently did not see his authority as an absolute authority. For, at the end of 1 Corinthians, he tells the Corinthians solemnly that they should love and be loyal to[2] the Lord or should

---

1. Eisenstadt and Roniger, *Patrons, Clients and Friends*, pp. 48-49.
2. In 1 Cor. 16.22, instead of using ἀγαπᾶν, Paul uses φιλεῖν which is found only here in the undisputed Pauline letters. Moffatt suggests the meaning of 'loyalty, whole-hearted devotion... inspired by personal gratitude' (*First Corinthians*, pp. 280-81). Many commentators are aware of the 'un-Pauline character' of φιλεῖν

become 'friends' of the Lord,[1] lest they come under God's curse (1 Cor. 16.22). This appears to be Paul's reminder to the Corinthians that they have an obligation neither to him, nor to any human authorities, but solely to the Lord. This piece of advice can be appreciated more fully against the background of the existing patron–client ties in the Christian community in Corinth.

As argued before, the immoral man who associated with his father's wife could have been one of the rich and powerful patrons in the church. If this was the case it would be easy to imagine that he was an influential patron in the church, and that not many would dare to take any action against him, even though there might have been people who disapproved of his behaviour.[2] After all, the immoral man could plausibly justify his action on the ground that all things were lawful (1 Cor. 6.12): as a spiritual person and a 'king' (1 Cor. 4.8), he is free to do what he wants (1 Cor. 6.12). It is thus understandable that there might actually be people in the church who supported and were proud of such a powerful patron (1 Cor. 5.2, 6; cf. 3.21).

But for Paul who saw himself and the church as belonging to a more powerful master, namely God, such approval was intolerable. Small wonder that Paul seems to be alarmed by the church's decision or perhaps indecision (1 Cor. 5.2). In the eyes of Paul the church was faltering in its loyalty to God. Hence the Corinthians are reminded that Christ, the paschal lamb, was sacrificed for them (1 Cor. 5.7), and that they ultimately belonged to God who had paid a price to ransom them, thus establishing a more powerful claim on them than that of any earthly patron (1 Cor. 6.20; 7.23). Consequently the

---

in 1 Cor. 16.22 (Fee, *First Corinthians*, p. 837). It has been suggested that Paul is quoting a traditional formula (e.g. Barrett, *First Corinthians*, p. 396; Käsemann, *New Testament Questions of Today*, pp. 69-70). But it should also be noted that φιλεῖν can carry patronal overtones (e.g. Jn 19.12) (Marshall, *Enmity*, p. 131; Garnsey and Saller, *Roman Empire*, pp. 148-50, 154-56).

1. Parry, *I Corinthians*, p. 251. Perhaps because of the patronal overtones, as Judge has observed, Paul seldom uses friendship language ('Social Identity', p. 214). Paul's use of φιλεῖν in 1 Corinthians thus looks especially striking. In the light of my reconstructed situation in Corinth, it is plausible that the uncommon use of φιλεῖν in 1 Corinthians was inspired by the situation Paul faced in Corinth.

2. That there were people who informed Paul orally about such an act of immorality may suggest that there were people in the church who disliked it (1 Cor. 5.1; cf. 1.11).

4. The Response of Paul

Corinthians are encouraged to live a new life in sincerity and truth which is worthy of their master (1 Cor. 5.8). It follows that they should drive the man out of the fellowship (1 Cor. 5.3-5; cf. 5.13).[1] If the immoral man was really a powerful patron, Paul's ruling here is highly significant.[2] The same may be said about Paul's response to the issue of the eating of idolatrous feasts.

If the idolatrous feasts in which some of the Corinthians took part were really feasts related to the imperial cult and held with the intention of acquiring public honour and power, as I argued in Chapter 3, this will provide us with another example of the conflict created by the demand to be loyal to God and the demand to be loyal to man. In order for people such as Erastus (if he really was the rising star who later became one of the *aediles* in the colony) to get ahead of other competitors or to bring honour to themselves,[3] it would be essential for them to take part in occasions which were designed to express loyalty to the Roman emperor, such as a feast in a pagan temple.

If it seemed acceptable to a patron in the church to join in such feasts, the idolatrous implications of such actions were simply too offensive to Paul. So Paul warns the Corinthians, perhaps the powerful patrons in particular,[4] that they are not stronger than the Lord (1 Cor. 10.22). Paul also asks the Corinthians to flee from idolatry (1 Cor. 10.14), because they cannot serve two masters. They cannot

---

1. Forkman, *Limits of the Religious Community*, p. 140.
2. If the man was a powerful patron, would Paul be able to drive him out easily? We have no certain answer to this question. But in view of the fact that Paul had to defend his authority again in 2 Cor. 10–13, it may be surmised that the conflict between Paul and some of the Corinthians was still unresolved some time after the writing of 1 Corinthians.
3. Perhaps we should not rule out the possibility that people such as Erastus were required to take part in idolatrous feasts because they had to fulfil their official duty. But the idolatrous implication of such an action probably would still make it unacceptable to Paul.
4. Some see ἰσχυρότεροι as an indirect reference to the 'strong' in the church (e.g. Barrett, *First Corinthians*, p. 238; Murphy-O'Connor, 'First Letter to the Corinthians', p. 808). But others do not think so (e.g. Conzelmann, *I Corinthians*, p. 174; Fee, *First Corinthians*, p. 474). Willis, for example, does not see ἰσχυρότεροι as alluding to a special group in Corinth, but 'to the concrete issue of participation in the pagan meals' (*Idol Meat*, p. 215). But if what I have argued is right, that is, the participants in idolatrous feasts were a few of the powerful patrons, it is just possible that Paul refers to such people here. Cf. 1 Cor. 4.10; 8.7, 10.

worship God and at the same time take part in feasts which honour demons (1 Cor. 10.14-22). On the contrary, they should do all things to the glory of the real master, namely God (1 Cor. 10.31).[1]

Paul's Defence

If the church's acceptance of the immoral man in their midst and the participation in the idolatrous feasts by some of the Corinthians indicate that they submitted themselves, not to God and Christ, but to more powerful men, then Paul's refusal to accept financial support from the church at Corinth would signify his unwillingness to be obligated to the powerful patrons in the church. As argued before, even if Paul's authority was not challenged by the church, he apparently was not on good terms with some of the people, presumably the powerful leaders in the church. His discussion in 1 Cor. 4.1-5 and 9.1-23 not only gives the impression that Paul was confronted by some of the people in the church, but also that Paul saw the need to assert his loyalty to God.

1 Cor. 4.1-5. Here Paul sounds as if he is counteracting some pressure from the Corinthians which could have undermined his loyalty to God. Paul emphasizes that he cares little if he is being investigated (ἀνακριθῶ) by the Corinthians (1 Cor. 4.3).[2] In the light of my previous reconstruction and the language Paul uses in this passage,[3] it

---

1. 1 Cor. 10.31 parallels 6.20 (Murphy-O'Connor, 'First Letter to the Corinthians', p. 808).
2. The use of the verb ἀνακρίνω suggests that Paul could have been examined or scrutinized by some of the people in the church at this stage (1 Cor. 4.3) (Barrett, *First Corinthians*, p. 101).
3. It is noteworthy that, in the undisputed letters of Paul, some of the words Paul uses in this passage appear only or predominantly in 1 Corinthians. They include ὑπηρέτης, ἀνάκρισις (ἀνακρίνω), βουλή. It is also worth pointing out that these words were often used in connection with the court and public life.
   (a) The word ὑπηρέτης could refer to a servant of the council in Athens (Demosthenes 47.35). According to Murphy-O'Connor, it acquired 'a technical connotation in the language of the courts and the public service, namely, that of "official witness" (Lk. 1.4)' (*I Corinthians*, p. 29). Compare οἰκονόμος which could also denote a position of power (1 Cor. 4.1; Rom. 16.23) (Murphy-O'Connor, *I Corinthians*, p. 29).
   (b) The process of ἀνάκρισις could refer to the preliminary examination in a legal

4. The Response of Paul

is natural to surmise that those to whom Paul gives his answer were some of the more powerful patrons in the church. In his reply Paul suggests that to him the one who really matters is not man but the Lord, the judge who will come to reveal what is in man's heart. The praise (ἔπαινος) which comes from his master is worth more than that which is dispatched by a human council.[1] For Paul sees himself as a servant (ὑπηρέτης) and a steward (οἰκονόμος) in the household of God. As such it is important for him to be faithful to God, the master in the house, not to the Corinthians, not even to himself.[2] Paul's declaration of his ultimate loyalty to God in 1 Cor. 4.1-5 is clear.

1 Cor. 9.1-23. In 1 Corinthians 9 Paul again has to defend himself against those in the church who might have investigated him.[3] It looks likely that they were those in the church who provided material support for other apostles (1 Cor. 9.12a), that is, the rich patrons who had money to spend on their inferiors.[4] According to Hock[5] it is also likely that there were other apostles who accepted pay (μισθός) from the rich patrons and, consequently, were beholden to them as clients. If so, Paul's refusal to accept support from the church, in effect,

---

proceeding (Isaeus 6.12-13; D.M. MacDowell, *The Law in Classical Athens* [London: Thames & Hudson, 1978], pp. 235-59) or to the δοκιμασία of the Athenian archons before they took office (Aristotle, *Ath.* 45.3; 55.2-4; P.J. Rhodes, *The Athenian Boule* [Oxford: Clarendon Press, 1972], pp. 176-78).

(c) The word βουλή could refer, perhaps not so directly here, to a 'council' or 'senate' in which matters related to 'public honour' (ἔπαινος) are decided (Smallwood, *Documents*, no. 401 = Braund, *Augustus to Nero*, no. 673) or public magistrates scrutinized (Aristotle, *Ath.* 55.2).

The concentrated use of these uncommon words which suggest a setting in the court and public life demands an explanation. The image of the court suggests that Paul might have seen himself as being challenged by some of the people in the church. But, as argued before, it is possible that some of the people in the church might have been connected to the municipal authorities (Rom. 16.23). If this is correct, it may be surmised that Paul could have these people in mind when he introduces these words.

1. B. Winter, 'The Public Honouring of Christian Benefactors: Romans 13.3-4 and I Peter 2.14-15', *JSNT* 34 (1988), pp. 87-103.
2. Parry, *I Corinthians*, p. 74.
3. Note the use of ἀνακρίνω again in 1 Cor. 9.3.
4. Judge, 'Cultural Conformity and Innovation', p. 15.
5. Hock, *Social Context*, p. 61.

would amount to a rejection of the claim of these patrons on him. It is also conceivable, as Marshall has suggested,[1] that Paul in so doing would have offended some of the powerful patrons in the church.

In any case it is noteworthy that Paul's apology reads like a declaration of his acceptance of the claim of God on his life. He tells the Corinthians how he exercises his apostolic right. Paul asserts that he is an apostle of Christ to the Corinthians if not also to others (1 Cor. 9.1-2). He therefore has the right to claim material support from the church, just as other apostles did (1 Cor. 9.3-14). However, Paul states clearly that it is not in order to exercise that right that he has argued his case before the church (1 Cor. 9.12, 15). Paul's argument in 1 Cor. 9.15-18 is not easy to follow.[2] The thrust of the passage appears to suggest that he is a man under compulsion to serve or a slave of God in Christ.[3] In other words, he has a duty to serve the interest of God (1 Cor. 9.16-17).[4] Hence he can only do what the master has asked him to do, that is, to preach the gospel (1 Cor. 9.12, 23). Moreover, he can expect no pay for his preaching from man.[5] In this way Paul once again has made clear to whom he owes his ultimate loyalty.

In the light of Paul's response to the challenge from the church and his reaction to the problems of immorality and idolatry in the church, as described above, it may be appropriate therefore to compare 1 Corinthians to a one-sided record of a battle in which Paul fought hard to win the Corinthians' loyalty back, as he would have seen it, for God. The conflicts between Paul and some of the Corinthians were probably generated by two conflicting loyalty claims. One demands loyalty to God the father, the other loyalty to human authorities. In

---

1. Marshall, *Enmity*, pp. 257-58.
2. For a most helpful discussion, see Käsemann, *New Testament Questions of Today*, pp. 217-35.
3. Moffatt, *First Corinthians*, pp. 120-21; Barrett, *First Corinthians*, pp. 209-10; Conzelmann, *I Corinthians*, pp. 157-58; Marshall, *Enmity*, pp. 295-306.
4. On ἀνάγκη, Käsemann's comment is pertinent: '*Ananke* describes here the power of the divine will which radically and successfully challenges man and makes its servant its instrument. This definition, then, makes it clear that, simply in his capacity as a Jew, Paul cannot be speaking, like the Greek with his *ananke* or the Roman with his *fatum*, of an impersonal force of blind ill-omen or chance' (*New Testament Questions of Today*, p. 230).
5. Barrett, *First Corinthians*, pp. 209-10; Fee, *First Corinthians*, p. 423.

4. The Response of Paul

face of these two claims, it is understandable that members of the Christian community in Corinth would have found it hard to get the balance right. It is also natural for some have acted in accordance with the traditional norms, that is, to pledge loyalty to the human patrons. But in the eyes of Paul such decisions under certain circumstances were likely to be incompatible with the higher loyalty owed to their newly found master. They should be faithful to God, not to man.

Paul's Directives

In asking the Corinthians to submit themselves to God, the higher authority, the authority of the human patrons in the church would be relativized. Are there other indications in 1 Corinthians which suggest that Paul attempted to counteract the influence of the patrons in the church? It has been noted that Paul claims to be the father to the Corinthians (1 Cor. 4.15), that is, an authority in the church. Could Paul have asserted his authority only to serve his own interest? Or was it used to protect the interests of the weak in the church?

To answer this question I will look more closely at Paul's directives in 1 Corinthians, especially those regarding the organization of human relationships in the church.[1] I will first locate an overall guiding concept in 1 Corinthians for organizing human relationships inside the church. Then I will consider how it was applied when Paul handled some of the problems in the church. I hope that, through such a study, we will be able to see the implications of such directives on power relationships in the church.

The Body

If one is to choose a concept from 1 Corinthians to represent Paul's view regarding the organization of human relationships under God in Christ[2] the metaphor of the body is the almost inevitable choice

---

1. Here we would do well to note that 1 Corinthians basically was written to address issues raised in the life of the church, not to give a general discussion of ethical issues in the society at large. As a result, we have more information on how social relationships in the church should be organized and less on how the world should be changed. The reason for such a phenomenon may perhaps be related to Paul's eschatological outlook (J.C. Beker, *Paul the Apostle: The Triumph of God in Life and Thought* [Philadelphia: Fortress Press, 1980], pp. 303-304).

2. Another important image for the church in 1 Corinthians is ἐκκλησία. But it is

(1 Cor. 10.16-17; 12.12; 12.27).[1] As a metaphor,[2] it should be pointed out that the body is one which might carry strong political overtones[3] and could have been made to serve a patronage system.[4] In our previous discussion I suggested that some of the patrons in the church might have been connected to public life. If that is correct, then Paul's use of such a metaphor in 1 Corinthians might have carried additional significance.[5] What could have been Paul's intention in using the image of the body to describe the church? To maintain unity or diversity?[6] To preserve the status quo or what?

In 1 Corinthians the metaphor quite clearly is used with the aim of unifying a church that appears to be on the verge of dividing (1 Cor. 1.10, 13; 3.3; 11.18-19). Paul argues that individual differences should not hinder unity. On the contrary, interdependence and communal participation could actually enhance the proper functioning of the church as a body (1 Cor. 12.18-20).[7] Although the general import of the metaphor seems clear, its intended nuances in the context of the church at Corinth are more subtle. As it stands, the

---

a metaphor which describes more of man's relationship to God than man's relationship to man (Beker, *Paul*, p. 318).

1. Many studies have been made on Paul's idea of the body of Christ. The more significant ones are J.A.T. Robinson, *The Body: A Study in Pauline Theology* (London: SCM Press, 1952); E. Best, *One Body in Christ: A Study in the Relationship of the Church to Christ in the Epistles of the Apostle Paul* (London: SPCK, 1955). See also J.D.G. Dunn, *Jesus and the Spirit: A Study of the Religious and Charismatic Experience of Jesus and the First Christians as Reflected in the New Testament* (London: SCM Press, 1975), pp. 259-300; Beker, *Paul*, pp. 305-15.

2. The body of Christ is basically a metaphor (Meeks, *First Urban Christians*, p. 89), even though some scholars have tried to go beyond this basic understanding (e.g. E. Käsemann, *Perspectives on Paul* [London: SCM Press, 1971], pp. 102-21).

3. Scholars have long recognized the use of the metaphor for political relationships. The classic example is found in Livy 2.32. For more examples, see Conzelmann, *I Corinthians*, p. 211 nn. 7, 8.

4. Seneca, *De Clementia* 1.3.5; 1.4.3; 1.5.1. Seneca suggests that the emperor is the head while the Empire is the body, and that the body needs the head.

5. Note that the only other place in the undisputed Pauline letters where the image of the body = community is found is Romans 12.4-5.

6. Hurd, *I Corinthians*, pp. 190-93.

7. Beker, *Paul*, p. 307; Meeks, *First Urban Christians*, p. 90. Shaw's interpretation may have overemphasized the dimension of unity and missed Paul's point (*Cost of Authority*, p. 91).

4. The Response of Paul

metaphor can be made to work in two different directions. It can be so interpreted that the status quo is maintained,[1] possibly in the interests of the powerful. But it can also be interpreted in such a way that the differences between the more powerful and the less powerful are relativized.[2] In which of the two directions could Paul have intended to go in using the metaphor in 1 Corinthians? A final and definite answer is difficult to obtain. But several observations based on Paul's discussion in 1 Cor. 12.12-27 seem to suggest that the latter is likely to be the case.

First, it is important to note that the image of God as one who is ultimately in control of everything is preserved even in Paul's use of the body metaphor in 1 Corinthians. God is the one who arranged the organs in the body according to his will (1 Cor. 12.18). But the idea that Christ is the head of the body, which looms large in later Epistles (Col. 1.18; 2.19; Eph. 1.22; 4.15; 5.23) is absent. Actually, the head appears to be part of the body in Paul's depiction of the body (1 Cor. 12.21). The image of God as the ultimate master is striking. Since God is the one who creates individual differences, it is therefore justifiable to have diversity in the church (1 Cor. 12.18). Paradoxically, Paul suggests, it is this diversity which, in turn, helps to build up the church as a rich unity or a body (1 Cor. 12.19-20). What then could be the intended function of this emphasis on God as the master of human relationships? Could Paul be trying to remind those in the church who were prominent not to be proud? Or could Paul be seeking to support those in the church who appear to be weak? This leads us to my second observation.

The important point which Paul seems to emphasize is that God has created a new situation. Under one God in one Spirit those who are in the church, regardless of their racial (Jews and Greeks) and social (slaves and free) differences, have been made into one body (1 Cor. 12.13). In the light of this explication the accent of the metaphor apparently aims at playing down, if not breaking down, ethnic and social barriers. For it is God's intention, Paul suggests, that members of the church should not be divided. On the contrary, they should care

---

1. Cf. Livy 2.32. According to Käsemann, the idea of the body of Christ has been used to legitimize the hierarchical structure of the Catholic church (*Perspectives*, p. 107).
2. Cf. C. Rowland, *Christian Origins* (London: SPCK, 1985), pp. 255-56.

for one another and live harmoniously together (1 Cor. 12.25-26). But who is to take care of whom? This question brings me to consider my third point.

It is most noteworthy that a discussion of the body of Christ leads to an apologia for the inclusion of the weak members in the make-up of the body (1 Cor. 12.22-26). Paul argues that the presence of the weaker parts is necessary in order to have a sound body. God not only places the necessary weaker members in the body, but also gives more honour to them (1 Cor. 12.24). In contrast, the already presentable parts have no need of such honouring (1 Cor. 12.24). As some of the words[1] used to designate the weak in this passage clearly recall earlier usages in contexts where the socially strong are addressed, it is feasible to suggest that the socially strong were the intended audience.[2] In other words, the metaphor of the body may have been used by Paul to fight for the rights of the socially weak in the church.[3] That is to say,

1. So ἀσθενέστερα (1 Cor. 12.22) = ἀσθενῆ (1 Cor. 1.27; 4.10; 8.10; 9.22); ἀτιμότερα (1 Cor. 12.23) = ἄτιμοι (1 Cor. 4.10).

2. The feasibility of this cannot be proven from this distance, but it may be worth considering.

(a) As argued before, it was not uncommon in Corinth and elsewhere for men of influence to assume both political and religious roles (see discussion in Chapter 1 and Chapter 3 above). I have also sought to show that some of the rich and powerful patrons could have been among those who underwent baptism for the dead. If my argument is correct, it may be inferred that the powerful men in the church could also have been people who were interested in religious power.

(b) Those who spoke in tongues spoke of mysteries (1 Cor. 14.2). It is noteworthy that Paul seems to be defending himself against some people in the church who claimed to know mysterious wisdom (1 Cor. 2.1, 7; 4.1; 13.2). As argued all along, it is likely that Paul's opponents in the church could have been some of the socially powerful people in the church. It is thus tempting to ask if they could also be among those who boasted of their spiritual gifts, even tongues, and if the mysterious speaking in tongues might be used by them to further their power? It may be added that the speaking in tongues apparently could be voluntarily controlled (1 Cor. 14.28) (Keck, *Paul and his Letters*, p. 99). In other words, it is not impossible for a person to manipulate this 'gift' for their own purpose. But whether such a 'gift' could have been manipulated by some of the Corinthians we have no way of knowing. For a discussion of how some people in ancient Corinth might have acquired power through manipulating a special 'miraculous' phenomenon, see C. Bonner, 'A Dionysiac Miracle at Corinth', *AJA* 33 (1929), pp. 368-75.

3. If Paul's use of the metaphor here was meant to be a defence for the socially inferior before the socially superior, it would be a reversal of the use of the metaphor

4. The Response of Paul

unity in the church should be preserved precisely through protecting the existence of the weak. In which case, Paul could have been speaking for the weak in the church.

From the above observations, a hint or two of the implication of Paul's directives in terms of horizontal relationships among men have emerged. The solidarity of God's people under him, despite racial and social differences, appears to be one of the important implications to be drawn from Paul's use of the metaphor of a body. Since the weak can easily be disregarded in a world often dominated by the strong, unity in the body should be maintained, but not at the expense of diversity. Instead, different members should care for one another. Or to be more precise, the strong should serve the weak in the upbuilding of a church under God. If patron–client ties undermine horizontal relationship, could Paul's idea of the interdependence of the body have been intended to subvert the strength of such ties?

The Community
It is my belief that the course of action a person chooses to follow may indicate adequately, if not better than the image projected by that person's rhetoric, the convictions which that person at a certain point in time has. Hence to ascertain further if Paul's concern could have been to strengthen horizontal relationships among men which, in effect, would undermine the vertical relationship between the patron and the clients, I will examine the courses of action Paul proposes in 1 Corinthians for handling some of the problems in the church. They include the disciplining of the immoral man, the way to settle disputes inside the church, the eating of food offered to idols, the observance of the Lord's supper, the order of worship and the organization of the collection for the poor in Jerusalem.

Church discipline (1 Cor. 5.1-13). The noteworthy feature of Paul's exhortation in 1 Corinthians 5 is his apparent concern to build up the Corinthian church as a community under God in Christ. Thus Paul seems to have shown more immediate concern for the church than for

---

in Livy's context where it is used in an appeal to the plebs not to withdraw their services to the patricians.

the wrongdoer.[1] After he has mentioned the case of immorality, he moves on to address the church (1 Cor. 5.1-5). Moreover, although Paul might have asserted his authority in the church[2] in speaking his mind concerning the immoral man, saying that the man should be removed from the community (1 Cor. 5.2, 3-5, 7, 13), he seems to have expected the church to solve the problem themselves at an earlier stage (1 Cor. 5.2), and gives his decision only when they have not. Even so, he apparently does not intend to impose his will on the church.[3] Instead, he appears to have encouraged the church, as a community, to deliver the immoral man to the realm of Satan with the power of the Lord Jesus when they gather together in the name of the Lord.[4] So the church was expected to take responsibility as a group in disciplining the deviant (1 Cor. 5.4-5).[5] For the action to purge out

1. Forkman, *Limits of the Religious Community*, p. 139; Fee, *First Corinthians*, p. 197.
2. Meeks, *First Urban Christians*, p. 128.
3. Barrett, *First Corinthians*, pp. 124-25.
4. The syntax of 1 Cor. 5.3-5 is difficult. Conzelmann has listed six possible constructions (*I Corinthians*, p. 97). Barrett's rendering seems to make the best sense and is adopted here (*First Corinthians*, pp. 123-25).
5. Not all scholars agree that the church has a role to play in consigning the immoral man to the realm of Satan. Conzelmann seems to believe that the action is solely Paul's (*I Corinthians*, pp. 97-98). It may be granted that Paul might want to exercise his apostolic authority in expelling the immoral man when the church failed to do so (Meeks, *First Urban Christians*, p. 128). But it does not follow that the church is denied its responsibility in this case (e.g. Moffatt, *First Corinthians*, p. 56; Käsemann, *New Testament Questions of Today*, p. 71; Barrett, *First Corinthians*, p. 124; Dunn, *Jesus*, p. 278; J. Murphy-O'Connor, 'I Corinthians, V, 3-5', *RB* 84 [1977], pp. 239-45; Fee, *First Corinthians*, pp. 203-13). It is worth pointing out that Paul's exhortation in 1 Cor. 5 presupposes that the Corinthian church as a community under God has a responsibility to discipline its deviant members, in this case, to remove the immoral man from their midst (Forkman, *Limits of Religious Community*, p. 140). This responsibility is made especially clear in two places. In 1 Cor. 5.2, Paul expresses his surprise at the church's uncritical acceptance of the immoral man in their midst without taking appropriate action. In 1 Cor. 5.12, Paul clearly emphasizes that it is the responsibility of the Corinthians to judge the insiders. Besides, it is within their capacity to pass judgment as a community (1 Cor. 6.2-3). Furthermore, specific ruling is given to help the church to discipline the nominal brother (1 Cor. 5.11). Hence, it seems preferable to see Paul's exhortation here as a way to encourage the church to take up their responsibility in disciplining the immoral man.

4. The Response of Paul

the old leaven, Paul goes on to suggest, is for the well-being of the group as a whole, lest the whole lump of dough be infected (1 Cor. 5.6-7). Moreover, it is the church's responsibility to discipline those inside the church (1 Cor. 5.12). The community again seems to have been in Paul's mind.

Church arbitration (1 Cor. 6.1-6). Paul's exhortation in response to the action of a member in the church who brought a lawsuit against another brother before the pagan magistrate may also be read as an encouragement for communal action.[1] Apparently Paul does not entertain the idea of a Christian brother bringing a case before the formal court against another brother.[2] In suggesting that the Christians in Corinth are worthy or capable of forming a court[3] for handling trivial cases such as the one they took to the pagan magistrate (1 Cor. 6.2)[4] and in chiding the Corinthians for not being able to find a wise man among them to settle disputes between brothers (1 Cor. 6.5),[5] Paul may be saying that the church should establish some kind of internal mechanism for settling disputes among brothers. If such

---

1. Meeks, *First Urban Christians*, p. 104. Delcor's suggestion that there was already a kind of church court in Corinth is possibly too far-fetched ('The Courts of the Church of Corinth', p. 70). On the matter of internal arbitration, many scholars like to look into Jewish parallels, but that is not my immediate concern here.

2. Paul's indignation is shown in the use of the strong word τολμᾷ (1 Cor. 6.1) (Robertson and Plummer, *First Corinthians*, p. 110; Barrett, *First Corinthians*, p. 135).

3. This is the image suggested by the word κριτήριον (1 Cor. 6.2) (Lightfoot, *Notes*, p. 211). Although not a comment on this word, Barrett's description of the church as 'a society consisting of potential judges in God's tribunal' is apt (*First Corinthians*, p. 137).

4. On taking ἐλαχίστων as trivial money matters, see Fuller, 'First Corinthians 6.1-11', p. 99.

5. According to Barrett, 1 Cor. 6.4 can be translated as follows: 'If it is absolutely necessary to have suits dealing with everyday affairs, show your contempt for them by singling out the meanest and most despised members of the church and appointing them as judges' (*First Corinthians*, p. 137). Although such a translation fits καθίζειν better, Barrett finds it difficult to imagine that Paul could speak of some Christians as τοὺς ἐξουθενημένους. But, as the usage does appear earlier in 1 Cor. 1.26 apparently with reference to the socially weak, so Paul could have spoken ironically against the strong in the church here (cf. 1 Cor. 6.5) (Murphy-O'Connor, 'I Corinthians', p. 803).

was Paul's intention, his suggestion may not be unimportant. For in view of the way the Roman court was structured in favour of the powerful, especially if the case was one which actually profited the strong in the church,[1] Paul's advice for the Corinthians to settle disputes before the saints would probably benefit the weaker party more than a formal court.

The eating of food offered to idols (1 Cor. 8.7-13). On the problem of the eating of food offered to idols, no explicit ruling for communal action is laid down in Paul's discussion. However the underlying concern appears to be the same, that is, the upbuilding of the church as a community under God in Christ (1 Cor. 10.23-24). For this purpose, the strong or those who eat food offered to idols or at table in an idol's temple without scruples are urged to accommodate the weak whose conscience might be offended by their behaviour (1 Cor. 8.9). Consideration for others thus becomes an important criterion for dealing with interpersonal relationships in the church.[2]

The ground on which the strong are warned is also interesting. Paul suggests that by becoming a stumbling block to the weak, thus wrecking their lives, the strong are sinning against Christ who died for the weak (1 Cor. 8.11-12). Hence, for the sake of Christ, the strong should give up the eating of food offered to idols (1 Cor. 8.13), lest the weak who belong to Christ may be ruined. Such logic makes most sense against the background of a patronage system. Since Christ died for the weak brothers and is their Lord, they therefore belong to Christ and are under his protection (1 Cor. 8.11). Thus the harm done to the weak brother by the strong can be seen as harm done to Christ (1 Cor. 8.12). In other words the weak brother is to be cared for not only because he is a human being, but because he is a person under

1. J.P. Sampley's comment may be added here: 'It was a commonplace of the times. . . that civil courts were not to be trusted for justice' (*Pauline Partnership in Christ* [Philadelphia: Fortress Press, 1980], p. 3). Hence, it may not be necessary to defend the justice of the Roman legal system and to smooth the sharpness of Paul's use of ἄδικοι (1 Cor. 6.1) when referring to the pagan magistrates, as some commentators have tried to do (e.g. Barrett, *First Corinthians*, p. 135; Fuller, 'First Corinthians 6.1-11', p. 98). Shaw's suggestion that Paul tried to stop the church from seeking justice in the court (*Cost of Authority*, p. 72) has also failed to take into consideration the reality of the legal system in Paul's days.
2. Horsley, 'Consciousness and Freedom', pp. 586-87.

4. The Response of Paul 183

Christ. So, under God in Christ, a Christian is obliged to care for another Christian.

The observance of the Lord's supper (1 Cor. 11.17-34). In theory, the eating of the Lord's supper should be the place where the ideal, that is, the church as the body of Christ, is lived out. In reality however, the Corinthians fell far short of the ideal. The eating of the Lord's supper became an occasion where the poor were humiliated by the rich. In response to this situation Paul clearly was indignant about the disrespect some of the rich Corinthians showed towards the poor in the church (1 Cor. 11.21-22). Significantly, in his reply, Paul asks the Corinthians to discern the body, that is, to evaluate their relationships to others in the church when they observe the Lord's supper (1 Cor. 11.29).[1] Two further points in Paul's recommendations are to be noted (1 Cor. 11.33-34). First, Paul suggests that the Corinthians should wait for one another when eating the Lord's supper (1 Cor. 11.33). This fits in well with Paul's concern to build up a community (cf. 1 Cor. 11.22).[2] Secondly, since those who did not wait and ate first were probably some of the rich members, it seems best to see Paul's advice to wait as addressed to these people.[3] If this was the case, Paul would look very much like one who defended the dignity of the poor in the church, and his directives here also stand in strong contrast to the rules set down by the association at Lanuvium which seem to protect and honour the leaders.

The order of worship service (1 Cor. 14.1-33). Paul's concern for building up the community as a whole is seen again in his advice for organizing the worship service. In accordance with the central

---

1. Murphy O'Connor, *I Corinthians*, pp. 113-14.
2. Barrett's comment is intriguing: 'Paul does not say, Wait for so-and-so, or for such-and-such an official, to preside over your gathering, though this might seem to have been the easiest way of reducing the chaotic Corinthian assembly to order' (*First Corinthians*, p. 276). The importance of the community apparently takes precedence over the individual leaders. But can it be because the leaders were the ones who did not wait for other people that Paul asked no leader to preside in the meal?
3. Theissen, *Social Setting*, p. 150. *Contra* Conzelmann who seems to understand him who was hungry in 1 Cor. 11.3 literally as 'a man who has worked all day comes hungry to the meeting direct from his work' (*I Corinthians*, p. 203 n. 119).

concern to build up a community, two points are underscored. First, worshipping acts in public service should aim at benefiting the whole group, not oneself. Thus Paul states clearly that he prefers prophecy to glossolalia. For prophecy which is readily understandable benefits more people than glossolalia which is unintelligible without interpretation (1 Cor. 14.1-5). Glossolalia can be accepted in public worship on the condition that there is interpretation (1 Cor. 14.12-13, 17-19). Secondly, all members of the church are expected to participate in the worship in an orderly manner. So Paul encourages all the Corinthians[1] to strive for the gift of prophecy, that is, the gift of speaking words of edification, encouragement and consolation (1 Cor. 14.1, 3). This, however, does not mean that other contributions, such as hymns, teaching, even speaking in tongues, are to be suppressed (1 Cor. 14.26). On the contrary, each should be ready to join in. But they should also evaluate what is said (1 Cor. 14.29).

As far as Paul's advice on public worship is concerned, the concern for building a community may be relatively easy to see. But Paul's preference of prophecy over glossolalia is most interesting. Since speaking in tongues is mysterious and can give one special recognition,[2] it can easily be used to serve one's own interest and to create a difference between members in a group. In asking for tongues to be interpreted and in encouraging all to prophesy, it might have been Paul's intention to play down the danger of making distinctions within the group. This would be all the more significant if speaking in

---

1. Barrett quoting Schlatter's view (*First Corinthians*, p. 314). In the light of this emphasis, two other related passages may be considered.
(a) *1 Cor. 11.2-16*. The point of this passage is not to forbid women from prophesying in public worship, but to emphasize that it should be done in an orderly manner (O.L. Yarbrough, *Not Like the Gentiles: Marriage Rules in the Letters of Paul* [Atlanta: Scholars Press, 1985], pp. 115-16; Fiorenza, *In Memory of Her*, pp. 226-35). In other words, men and women, though different, are equal in the church.
(b) *1 Cor. 14.34-35*. This is a difficult passage. Since the import of this passage obviously contradicts that of 1 Cor. 11.2-16, it has been suggested that this may be an interpolation. For a discussion which argues strongly for this view, see Fee, *First Corinthians*, pp. 699-705. If such is the case, we have no need to include this passage in our discussion.
2. Meeks, *First Urban Christians*, pp. 119-20; Murphy-O'Connor, *I Corinthians*, p. 128.

tongues could have been used by the powerful to denigrate the less spiritual people in the church.

The collection (1 Cor. 16.1-4). Another case which could have reflected Paul's concern to build up horizontal relationships under God in Christ with due respect for the weak is Paul's directive for collecting money to give to 'the saints' or the church in Jerusalem.[1] Paul's instructions on matters related to both the collection and the delivery of the money may be revealing. With regard to Paul's actual instructions on how the money was to be collected, two points may be highlighted. First, Paul seems to expect every member of the community to take part in this project,[2] but only on a voluntary basis[3] and in accordance with the ability to give.[4] Since each is asked to contribute something, perhaps some may want to argue that Paul's suggestion is less than fair and asks more of the poor than of the rich. However, if each is to give on a voluntary basis, this should cause no great problem. Secondly, Paul suggests that the money should be saved up bit by bit in keeping with one's gains[5] until he comes. When this aspect of Paul's instruction is considered in the light of the situation in the church, as reconstructed before, it appears to be quite significant. For it is quite possible that there were several rich and powerful patrons in the church at that time who were willing to give Paul financial support and might even be offended by Paul's refusal of their offer. However, in asking members of the church to save up in order to give to the collection, Paul gives the impression that his audience is not very well off,[6] and may include poorer people and slaves

---

1. Barrett, *First Corinthians*, p. 386; Conzelmann, *I Corinthians*, p. 295; Fee, *First Corinthians*, p. 810.
2. So the use of ἕκαστος ὑμῶν (1 Cor. 16.2).
3. Robertson and Plummer, *First Corinthians*, p. 384; Conzelmann, *I Corinthians*, p. 295.
4. Fee, *First Corinthians*, p. 814.
5. This is the meaning of θησαυρίζων ὅ τι ἐὰν εὐοδῶται (BAGD, p. 361).
6. Based on Paul's impressionistic sketch here, Meeks gives the following picture of the early Christians: 'This bespeaks the economy of small people, not destitute, but not commanding capital either. This, too, would fit the picture of fairly well-off artisans and tradespeople as the typical Christians' (*First Urban Christians*, p. 65).

who may not have stated income.¹ Why does Paul speak in this way? The most probable reason is that Paul saw the church as a community with equal rights and honour and would want to build up the church as such. So, instead of asking one or two rich leaders to demonstrate their readiness for benefaction and thereby to reap a harvest of honour, Paul insisted on having everyone, even the poorer members if they could, contribute to the project. In this way Paul's directive for the collection appears to be consistent with the ideal of the body, as explicated above.²

Of equal significance may be Paul's instructions concerning the delivery of the money to Jerusalem. Paul first asks the church to select their own delegates to deliver the money (1 Cor. 16.3).³ He then adds that he would go too if it is appropriate for him⁴ to do so (1 Cor. 16.4). The main reason for asking the church to select their own representatives to deliver the monetary gift is probably to avoid suspicion or slander.⁵ But the actual effect on the church in going through the process of approving its representatives should not be overlooked either. For it could become another occasion for the church to learn to live as a community through the choosing of a representative. If Paul's uncertainty expressed in 1 Cor. 16.4 does to some extent suggest a request for advice from the church, can we see this as Paul setting another example for the strong in the church?

---

1. Findlay, 'First Epistle to the Corinthians', p. 945; Fee, *First Corinthians*, p. 814.
2. The collection certainly carries a much wider implication. For it might have been designed to bring about a union of the Jews and the Greeks. For further discussion, see, e.g., K.F. Nickle, *The Collection: A Study in Paul's Strategy* (London: SCM Press, 1966), pp. 111-29.
3. The delegates should first be scrutinized or approved (δοκιμάσητε) by the church. On the process of δοκιμασία in Athenian politics, see Rhodes, *Athenian Boule*, pp. 176-78.
4. ἐὰν δὲ ἄξιον ᾖ τοῦ κἀμὲ πορεύεσθαι is ambiguous. Some take it to mean 'if the sum is worthy', that is, big enough (e.g. Findlay, 'First Epistle to the Corinthians', p. 946). But it seems better to take it as suggesting that Paul's travel plan was still to be fixed (so Barrett, *First Corinthians*, p. 387). But there can also be another shade of meaning, that is, if the church thinks Paul should go he will go (Conzelmann, *I Corinthians*, p. 294 n. 5).
5. See, e.g., Barrett, *First Corinthians*, p. 387; Fee, *First Corinthians*, p. 815.

Conclusion

Paul certainly sought to assert his authority in the church. The question is how and for what purpose that authority was exercised. If his authority was exercised to have the immoral man removed from the church and to discourage the idolaters from eating at table in an idol's temple, and if I am right in suggesting that such people included some of the richer and more powerful patrons in the church, then Paul's authority was being used to challenge the strong for their lack of care for others. This insight also helps to explain certain features of Paul's approach in 1 Corinthians, in particular, the emphasis on the need to be 'friends' to the Lord and to give due respect to the place of the weak in the church. The Corinthians are encouraged to settle their disputes inside the church and to treat the poor and the lowly respectfully at the Lord's table. Likewise, the less rich are asked to contribute to the collection for Jerusalem.

The import of Paul's directives discussed above supplements what is implicit in Paul's use of the body metaphor, that is, unity in the church should be preserved through protecting the weak. It points further to the conclusion that Paul was deliberately offering the metaphor as an alternative model of relationships to the more oppressive patron–client ties which were built to be vertical and unequal. In this sense the directives of Paul can be seen as carrying subversive implications.

CONCLUSION

I began this study with the presupposition that an understanding of the historical social situation in which Paul and the early Christians worked and lived would help us understand them and their mutual relationships better. I have therefore chosen to consider Paul's interaction with the Christian community in Corinth, as reflected in 1 Corinthians, in the light of the convention of patronage in first-century Corinth. I can now summarize the discussion and draw out some wider implications.

I have sought to establish a picture of the functioning of patronage in first-century Corinth through a study of epigraphical and other evidence. If my study is correct, I have contributed to a better understanding of an important aspect of social life in first-century Corinth. I may also say that patronage was *one* of the important ways through which relationships in first-century Corinth were structured. Such patron–client relations were vertical relations and could be formed in both public life between the emperor and his officials and in semi-public life between a rich patron and members of an association or of a household. Through these patron–client ties resources were exchanged. The rich and powerful could dispatch different kinds of favours. These could be material goods, such as food in times of famine and beautification of the city, or political benefits, such as citizenship and promotion to higher offices, or legal assistance and protection. In return they could expect to be honoured and supported by their dependents who might be citizens of the colony or dependents in a household.

When the problems inside the church dealt with in 1 Corinthians are viewed in the light of the convention of patronage in Roman Corinth, we can attribute important aspects of these problems to the presence, influence and activity of some who functioned as patrons of the church. It is likely that Paul's conflict with some of the Corinthians resulted partly from Paul's refusal to accept money from the church which, in effect, constituted a violation of the convention of friendship or patronage and which would therefore be seen by some at least to bring dishonour to the rich patrons in the church. The divisions at the Lord's table probably reflect something of the same distinctions between patrons and inferiors. It may also be assumed that the tensions in the church were caused or exacerbated to some extent by competition among patrons in the church.

Similarly, the puzzling features of other problems discussed in 1 Corinthians which so far have not been given sufficient attention or adequately explained by more traditional theological investigations can be explained by the assumed presence and activity of some relatively richer and powerful patrons in the church. It is possible that the litigants were powerful patrons who had a better chance of redressing damage or making personal gains through litigation. The case of immorality might have arisen when a rich and influential patron sought to acquire more wealth through uniting with his stepmother. The man's influential position as a patron would also help to explain partially why the church appears to be proud of him. It has been argued in a convincing way by Theissen that those in the church who ate meat were members of the patronal class. I suggest further that those who ate at table in an idol's temple were likely also to be some powerful people in the church who, for reasons of ambition and/or obligation, found it difficult to give up their connections with more powerful patrons in the colony. In addition, the practice of a vicarious baptism for the dead may also be understood in the light of a society in which favours were secured through powerful patrons. It is even conceivable that some powerful patrons were among those who underwent the rite for the dead.

Many of the above problems have been approached from a theological perspective in the past and, more recently, from a sociological perspective with good results. If I have succeeded in achieving my purpose, that is, in showing the relationship between many of the problems behind 1 Corinthians and the activity of some powerful patrons in the Corinthian church, I will have provided a helpful complement to these earlier theological and sociological investigations into the problems in Corinth. Apparently there were some relatively powerful patrons in the church at Corinth who had no scruples in exercising their power and their rights, even if it did damage to the weaker people in the church.

Even when we take the historical social context of the Corinthian church into account as fully as possible, our understanding of Paul will be open to different interpretations. Paul has therefore been seen as the father of patriarchalism or as a manipulator. However, this investigation of the situation in the church has led us to appreciate the difficult situation Paul was facing and not least in his reply in 1 Corinthians. Far from being a dominating authority, Paul's position in the church, in comparison with the powerful foes in the church, appears to have been quite precarious. In 1 Corinthians Paul asserts his authority, paradoxically, by stressing his servanthood under God in Christ. This emphasis was probably intended to counteract the influence of some dominating authorities, that is, some of the more powerful patrons in the church. Against this background it is therefore not surprising that, before long, Paul had to assert his authority once again in 2 Corinthians. My study of Paul's directives in 1 Corinthians also suggests that Paul sided with the socially weak in the church. Moreover Paul's directives were aimed at strengthening the horizontal relationships in the church and these directives, in effect, carried subversive implication for vertical patron–client ties in the church.

BIBLIOGRAPHY

1. Ancient Texts and Translations

Braund, D.C., *Augustus to Nero: A Sourcebook on Roman History, 31 BC–AD 68* (London: Croom Helm, 1985).
Brunt, P.A., and J.M. Moore (eds.), *Res Gestae Divi Augusti: The Achievements of the Divine Augustus* (Oxford: Oxford University Press, 1967).
Cornford, F.M., *The Republic of Plato* (Oxford: Clarendon Press, 1941).
Dessau, H., *Inscriptiones latinae selectae* (3 vols.; Berlin: Weidmann, 1882–1916).
Ehrenberg, V., and A.H.M. Jones, *Documents illustrating the Reigns of Augustus and Tiberius* (Oxford: Clarendon Press, 2nd edn, 1955).
Grant, M., *Tacitus: The Annals of Imperial Rome* (Harmondsworth: Penguin Books, rev. edn, 1971).
Graves, R., *Suetonius* (rev. M. Grant; Harmondsworth: Penguin Books, 1979).
Kent, J.H., *The Inscriptions, 1926–1950. Corinth: Results*, VIII.3 (Princeton: American Schools of Classical Studies at Athens, 1966).
Lewis, N., and M. Reinhold, *Roman Civilization* (2 vols.; New York: Harper & Row, 1951, 1966).
Lutz, C.E., 'Musonius Rufus "The Roman Socrates"', *YCS* 10 (1947), pp. 3-147.
Malherbe, A.J. (ed.), *The Cynic Epistles* (Missoula, MT: Scholars Press, 1977).
—'Ancient Epistolary Theorists', *Ohio Journal of Religious Studies* 5 (1977), pp. 3-77.
Meritt, B.D., *Greek Inscriptions, 1896–1927. Corinth: Results*, VIII.1 (Cambridge, MA: Harvard University Press, 1931).
Mommsen, T., et al. (eds.), *Corpus inscriptionum latinarum* (Berlin: Deutsche Akademie der Wissenschaften, 1863–).
Rhodes, P.J., *Aristotle: The Athenian Constitution* (Harmondsworth: Penguin Books, 1984).
Rudd, N., *Horace: Satires and Epistles; Persius: Satires* (Harmondsworth: Penguin Books, 1979).
Sandars, T.C., *The Institutes of Justinian* (London: Longmans, 1952).
Sherk, R.K., *Rome and the Greek East to the Death of Augustus* (Cambridge: Cambridge University Press, 1984).
—*The Roman Empire: Augustus to Hadrian* (Cambridge: Cambridge University Press, 1988).
Smallwood, A.H., *Documents illustrating the Principates of Gaius, Claudius and Nero* (Cambridge: Cambridge University Press, 1967).
Smith, M.S., *Petronius: Cena Trimalchionis* (Oxford: Clarendon Press, 1975).

Sullivan, J.P., *Petronius: The Satyricon and Seneca: The Apocolocyntosis* (Harmondsworth: Penguin Books, rev. edn, 1986).
West, A.B., *Latin Inscriptions, 1896-1926. Corinth: Results*, VIII.2 (Cambridge, MA: Harvard University Press, 1931).

2. Modern Studies

Abbott, F.F., and A.C. Johnson, *Municipal Administration in the Roman Empire* (Princeton: Princeton University Press, 1926).
Abercrombie, N., and S. Hill., 'Paternalism and Patronage', *BJS* 27 (1976), pp. 413-29.
Adams, B.N., 'Interaction Theory and the Social Network', *Sociometry* 30 (1967), pp. 64-78.
Adkins, A.W.H., ' "Friendship" and "Self-Sufficiency" in Homer and Aristotle', *CQ* 13 (1963), pp. 33-45.
Alexander, C., 'Abstract of the Articles on the Bacchic Inscription in the Metropolitan Museum', *AJA* 37 (1933), pp. 264-70.
Alföldy, G., *The Social History of Rome* (trans. D. Braund and F. Pollock; London: Routledge, rev. edn, 1988).
Allo, E.-B., *Saint Paul: Première épître aux Corinthiens* (Paris: Gabalda, 1934).
Altheim, F., *A History of Roman Religion* (trans. H. Mattingly; London: Methuen, 1938).
Altman, M., 'Ruler Cult in Seneca', *CP* 33 (1938), pp. 198-204.
Anderson, G., *Philostratus: Biography and Belles Lettres in the Third Century AD* (London: Croom Helm, 1986).
Angus, S., *The Mystery Religions: A Study in the Religious Background of Early Christianity* (New York: Dover, 1975).
Arai, S., 'Die Gegner des Paulus im 1. Korintherbrief und das Problem der Gnosis', *NTS* 19 (1973), pp. 430-37.
Arnold, W.T., *The Roman System of Provincial Administration to the Accession of Constantine the Great* (rev. E.S. Bouchier; Oxford: Basil Blackwell, 3rd edn, 1914).
Aronson, D.R. (ed.), 'Social Networks', *The Canadian Review of Sociology and Anthropology* special issue 7 (1970), pp. 221-86.
Aune, D.E., *Prophecy in Early Christianity and the Ancient Mediterranean World* (Grand Rapids: Eerdmans, 1983).
—*The New Testament in its Literary Environment* (Philadelphia: Westminster Press, 1987).
Badian, E., *Foreign Clientele (264-70 BC)* (Oxford: Clarendon Press, 1958).
Bagdikian, A., 'The Civic Officials of Roman Corinth' (unpublished MA thesis, University of Vermont, 1953).
Bailey, K.E., 'The Structure of I Corinthians and Paul's Theological Method with Special Reference to 4.17', *NTS* 25 (1983), pp. 152-81.
Baird, W., 'Letters of Recommendation: A Study of 2 Cor. 3.1-3', *JBL* 80 (1961), pp. 166-72.
—*1 Corinthians, 2 Corinthians* (Atlanta: John Knox, 1980).
Balch, D.L., 'I Cor. 7.32-35 and Stoic Debates about Marriage, Anxiety and Distraction', *JBL* 102 (1983), pp. 429-39.
Balsdon, J.P.V.D., *Roman Women* (London: Bodley Head, 1962).
—*Life and Leisure in Ancient Rome* (London: Bodley Head, 1969).

Bibliography

Banks, R., *Paul's Idea of Community: The Early House Churches in their Historical Setting* (Exeter: Paternoster Press, 1980).

Banton, M. (ed.), *The Relevance of Models for Social Anthropology* (New York: Praeger, 1965).

Barnes, J.A., 'Class and Committees in a Norwegian Island Parish', *Human Relations* 7 (1954), pp. 39-58.

—'Networks and Political Process', in *Social Networks in Urban Situations* (ed. J.C. Mitchell; Manchester: Manchester University Press, 1969).

Barnett, P.W., 'Opposition in Corinth', *JSNT* 22 (1984), pp. 3-17.

Barrett, C.K., *A Commentary on the Epistle to the Romans* (London: A. & C. Black, 1957).

—*A Commentary on the First Epistle to the Corinthians* (London: A. & C. Black, 1968).

—'Christianity at Corinth', in *Essays on Paul* (London: SPCK, 1982).

—'Cephas and Corinth', in *Essays on Paul* (London: SPCK, 1982).

—'Things Sacrificed to Idols', in *Essays on Paul* (London: SPCK, 1982).

—'Paul's Opponents in 2 Corinthians', in *Essays on Paul* (London: SPCK, 1982).

Barton, S.C., 'Paul and the Cross: A Sociological Approach', *Theology* 85 (1982), pp. 13-19.

—'Paul's Sense of Place: An Anthropological Approach to Community Formation in Corinth', *NTS* 32 (1986), pp. 225-46.

Barton, S.C., and G.H.R. Horsley, 'A Hellenistic Cult Group and the New Testament Churches', *JAC* 24 (1981), pp. 7-41.

Batey, R., 'Paul's Interaction with the Corinthians', *JBL* 84 (1965), pp. 139-46.

Baur, F.C., 'Die Christuspartei in der korinthischen Gemeinde, der Gegensatz des paulinischen und petrinischen Christentums in der ältesten Kirche, der Apostel Petrus in Rom', *Tübinger Zeitschrift für Theologie* 4 (1831), pp. 61-206.

—*Paul the Apostle of Jesus Christ* (2 vols.; London: Williams & Norgate, 1876).

Beasley-Murray, G.R., *Baptism in the New Testament* (London: Macmillan, 1962).

Beauvery, R., 'Πλεονεκτεῖν in I Thess. 4, 6a', *Verbum Domini* 33 (1955), pp. 273-86.

Beker, J.C., *Paul the Apostle: The Triumph of God in Life and Thought* (Philadelphia: Fortress Press, 1980).

—'Paul's Theology: Consistent or Inconsistent?', *NTS* 34 (1988), p. 364-77.

—'The Function of I Cor. 15 in the Structure of the Letter' (SNTS Seminar Paper, 1989).

Bell, H.I., 'Egypt under the Early Principate', in *Cambridge Ancient History*, X (ed. S.A. Cook, F.E. Adcock and M.P. Charlesworth; Cambridge: Cambridge University Press, 1934).

Belleville, L.L., 'Continuity or Discontinuity: A Fresh Look at 1 Corinthians in the Light of First-Century Epistolary Forms and Conventions', *EvQ* 59 (1987), pp. 15-37.

Benko, S., and J.J. O'Rourke (eds.), *Early Church History: The Roman Empire as the Setting of Primitive Christianity* (London: Oliphants, 1971).

Bernard, J.H., 'The Connexion between the Fifth and Sixth Chapters of 1 Corinthians', *Exp* 7.3 (1907), pp. 433-43.

Beshers, J.M. and Laumann, E.O., 'Social Distance: A Network Approach', *ASR* 32 (1967), pp. 225-36.

Best, E., *One Body in Christ: A Study in the Relationship of the Church to Christ in the Epistles of the Apostle Paul* (London: SPCK, 1955).

—*A Commentary on the First and Second Epistles to the Thessalonians* (London: A. & C. Black, 1972).

Betz, H.D., '2 Cor. 6.14–7.1: An Anti-Pauline Fragment?', *JBL* 92 (1973), pp. 88-108.
—*Galatians* (Philadelphia: Fortress Press, 1979).
Biers, W.R., and D.J. Geagan, 'A New List of Victors in the Caesarea at Isthmia', *Hesp* 39 (1970), pp. 79-93.
Blau, P.M., *Exchange and Power in Social Life* (New York: John Wiley & Sons, 1964).
—'A Macrosociological Theory of Social Structure', *AJS* 83 (1977), p. 26-54.
Blegen, C.W., *The North Cemetery. Corinth: Results*, XIII (Princeton: American School of Classical Studies at Athens, 1964).
Bloch, M., and S. Guggenheim, 'Compadrazgo, Baptism and the Symbolism of a Second Birth', *Man* ns 16 (1981), pp. 376-86.
Blok, A., 'Variations in Patronage', *Sociologische Gids* 16 (1969), pp. 365-78.
—'Rams and Billy-Goats: A Key to the Mediterranean Code of Honour', *Man* ns 16 (1981), pp. 427-40.
Boak, A.E.R., 'The Organisation of Gilds in Greco-Roman Egypt', *TAPA* 68 (1937), pp. 29-46.
Boer, W. den, 'Demography in Roman History: Facts and Impressions', *Mnemosyne* 26 (1973), pp. 29-46.
Boissevain, J., 'Patronage in Sicily', *Man* ns 1 (1966), pp. 8-33.
—'The Place of Non-Groups in the Social Sciences', *Man* ns 3 (1968), pp. 542-56.
—'Factions, Parties and Politics in a Maltese Village', in *Friends, Followers and Factions* (ed. S.C. Schmidt, L. Guasti, C.H. Landé and J.C. Scott; Berkeley: University of California, 1977).
—'When the Saints Go Marching Out: Reflections on the Decline of Patronage in Malta', in *Patrons and Clients in Mediterranean Societies* (ed. E. Gellner and J. Waterbury; London: Gerald Duckworth, 1977).
Boissevain, J., and J.C. Mitchell (eds.), *Network Analysis: Studies in Human Interaction* (The Hague: Mouton, 1973).
Bonner, C., 'A Dionysiac Miracle at Corinth', *AJA* 33 (1929), pp. 368-75.
Bonner, R.J., *Evidence in Athenian Courts* (New York: Arno, 1979).
Borgen, P., 'Catalogues of Vices, the Apostolic Decree, and the Jerusalem Meeting', in *The Social World of Formative Christianity and Judaism: Essays in Tribute to H.C. Kee* (Philadelphia: Fortress Press, 1988).
Bornkamm, G., *Early Christian Experience* (New York: Harper & Row, 1969).
—*Paul* (New York: Harper & Row, 1971).
Boswell, D.M., 'Personal Crises and the Mobilization of the Social Network', in *Social Networks in Urban Situation* (ed. J.C. Mitchell; Manchester: Manchester University Press, 1969).
Bott, E., 'Urban Families: Conjugal Roles and Social Networks', *Human Relations* 8 (1955), pp. 345-83.
—*Family and Social Networks* (London: Tavistock, 2nd edn, 1971).
Bowersock, G., 'Eurycles of Sparta', *JRS* 51 (1961), pp. 112-18.
—*Augustus and the Greek World* (Oxford: Clarendon Press, 1965).
—*Greek Sophists in the Roman Empire* (Oxford: Clarendon Press, 1969).
—'Greek Intellectuals and the Imperial Cult in the Second Century AD', in *Le culte des souverains dans l'empire romain* (ed. E. Bickerman; Geneva: Vandoeuvres, 1973).
Box, H., 'Roman Citizenship in Laconia', *JRS* 21 (1931), pp. 200-14.

Bibliography

Bradley, K.R., *Slaves and Masters in the Roman Empire: A Study in Social Control* (New York: Oxford University Press, 1987).
Bratcher, R.C., *A Translator's Guide to Paul's First Letter to the Corinthians* (London: United Bible Societies, 1982).
Broneer, O., 'Corinth. Center of Saint Paul's Missionary Work in Greece', *BA* 14 (1951), pp. 78-96.
—'The Apostle Paul and the Isthmian Games', *BA* 25 (1962), pp. 1-31.
—'Paul and the Pagan Cult at Isthmia', *HTR* 64 (1971), pp. 169-87.
Brown, G.B., *From Schola to Cathedral: A Study of Early Christian Architecture and its Relation to the Life of the Church* (Edinburgh: David Douglas, 1886).
Brown, P., *Society and the Holy in Late Antiquity* (London: Faber & Faber, 1982).
Bruce, F.F., *The Acts of the Apostles* (London: Tyndale Press, 2nd edn, 1952).
—*I and II Corinthians* (London: Oliphants, 1971).
—*1 and 2 Thessalonians* (Waco, TX; Word Books, 1982).
—*The Pauline Circle* (Grand Rapids: Eerdmans, 1985).
Brunt, P.A., 'Charges of Provincial Maladministration under the Early Principate', *Historia* 10 (1961), pp. 189-223.
—' "Amicitia" in the Late Roman Republic', *PCPhS* 191 (1965), pp. 1-20.
—'Procuratorial Jurisdiction', *Latomus* 25 (1966), pp. 461-89.
—'The Roman Mob', *PP* 35 (1966), pp. 3-27.
—'The Augustan Marriage Laws', in *Italian Manpower, 25 BC–AD 14* (Oxford: Clarendon Press, 1971).
—'Aspects of the Social Thought of Dio Chrysostom and the Stoics', *PCPhS* 19 (1973), pp. 9-34.
—'Stoicism and the Principate', *PBSR* 43 (1975), pp. 7-35.
—'The Administrators of Roman Egypt', *JRS* 65 (1975), pp. 124-47.
—'The Romanization of the Local Ruling Classes in the Roman Empire', in *Assimilation et résistance à la culture gréco-romaine dans le monde ancien* (ed. D.M. Pippidi; Paris: Editura Academiei, 1976).
—'From Epictetus to Arrian', *Athenaeum* 50 (1977), pp. 19-48.
Buckland, W.W., *A Textbook of Roman Law from Augustus to Justinian* (rev. P. Stein; Cambridge: Cambridge University Press, 3rd edn, 1963).
Büchsel, F., 'εἴδωλον κτλ.', *TDNT*, II, pp. 375-80.
Bünker, M., *Briefformula und rhetorische Disposition im 1. Korintherbrief* (Göttingen: Vandenhoeck & Ruprecht, 1983).
Bugh, G.R., 'An Emendation to the Prosopography of Roman Corinth', *Hesp* 48 (1979), pp. 45-53.
Bultmann, R., *Theology of the New Testament*, I (London: SCM Press, 1952).
—'Is Exegesis without Presuppositions Possible?', in *Existence and Faith* (ed. and trans. S. Ogden; New York: Meridian, 1960).
Burke, P., *Sociology and History* (London: George Allen & Unwin, 1980).
Burkert, W., *Greek Religion: Archaic and Classical* (Oxford: Basil Blackwell, 1985).
Burt, R., 'Position in Networks', *Social Forces* 55 (1976), pp. 93-122.
Burton, G., 'Powers and Functions of Proconsuls in the Roman Empire, 70–260 AD' (PhD dissertation, Oxford University, 1973).
—'Proconsuls, Assizes and the Administration of Justice under the Empire', *JRS* 65 (1975), pp. 92-106.

—'The curator rei publicae', *Chiron* 9 (1979), pp. 465-88.
Byrne, B., 'Sinning against One's Own Body: Paul's Understanding of the Sexual Relationship in 1 Corinthians 6.18', *CBQ* 45 (1983), pp. 608-16.
—'Ministry and Maturity in I Corinthians 3', *ABR* 35 (1987), pp. 83-87.
Cadbury, H.J., 'Erastus of Corinth', *JBL* 50 (1931), pp. 42-58.
—'The Macellum of Corinth', *JBL* 53 (1934), pp. 134-41.
Caird, G.B., 'Everything to Everyone: The Theology of the Corinthian Epistles', *Int* 13 (1959), pp. 387-99.
Callan, T., 'Prophecy and Ecstasy in Greco-Roman Religion and in I Corinthians', *NovT* 27 (1985), pp. 125-40.
Calvin, J., *The First Epistle of Paul the Apostle to the Corinthians* (Edinburgh: Saint Andrew Press, 1960).
Cameron, A., 'Inscriptions relating to Sacral Manumission and Confession', *HTR* 32 (1939), pp. 143-79.
Campbell, J.K., *Honour, Family and Patronage* (New York: Oxford University Press, 1964).
—'Honour, Family and Patronage: A Study of Institutions and Moral Values in a Greek Mountain Community', in *Friends, Followers and Factions* (ed. S.W. Schmidt, L. Guasti, C.H. Landé and J.C. Scott; Berkeley: University of California Press, 1977).
Campenhausen, H. von, *Tradition and Life in the Church* (London: Collins, 1968).
—*Ecclesiastical Authority and Spiritual Power in the Church of the First Three Centuries* (London: A. & C. Black, 1969).
Carr, W., 'The Rulers of This Age—I Corinthians II.6-8', *NTS* 23 (1976), pp. 20-35.
—*Angels and Principalities: The Background, Meaning and Development of the Pauline Use of hai archai kai hai exousiai* (Cambridge: Cambridge University Press, 1981).
Cartledge, P., and A. Spawforth, *Hellenistic and Roman Sparta: A Tale of Two Cities* (London: Routledge, 1989).
Cartwright, D., and F. Harary, 'Structural Balance: A Generalization of Heider's Theory', *Psychological Review* 63 (1956), pp. 277-93.
Cartwright, D., and A. Zander (eds.), *Group Dynamics: Research and Theory* (Evanston: Row Peterson, 2nd edn, 1960).
Cavallin, H.C.C., *Life After Death: Paul's Argument for the Resurrection of the Dead in I Cor. 15. Part I: An Enquiry into the Jewish Background* (Lund: Gleerup, 1974).
Chadwick, W.E., *The Social Teaching of St Paul* (Cambridge: Cambridge University Press, 1906).
Charlesworth, M.P., 'Tiberius', in *Cambridge Ancient History*, X (ed. S.A. Cook, F.E. Adcock and M.P. Charlesworth; Cambridge: Cambridge University Press, 1934).
—'Gaius and Claudius', in *Cambridge Ancient History*, X (ed. S.A. Cook, F.E. Adcock and M.P. Charlesworth; Cambridge, Cambridge University Press, 1934).
Church, F.F., 'Rhetorical Structure and Design in Paul's Letter to Philemon', *HTR* 71 (1978), pp. 17-31.
Coleman, J., E. Katz and H. Menzel, 'The Diffusion of an Innovation among Physicians', *SQ* 18 (1977), pp. 62-82.
Collins, A.Y., 'The Function of "Excommunication" in Paul', *HTR* 73 (1980), pp. 251-63.
Collins, J.J., 'Chiasmus, the "ABA" Pattern and the Text of Paul', in *Studiorum Paulinorum Congressus Internationalis Catholicus* (Analecta Biblica, 17; Rome: Biblical Institute Press, 1963).

Bibliography 197

Collins, R.F., 'The Unity of Paul's Paraenesis in I Thess. 4.3-8: I Cor. 7.1-7, a Significant Parallel', *NTS* 29 (1983), pp. 420-29.

Conzelmann, H., *I Corinthians* (Philadelphia: Fortress Press, 1975).

—*Acts* (Philadelphia: Fortress Press, 1987).

Corbett, P.E., *The Roman Law of Marriage* (Oxford: Clarendon Press, 1930).

Cotton, H., *Documentary Letters of Recommendation in Latin from the Roman Empire* (Königsten: Anton Hain, 1981).

Countryman, L.W., 'Patrons and Officers in Club and Church', in *SBL 1977 Seminar Papers* (ed. P.J. Achtemeier; Missoula, MT: Scholars Press, 1977).

—*The Rich Christian in the Church of the Early Empire: Contradictions and Accommodations* (New York: Edwin Mellen, 1980).

Craig, C.T., 'The First Epistle to the Corinthians: Introduction and Exegesis', in *The Interpreter's Bible*, X (New York: Abingdon Press, 1953).

Crawford, M.H. (ed), *Sources for Ancient History* (Cambridge: Cambridge University Press, 1983).

Crook, J.A., *Law and Life of Rome* (London: Thames & Hudson, 1967).

—'*Patria Potestas*', *CQ* 17 (1967), pp. 113-22.

—'Intestacy in Roman Society', *PCPhS* 19 (1973), pp. 38-44.

—'Women in Roman Succession', in *The Family in Ancient Rome* (ed. B. Rawson; London: Croom Helm, 1986).

Csillag, P., *The Augustan Laws on Family Relations* (Budapest: Akademiai Kiado, 1976).

Cullmann, O., *Baptism in the New Testament* (London: SCM Press, 1950).

Cummer, W.W., 'A Roman Tomb at Corinthian Kenchreai', *Hesp* 40 (1971), pp. 205-31.

Cumont, F., *After Life in Roman Paganism: Lectures delivered at Yale University on the Silliman Foundation* (New Haven: Yale University Press, 1932).

—'La grande inscription bachique du metropolitan museum, II', *AJA* 37 (1933), pp. 232-63.

Cuss, D., *Imperial Cult and Honorary Terms in the New Testament* (Fribourg: Fribourg University Press, 1974).

Dahl, M.E., *The Resurrection of the Body: A Study of I Corinthians 15* (London: SCM Press, 1962).

Dahl, N.A., 'Paul and the Church at Corinth according to I Cor. 1–4', in *Christian History and Interpretation* (ed. W.R. Farmer, C.F.D. Moule and R.R. Niebuhr; Cambridge: Cambridge University Press, 1967).

—'A Fragment and its Context: 2 Corinthians 6.14–7.1', in *Studies in Paul* (Minneapolis, MN: Augsburg, 1972).

Daniel, J.L., 'Anti-Semitism in the Hellenistic-Roman Period', *JBL* 98 (1979), pp. 45-65.

D'Arms, J.H., *Commerce and Social Standing in Ancient Rome* (Cambridge, MA: Harvard University Press, 1981).

Daube, D., 'Pauline Contributions to a Pluralistic Culture: Re-creation and Beyond', in *Jesus and Man's Hope* (ed. D.G. Miller and D.Y. Hadidian; Pittsburgh: Pittsburgh Theological Seminary, 1971).

Davies, W.D., *Paul and Rabbinic Judaism: Some Rabbinic Elements in Pauline Theology* (London: SPCK, 3rd edn, 1970).

—*Jewish and Pauline Studies* (Philadelphia: Fortress Press, 1984).

Davis, J.A., 'Structural Balance, Mechanical Solidarity and Interpersonal Relations', *AJS* 68 (1963), pp. 444-63.

—'Clustering and Structural Balance in Graphs', *Human Relations* 20 (1967), pp. 181-87.
Davis, J.A., *Wisdom and Spirit: An Investigation of 1 Corinthians 1.18-3.20 against the Background of Jewish Sapiential Traditions in the Greco-Roman Period* (Lanham, MD: University Press of America, 1984.
Dean, L.R., 'Latin Inscriptions from Corinth', *AJA* 22 (1918), pp. 189-97.
—'Latin Inscriptions from Corinth, II', *AJA* 23 (1919), pp. 163-74.
—'Latin Inscriptions from Corinth, III', *AJA* 26 (1922), pp. 451-76.
Deissmann, G.A., *Paul: A Study in Social and Religious History* (New York: Harper & Row, 2nd edn, 1957).
—*Light from the Ancient East: The New Testament Illustrated by Recently Discovered Texts of the Graeco-Roman World* (trans. L.R.M. Strachan; Grand Rapids: Baker Book House, rev. edn, 1965).
Delcor, M., 'The Courts of the Church of Corinth and the Courts of Qumran', in *Paul and Qumran: Studies in New Testament Exegesis* (ed. J. Murphy-O'Connor; London: Chapman, 1968).
Delling, G., 'πλεονέκτης κτλ.', *TDNT*, VI, pp. 266-74.
Denney, J., 'St Paul's Epistle to the Romans', in *The Expositor's Greek Testament*, II (Grand Rapids: Eerdmans, 1988).
D'Epinay, C.L., *Haven of the Masses: A Study of the Pentecostal Movement in Chile* (London: Lutterworth, 1969).
Detienne, M., and J. Vernant, *The Cuisine of Sacrifice among the Greeks* (trans. P. Wissing; Chicago: Chicago University Press, 1989).
Dibelius, M., *Paul* (London: Longmans, 1953).
Dill, S., *Roman Society from Nero to Marcus Aurelius* (London: Macmillan, 1905).
Dinkler, E., 'Zum Problem der Ethik bei Paulus: Rechtsnahme und Rechtsverzicht (1 Kor. 6.1-11)', *ZTK* 49 (1952), pp. 167-200.
Dixon, S., 'Polybius on Roman Women and Property', *AJP* 106 (1985), pp. 147-70.
Dobschütz, E. von, *Christian Life in the Primitive Church* (London: Williams & Norgate, 1904).
—*Die Thessalonicher-Briefe* (Göttingen: Vandenhoeck & Ruprecht, 7th edn, 1909).
Dodd, C.H., '"Εννομος Χριστοῦ', in *More New Testament Studies* (Manchester: Manchester University Press, 1968).
Doty, W.G., 'The Classification of Epistolary Literature', *CBQ* 31 (1969), pp. 183-99.
—*Letters in Primitive Christianity* (Philadelphia: Fortress Press, 1973).
Dow, S., and D. Gill, 'The Greek Cult of Table', *AJA* 69 (1965), pp. 103-14.
Duff, A.M., *Freedmen in the Early Roman Empire* (Oxford: Clarendon Press, 1928).
Dumont, L., *Homo Hierarchicus* (Chicago: Chicago University Press, 1980).
Duncan-Jones, R.P., 'Patronage and City Privileges: The Case of Giufi', *Epigraphische Studien* 9 (1973), pp. 12-16.
—*Economy of the Roman Empire* (Cambridge: Cambridge University Press, rev. edn, 1982).
Dungan, D.L., *The Sayings of Jesus in the Churches of Paul: The Use of the Synoptic Tradition in the Regulation of Early Church Life* (Philadelphia: Fortress Press, 1971).
Dunn, J.D.G., *Baptism in the Holy Spirit* (London: SCM Press, 1970).
—*Jesus and the Spirit: A Study of the Religious and Charismatic Experience of Jesus and the First Christians as Reflected in the New Testament* (London: SCM Press, 1975).
—*Unity and Diversity in the New Testament* (London: SCM Press, 1977).

—*Romans* (Waco, TX: Word Books, 1988).
—*Christology in the Making* (London: SCM Press, 2nd edn, 1989).
Duthoy, R., *The Taurobolium: Its Evolution and Terminology* (Leiden: Brill, 1969).
Easton, B.S., 'New Testament Ethical Lists', *JBL* 51 (1932), pp. 1-12.
Edlund, E.M.I., 'Invisible Bonds: Clients and Patrons through the Eyes of Polybius', *Klio* 59 (1977), pp. 129-36.
Edwards, K.N., *The Coins, 1896-1929. Corinth: Results*, VI (Cambridge, MA: Harvard University Press, 1933).
Ehrhardt, A., 'Social Problems in the Early Church', in *The Framework of the New Testament Stories* (Manchester: Manchester University Press, 1964).
Eisenstadt, S.N., 'Ritualized Personal Relations', *Man* 96 (1956), pp. 90-95.
—'Anthropological Studies of Complex Societies', *Current Anthropology* 2 (1961), p. 201-22.
Eisenstadt, S.N., and R. Lemarchand (eds.), *Political Clientelism: Patronage and Development* (London: Sage, 1981).
Eisenstadt, S.N., and L. Roniger, 'Patron–Client Relations as a Model of Structuring Social Exchange', *CSSH* 22 (1980), pp. 42-77.
—'The Study of Patron-Client Relations and Recent Developments in Sociological Theory', in *Political Clientelism* (ed. S.N. Eisenstadt and R. Lemarchand; London: Sage, 1981).
—*Patrons, Clients and Friends: Interpersonal Relations and the Structure of Trust in Society* (Cambridge: Cambridge University Press, 1984).
Ellicott, C.J., *St Paul's First Epistle to the Corinthians* (London: Longmans, 1887).
Elliott, J.H., *Social-Scientific Criticism of the New Testament and its Social World* (Semeia, 35; Decatur: Scholars Press, 1986).
Ellis, E.E., 'Paul and his Co-Workers', *NTS* 17 (1971), pp. 437-52.
—'Paul and his Opponents', in *Christianity, Judaism, and Other Greco-Roman Cults*, I (ed. J. Neusner; Leiden: Brill, 1975).
—*Prophecy and Hermeneutics in Early Christianity: New Testament Essays* (Tübingen: Mohr, 1978).
—'The Silenced Wives of Corinth (I Cor. 14.34-35)', in *New Testament Textual Criticism: Its Significance for Exegesis, Essays in Honour of B.M. Metzger* (ed. E.J. Epp and G.D. Fee; Oxford: Clarendon Press, 1981).
—'Traditions in I Corinthians', *NTS* 32 (1986), pp. 481-502.
Engberg-Pedersen, T., 'The Gospel and Social Practice according to I Corinthians', *NTS* 33 (1987), pp. 557-84.
Engels, F., 'On the History of Early Christianity', in *On Religion* (Moscow: Progress, 1975).
Enslin, M.S., *The Ethics of Paul* (New York: Abingdon Press, 1957).
—'Once again, Luke and Paul', *ZNW* 61 (1970), pp. 253-71.
Epstein, A.L., 'The Networks and Urban Social Organization', in *Social Networks in Urban Situations* (ed. J.C. Mitchell; Manchester: Manchester University Press, 1969).
—'Gossip, Norms and Social Network', in *Social Networks in Urban Situations* (ed. J.C. Mitchell; Manchester: Manchester University Press, 1969).
Esler, P.F., *Community and Gospel in Luke–Acts: The Social and Political Motivations of Lucan Theology* (Cambridge: Cambridge University Press, 1987).

Evans, E., *The Epistles of Paul the Apostle to the Corinthians* (Oxford: Clarendon Press, 1930).
Ewald, G.H., *Die Sendschreiben des Apostels Paulus übersetzt und erklärt* (Göttingen: Verlag der Dieterichschen Buchhandlung, 1857).
Fascher, E., *Der erste Brief des Paulus an die Korinther. I. Einführung und Auslegung der Kapitel 1–7* (Berlin: Evangelische Verlagsanstalt, 1980).
Feaver, D.D., 'Historical Development in the Priesthoods of Athens', *YCS* 15 (1957), pp. 123-58.
Fee, G.D., 'II Corinthians VI.14–VII.1 and Food Offered to Idols', *NTS* 23 (1977), pp. 140-61.
—'Εἰδωλόθυτα Once Again: An Interpretation of I Corinthians 8–10', *Bib* 61 (1980), pp. 172-97.
—*The First Epistles to the Corinthians* (Grand Rapids: Eerdmans, 1987).
Ferguson, J., *The Religions of the Roman Empire* (London: Thames & Hudson, 1970).
Feuillet, A., 'La profession de foi monotheiste der 1 Cor. viii, 4-6', *Studii Biblici Franciscani Liber Annus* 13 (1962–63), pp. 7-32.
Filson, F.V., 'The Significance of the Early House Churches', *JBL* 58 (1939), pp. 105-12.
Findlay, G.G., 'The Letter of the Corinthian Church to St Paul', *Exp* 6.1 (1900), pp. 401-407.
—'St Paul's First Epistle to the Corinthians', in *The Expositor's Greek Testament*, II (Grand Rapids: Eerdmans, 1988).
Finley, M.I., 'The City from Fustel de Coulanges to Max Weber and Beyond', *CSSH* 19 (1977), pp. 305-27.
—*Democracy Ancient and Modern* (London: Hogarth, 2nd edn, 1985).
—*The Ancient Economy* (London: Hogarth, 2nd edn, 1985).
—*Ancient History: Evidence and Models* (London: Chatto and Windus, 1985).
Fiore, B., ' "Covert Allusion" in I Cor. 1–4', *CBQ* 47 (1985), pp. 85-102.
Fiorenza, E.S., *In Memory of Her: A Feminist Theological Reconstruction of Christian Origins* (New York: Crossroad, 1983).
—*Bread Not Stone: The Challenge of Feminist Biblical Interpretation* (Boston: Beacon, 1984).
—'Rhetorical Situation and Historical Reconstruction in I Corinthians', *NTS* 33 (1987), pp. 386-403.
—'I Corinthians', in *Harper's Bible Commentary* (New York: Harper & Row, 1988).
Fischer, C.S., *Networks and Places* (New York: Free Press, 1977).
—*To Dwell among Friends* (Chicago: Chicago University Press, 1982).
Fitzgerald, J.T., *Cracks in an Earthen Vessel: An Examination of the Catalogues of Hardships in the Corinthian Correspondence* (Missoula, MT: Scholars Press, 1988).
Foerster, W., 'κύριος κτλ.', *TDNT*, III, pp. 1039-98.
Forbes, C., 'Comparison, Self-Praise and Irony: Paul's Boasting and the Conventions of Hellenistic Rhetoric', *NTS* 32 (1986), pp. 1-30.
Forkman, G., *The Limits of Religious Community: Expulsion from the Religious Community within the Qumran Sect, within Rabbinic Judaism, and within Primitive Christianity* (Lund: Gleerup, 1972).
Foschini, B.M., 'Those who are Baptised for the Dead. I Cor. 15.29', *CBQ* 12 (1950), pp. 260-70, 379-88; 13 (1951), pp. 46-78, 172-98, 276-83.

Bibliography

Foster, G.M., 'The Dyadic Contract: A Model for the Social Structure of a Mexican Peasant Village', *American Anthropologist* 65 (1963), pp. 1173-92.

—'The Dyadic Contract in Tzintzuntzan, II: Patron–Client Relationships', *American Anthropologist* 65 (1963), pp. 1280-94.

—'Godparents and Social Networks in Tzintzuntzan', *Southwestern Journal of Anthropology* 25 (1969), pp. 261-78.

Fowler, W.W., *The Roman Festivals of the Period of the Republic: An Introduction to the Study of the Religion of the Romans* (London: Macmillan, 1899).

Frame, J.E., *A Critical and Exegetical Commentary on the Epistles of St Paul to the Thessalonians* (Edinburgh: T. & T. Clark, 1912).

Frank, R.I., 'Augustus' Legislation on Marriage and Children', *CSCA* 8 (1975), pp. 41-52.

Freeborn, J.C.K., 'The Development of Doctrine at Corinth', in *Studia Evangelica*, IV (Berlin: Akademie Verlag, 1968).

Frid, B., 'The Enigmatic ἀλλά in I Corinthians 2.9', *NTS* 31 (1985), pp. 603-11.

Fridrichsen, A., 'Peristasenkatalog und res gestae. Nachtrag zu 2 Cor. 11.23ff.', *SO* 8 (1929), pp. 78-82.

—*The Apostle and his Message* (Uppsala: Lundequistska Bokhandeln, 1947).

Friedländer, L., *Roman Life and Manners under the Early Empire* (trans. J.H. Freese; London: Routledge, 1908–13).

Fuller, R.H., *The New Testament in Current Study* (New York: Charles Scribner's Sons, 1962).

—'An Exegetical Paper: I Corinthians 6.1-11', *Ex Auditu* 2 (1986), pp. 96-104.

Funk, R.W., 'Word and Word in I Corinthians 2.6-16', in *Language, Hermeneutic and Word of God: The Problem of Language in the New Testament and Contemporary Theology* (New York: Harper & Row, 1966).

—'The Apostolic *PAROUSIA*: Form and Significance', in *Christian History and Interpretation* (ed. W.R. Farmer, C.F.D. Moule and R.R. Niebuhr; Cambridge: Cambridge University Press, 1967).

Furnish, V.P., 'Fellow Workers in God's Service', *JBL* 80 (1961), pp. 364-70.

—'Development in Paul's Thought', *JAAR* 38 (1970), pp. 289-303.

—*II Corinthians* (New York: Doubleday, 1984).

—'Corinth in Paul's Time: What can Archaeology tell Us?', *BARev* 14 (1988), pp. 14-27.

Gager, J.G., *Kingdom and Community: The Social World of Early Christianity* (Englewood Cliffs: Prentice–Hall, 1975).

—'Review of Recent Works by Robert M. Grant, A.J. Malherbe and G. Theissen', *Religious Studies Review* 5 (1979), pp. 179-80.

—'Shall We Marry Our Enemies? Sociology and the New Testament', *Int* 37 (1982), pp. 256-65.

Galinsky, K., 'Augustus' Legislation on Morals and Marriages', *Philologus* 125 (1981), pp. 126-44.

Gallagher, E.V., 'The Social World of Saint Paul', *Religion* 14 (1984), pp. 91-99.

Galt, A.H., 'Rethinking Patron–Client Relationships: The Real System and the Official System in Southern Italy', *AQ* 47 (1974), pp. 182-202.

Gamble, H.A., Jr, *The Textual History of the Letter to the Romans: A Study in Textual and Literary Criticism* (Grand Rapids: Eerdmans, 1977).

Gardiner, E.N., *Greek Athletic Sports and Festivals* (London: Macmillan, 1910).

Gardner, J.F., *Women in Roman Law and Society* (London: Croom Helm, 1986).
Garnsey, P., 'The *Lex Julia* and Appeal under the Empire', *JRS* 56 (1966), pp. 167-89.
—*Social Status and Legal Privilege in the Roman Empire* (Oxford: Clarendon Press, 1970).
—*Famine and Food Supply in the Graeco-Roman World: Responses to Risk and Crisis* (Cambridge: Cambridge University Press, 1988).
Garnsey, P., and R.P. Saller, *The Roman Empire: Economy, Society and Culture* (London: Gerald Duckworth, 1987).
Geagan, D.J., *The Athenian Constitution after Sulla* (Hesperia Supplement, XII; Princeton: American School of Classical Studies at Athens, 1967).
—'Notes on the Agonistic Institutions of Roman Corinth', *GRBS* 9 (1968), pp. 69-80.
—'Roman Athens: Some Aspects of Life and Culture, I, 86 BC–AD 267', *ANRW* II.7 (1979), pp. 371-437.
Gellner, E., 'The Great Patron: A Reinterpretation of Tribal Rebellions', *AES* 10 (1969), pp. 61-69.
Gellner, E., and J. Waterbury (eds.), *Patrons and Clients in Mediterranean Societies* (London: Duckworth, 1977).
Gelzer, M., *The Roman Nobility* (Oxford: Basil Blackwell, 1969).
Georgi, D., 'I Corinthians', in *The Interpreter's Dictionary of the Bible*, Supplementary Volume (Nashville: Abingdon Press, 1976).
—*The Opponents of Paul in Second Corinthians* (Edinburgh: T. & T. Clark, 1987).
Gill, D., '*Trapezomata*: A Neglected Aspect of Greek Sacrifice', *HTR* 67 (1974), pp. 117-37.
Gill, D.W.J., 'Roman Corinth: A Pluralistic Society?' (Tyndale New Testament/Biblical Archaeology Study Groups Paper, 1989).
Gluckmann, M., *Essays on the Ritual of Social Relations* (Manchester: Manchester University Press, 1962).
—'Gossip and Scandal', *Current Anthropology* 4 (1963), pp. 307-16.
Godet, F., *Commentary on First Corinthians* (Grand Rapids: Kregel, 1977).
Gooch, P.W., ' "Conscience" in I Corinthians 8 and 10', *NTS* 33 (1987), pp. 244-54.
Goppelt, L., *Apostolic and Post-Apostolic Times* (London: A. & C. Black, 1970).
Gordon, M.L., 'The Freedman's Son in Municipal Life', *JRS* 21 (1931), pp. 65-77.
Goudge, H.L., *The First Epistle to the Corinthians* (London: Methuen, 1903).
Goulder, M., 'ΣΟΦΙΑ in I Corinthians' (SNTS Seminar Paper, 1989).
Gouldner, A., 'The Norm of Reciprocity: A Preliminary Statement', *ASR* 25 (1960), pp. 161-78.
Graindor, P., 'Inscriptions attiques d'époque romaine', *BCH* 51 (1927), pp. 247-328.
Granovetter, M.S., 'The Strength of Weak Ties', *AJS* 78 (1973), pp. 1360-80.
Grant, R.M., 'Pliny and the Christians', *HTR* 41 (1948), pp. 273-74.
—'The Wisdom of the Corinthians', in *The Joy of Study: Papers on New Testament and Related Subjects Presented to Honor Frederick Clifton Grant* (ed. S.E. Johnson; New York: Macmillan, 1951).
—*Early Christianity and Society: Seven Studies* (New York: Harper & Row, 1977).
Graziano, L., 'Patron–Client Relationships in Southern Italy', in *Friends, Followers and Factions* (ed. S.W. Schmidt, L. Guasti, C.H. Landé and J.C. Scott; Berkeley: University of California, 1977).
Grosheide, F.W., *Commentary on the First Epistle to the Corinthians* (Grand Rapids: Eerdmans, 1953).

Güttgemanns, E., *Der leidende Apostel und sein Herr: Studien zur paulinischen Christologie* (Göttingen: Vandenhoeck & Ruprecht, 1966).
Gunther, J.J., *St Paul's Opponents and their Background: A Study of Apocalyptic and Jewish Sectarian Teachings* (Leiden: Brill, 1973).
Gutkind, P.C.W., 'African Urbanism: Mobility and Social Networks', *International Journal of Comparative Sociology* 6 (1965), pp. 48-60.
Haenchen, E., *The Acts of the Apostles* (Philadelphia: Westminster Press, 1971).
Hall, A., 'Patron–Client Relations', *Journal of Peasant Studies* 1 (1974), pp. 506-508.
Hallett, J.P., *Fathers and Daughters in Roman Society: Women and the Elite Family* (Princeton: Princeton University Press, 1984).
Hands, A.R., *Charities and Social Aid in Greece and Rome* (London: Thames & Hudson, 1968).
Hardy, E.G., *Christianity and the Roman Government* (London: George Allen & Unwin, 1894).
Harnack, A. von, *Mission and Expansion of Christianity in the First Three Centuries* (London: Williams & Norgate, 1908).
Harrington, D.J., 'Sociological Concepts and the Early Church: A Decade of Research', *TS* 41 (1980), pp. 181-90.
Harris-Jones, P., ' "Home-Boy" Ties and Political Organization in a Copperbelt Township', in *Social Networks in Urban Situations* (ed. J.C. Mitchell; Manchester: Manchester University Press, 1969).
Harrison, P.N., 'Erastus and his Pavement', in *Paulines and Pastorals* (London: Villiers, 1964).
Harvey, A.E., 'The Opposition to Paul', in *Studia Evangelica*, IV (ed. F.L. Cross: Berlin: Akademie-Verlag, 1968).
Hasler, V., 'Das Evangelium des Paulus in Korinth. Erwägungen zur Hermeneutik', *NTS* 30 (1984), pp. 109-29.
Hatch, E., *The Organization of the Early Christian Church* (London: Longmans, Green, 1892).
—*The Influence of Greek Ideas on Christianity* (New York: Harper & Row, 1957).
Hauck, F., and S. Schulz, 'πόρνη κτλ.', *TDNT*, VI, pp. 579-95.
Hawthorne, J.G., 'The Myth of Palaemon', *TAPA* 89 (1958), pp. 92-98.
Heider, F., 'Attitudes and Cognitive Organization', *Journal of Psychology* 21 (1946), pp. 107-12.
Heinrici, C.F., 'Die Christengemeinden Korinths und die religiösen Genossenschaften der Griechen', *Zeitschrift für wissenschaftliche Theologie* 19 (1876), pp. 465-526.
Hengel, M., *Property and Riches in the Early Church: Aspects of a Social History of Early Christianity* (Philadelphia: Fortress Press, 1974).
—*Acts and the History of Earliest Christianity* (London: SCM Press, 1979).
Héring, J., *The First Epistle of Saint Paul to the Corinthians* (London: Epworth, 1962).
Herman, G., *Ritualized Friendship and the Greek City* (Cambridge: Cambridge University Press, 1987).
Hill, B.H., 'Excavations at Corinth, 1925: Preliminary Report', *AJA* 30 (1926), pp. 44-49.
Hock, R.F., 'Paul's Tentmaking and the Problem of his Social Class', *JBL* 97 (1978), pp. 555-64.
—'The Workshop as a Social Setting for Paul's Missionary Preaching', *CBQ* 41 (1979), pp. 438-50.

—*The Social Context of Paul's Ministry: Tentmaking and Apostleship* (Philadelphia: Fortress Press, 1980).

Holladay, A.J., 'The Elections of Magistrates in the Early Principate', *Latomus* 37 (1978), pp. 874-93.

Holladay, C.R., *The First Letter of Paul to the Corinthians* (Austin, TX: Sweet, 1979).

Hollmann, G., *Urchristentum in Korinth* (Leipzig: Hinrichs, 1903).

Holmberg, B., *Paul and Power: The Structure of Authority in the Primitive Church as Reflected in the Pauline Epistles* (Philadelphia: Fortress Press, 1978).

—'Sociological versus Theological Analysis of the Question concerning a Pauline Church Order', in *Die Paulinische Literatur und Theologie: Anlässlich der 50. jährigen Gründungs-Feier der Universität von Aarhus* (Herausgegeben von Sigfred Pedersen; Arhus: Forlaget Aros, 1980).

Homans, G.C., *Social Behaviour: Its Elementary Forms* (London: Routledge & Kegan Paul, 1961).

Hooker, M.D., ' "Beyond the Things which are Written": An Examination of I Cor. IV.6', *NTS* 10 (1963), pp. 127-32.

Hopkins, M.K., 'The Age of Roman Girls at Marriage', *Population Studies* 18 (1965), pp. 309-27.

—'Elite Mobility in the Roman Empire', *PP* 32 (1965), pp. 12-26.

—'Taxes and Trade in the Roman Empire (200 BC–AD 400)', *JRS* 70 (1970), pp. 101-25.

—*Conquerors and Slaves: Sociological Studies in Roman History*, I (Cambridge: Cambridge University Press, 1978).

—*Death and Renewal: Sociological Studies in Roman History*, II (Cambridge: Cambridge University Press, 1983).

Horsley, R.A., 'Pneumatikos vs. Psychikos: Distinctions of Spiritual Status among the Corinthians', *HTR* 69 (1976), pp. 269-88.

—'Wisdom of Word and Words of Wisdom in Corinth', *CBQ* 39 (1977), pp. 224-39.

—'The Background of the Confessional Formula in 1 Kor. 8.6', *ZNW* 69 (1978), pp. 130-35.

—'Consciousness and Freedom among the Corinthians: 1 Corinthians 8–10', *CBQ* 40 (1978), pp. 574-89.

—' "How Can Some of You Say there is no Resurrection of the Dead?" Spiritual Elitism in Corinth', *NovT* 20 (1978), pp. 203-31.

—'Spiritual Marriage with Sophia', *VC* 33 (1979), pp. 30-54.

—'Gnosis in Corinth: 1 Corinthians 8.1-6', *NTS* 27 (1980), pp. 32-51.

House, H.W., 'Tongues and the Mystery Religions of Corinth', *BSac* 140 (1985), pp. 134-50.

Hurd, J.C., 'Pauline Chronology and Pauline Theology', in *Christian History and Interpretation* (ed. W.R. Farmer, C.F.D. Moule and R.R. Niebuhr; Cambridge: Cambridge University Press, 1967).

—*The Origins of I Corinthians* (Macon, GA: Mercer University Press, 2nd edn, 1983).

Isenberg, S.R., 'Some Uses and Limitations of Social Scientific Methodology in the Study of Early Christianity', in *SBL 1980 Seminar Papers* (ed. P.J. Achtemeier; Chico, CA: Scholars Press, 1980).

Jeremias, J., ' "Flesh and Blood Cannot Inherit the Kingdom of God" (1 Cor. XV.50)', *NTS* 2 (1955–56), pp. 151-59.

Jewett, R., *Paul's Anthropological Terms: A Study of their Use in Conflict Settings* (Leiden: Brill, 1971).
—*Dating Paul's Life* (London: SCM Press, 1979).
—'Paul, Phoebe, and the Spanish Mission', in *The Social World of Formative Christianity and Judaism: Essays in Tribute to H.C. Kee* (Philadelphia: Fortress Press, 1988).
Johnson, F.P., 'The Imperial Portraits at Corinth', *AJA* 30 (1926), pp. 158-76.
—*Sculpture, 1896–1923. Corinth: Results*, IX, Pt. 1 (Cambridge, MA: Harvard University Press, 1931).
Jolowicz, H.F., *Historical Introduction to the Study of Roman Law* (Cambridge: Cambridge University Press, 2nd edn, 1952).
Jones, A.H.M., *The Greek City from Alexander to Justinian* (Oxford: Clarendon Press, 1940).
—*The Criminal Courts of the Roman Republic and Principate* (Oxford: Basil Blackwell, 1972).
Jones, C.P., *The Roman World of Dio Chrysostom* (Cambridge, MA: Harvard University Press, 1978).
Judge, E.A., *The Social Pattern of the Christian Groups in the First Century: Some Prolegomena to the Study of New Testament Ideas of Social Obligation* (London: Tyndale Press, 1960).
—'The Early Christians as a Scholastic Community', *JRH* (1960–61), pp. 4-15, 125-37.
—'Paul's Boasting in Relation to Contemporary Professional Practice', *ABR* 16 (1968), pp. 37-50.
—'St Paul and Classical Society', *JAC* 15 (1972), pp. 19-36.
—'Paul as a Radical Critic of Society', *Interchange* 16 (1974), pp. 191-203.
—' "Antike und Christentum": Towards a Definition of the Field: A Bibliographical Survey', *ANRW* II.23.1 (1979), pp. 3-58.
—'The Social Identity of the First Christians: A Question of Method in Religious History', *JRH* 11 (1980), pp. 201-17.
—*Rank and Status in the World of the Caesars and St Paul* (The Broadhead Memorial Lecture, 1981; Christchurch: University of Canterbury, 1982).
—'Cultural Conformity and Innovation in Paul: Some Clues from Contemporary Documents', *TynBul* 35 (1984), pp. 3-24.
Käsemann, E., 'The Disciples of John the Baptist in Ephesus', in *Essays on New Testament Themes* (London: SCM Press, 1964).
—'Sentences of Holy Law in the New Testament', in *New Testament Questions of Today* (London: SCM Press, 1969).
—'On the Subject of Primitive Christian Apocalyptic', in *New Testament Questions of Today* (London: SCM Press, 1969).
—'The Theological Problem Presented by the Motif of the Body of Christ', in *Perspectives on Paul* (London: SCM Press, 1971).
Kane, J.P., 'The Mithraic Cult Meal in its Greek and Roman Environment', in *Mithraic Studies: Proceedings of the First International Congress of Mithraic Studies* (ed. J.R. Hinnels; Manchester: Manchester University Press, 1975).
Kapferer, B., 'Norms and Manipulation of Relationships in a Work Context', in *Social Networks in Urban Situations* (ed. J.C. Mitchell; Manchester: Manchester University Press, 1969).

Kaufmann, R., 'The Patron–Client Concept and Macropolitics: Prospects and Problems', *CSSH* 16 (1974), pp. 284-308.
Kautsky, K., *The Foundations of Christianity* (New York: Russell & Russell, 1953).
Keck, L.E., 'On the Ethos of Early Christianity', *JAAR* 42 (1974), pp. 435-52.
—*Paul and his Letters* (Philadelphia: Fortress Press, 2nd edn, 1988).
Kee, H.C., *Christian Origins in Sociological Perspective* (London: SCM Press, 1980).
Kelly, J.M. *Roman Litigation* (Oxford: Clarendon Press, 1966).
Kempthorne, R., 'Incest and the Body of Christ: A Study of I Corinthians VI.12-20', *NTS* 14 (1968), pp. 568-74.
Kennedy, G., *New Testament Interpretation through Rhetorical Criticism* (Chapel Hill, NC: University of North Carolina, 1984).
Kenny, M., 'Patterns of Patronage in Spain', *AQ* 33 (1960), pp. 14-23. Reprinted in *Friends, Followers and Factions* (ed. S.W. Schmidt, L. Guasti, C.H. Landé and J.C. Scott; Berkeley: University of California, 1977).
—*A Spanish Tapestry: Town and Country in Castile* (Bloomington: University of Indiana Press, 1962).
Keyes, C.W., 'The Greek Letter of Introduction', *AJP* 56 (1935), pp. 28-44.
Kim, C.H., *Form and Structure of the Familiar Greek Letter of Recommendation* (Missoula, MT: Scholars Press, 1972).
—'The Papyrus Invitation', *JBL* 94 (1975), pp. 391-402.
Klauck, H.-J., *Hausgemeinde und Hauskirche im frühen Christentum* (Stuttgart: Verlag Katholisches Bibelwerk, 1981).
—*Herrenmahl und hellenistischer Kult: Eine religionsgeschichtliche Untersuchung zum ersten Korintherbrief* (Münster: Aschendorff, 1982).
—'Gemeindestrukturen im ersten Korintherbrief', *Bibel und Kirche* 40 (1985), pp. 9-15.
Kleiner, D.E.E., *Roman Group Portraiture: The Funerary Reliefs of the Late Republic and Early Empire* (New York: Garland, 1977).
Knowling, R.J., 'The Acts of the Apostles', in *The Expositor's Greek Testament*, II (Grand Rapids: Eerdmans, 1988).
Knox, J., 'The Pauline Chronology', *JBL* 58 (1939), pp. 15-29.
—*Chapters in a Life of Paul* (London: A. & C. Black, 1954).
Koester, H., '*GNOMAI DIAPHOROI*: The Origin and Nature of Diversification in the History of Early Christianity', in *Trajectories through Early Christianity* (ed. J.M. Robinson and H. Koester; Philadelphia: Fortress Press, 1971).
—*Introduction to the New Testament* (2 vols.; New York: de Gruyter, 1982).
Kreissig, H., 'Zur sozialen Zusammensetzung der frühchristlichen Gemeinden in ersten Jahrhundert u. Z.', *Eirene* 6 (1967), pp. 91-100.
Kümmel, W.G., *Introduction to the New Testament* (London: SCM Press, rev. edn, 1975).
Kyrtatas, D.J., *The Social Structure of the Early Christian Communities* (London: Verso, 1987).
Lacey, W.K., '2 BC and Julia's Adultery', *Antichthon* 19 (1980), pp. 127-42.
—'*Patria Potestas*', in *The Family in Ancient Rome: New Perspective* (ed. B. Rawson; London: Croom Helm, 1986).
La Fontaine, J.S., 'Unstructured Social Relations', *West African Journal of Sociology and Political Science* 1 (1975), pp. 51-81.
Lambrecht, J., 'Paul's Christological Use of Scripture in I Cor. 15.20-28', *NTS* 28 (1982), pp. 502-27.

Lampe, G.W.H., 'Church Discipline and the Interpretation of the Epistles to the Corinthians', in *Christian History and Interpretation* (ed. W.R. Farmer, C.F.D. Moule and R.R. Niebuhr; Cambridge: Cambridge University Press, 1967).

Landé, C.H., 'Networks and Groups in Southeast Asia: Some Observations on the Group Theory of Politics', *American Political Science Review* 67 (1973), pp. 103-27. Reprinted in *Friends, Followers and Factions* (ed. S.W. Schmidt, L. Guasti, C.H. Landé and J.C. Scott; Berkeley: University of California, 1977).

—'Introduction: The Dyadic Basis of Clientelism', in *Friends, Followers and Factions* (ed. S.W. Schmidt, L. Guasti, C.H. Landé and J.C. Scott; Berkeley: University of California, 1977).

Lang, F., *Die Briefe an die Korinther* (Göttingen: Vandenhoeck & Ruprecht, 1986).

Larsen, J.A.O., 'Roman Greece', in *An Economic Survey of Ancient Rome*, IV (ed. T. Frank; Baltimore: Johns Hopkins University Press, 1938).

Lattimore, O., *Inner Asian Frontiers of China* (Boston: Beacon, 1962).

Laumann, E.O., *Bonds of Pluralism: The Form and Structure of Urban Social Networks* (New York: John Wiley & Sons, 1972).

Lemarchand, R., 'Comparative Political Clientelism: Structure, Process and Optic', in *Political Clientelism: Patronage and Development* (ed. S.N. Eisenstadt and R. Lemarchand; London: Sage, 1981).

Lemarchand, R., and K. Legg, 'Political Clientelism and Development: A Preliminary Analysis', *Comparative Politics* 4 (1972), pp. 149-78.

Leinhardt, S. (ed.), *Social Networks: A Developing Paradigm* (New York: Academic, 1977).

Levick, B., 'Imperial Control of the Elections under the Early Principate: *Commendatio*, *Suffragatio* and *"Nominatio"* ', *Historia* 16 (1967), pp. 207-30.

—*Tiberius the Politician* (London: Thames & Hudson, 1976).

Liebeschütz, J.H.W.G., *Continuity and Change in Roman Religion* (Oxford: Clarendon Press, 1979).

Lietzmann, H., *An die Korinther I-II* (Tübingen: Mohr, 5th edn, 1969).

Lightfoot, J.B., *Notes on Epistles of St Paul* (London: Macmillan, 1895).

Lim, T.H., 'Not in Persuasive Words of Wisdom, but in the Demonstration of the Spirit and Power', *NovT* 29 (1987), pp. 137-49.

Lincoln, A.T., *Paradise Now and Not Yet: Studies in the Role of the Heavenly Dimension in Paul's Thought with Special Reference to his Eschatology* (Cambridge: Cambridge University Press, 1981).

Lisle, R., 'The Cults of Corinth' (PhD dissertation, Johns Hopkins University, 1955).

Lohmeyer, E., *Soziale Fragen im Urchristentum* (Leipzig: Quelle & Meyer, 1921).

Lüdemann, G., *Paul, Apostle to the Gentiles: Studies in Chronology* (Philadelphia: Fortress Press, 1984).

Lütgert, W., *Freiheitspredigt und Schwarmgeister in Korinth* (Gütersloh: Bertelsmann, 1908).

Lyall, F., 'Roman Law in the Writings of St Paul: The Slave and the Freedman', *NTS* 17 (1970), pp. 73-79.

MacArthur, S.D., ' "Spirit" in Pauline Usage: I Corinthians 5.5', in *Studia Biblica 1978*, III (ed. E.A. Livingstone; Sheffield: JSOT Press, 1980).

MacDonald, M.Y., *The Pauline Churches: A Socio-Historical Study of Institutionalization in the Pauline and Deutero-Pauline Writings* (Cambridge: Cambridge University Press, 1988).
MacDowell, D.M., *Andokides: On the Mysteries* (Oxford: Oxford University Press, 1962).
—*The Law in Classical Athens* (London: Thames & Hudson, 1978).
—*Spartan Law* (Edinburgh: Scottish Academic, 1986).
MacMullen, R., *Enemies of Roman Order* (Cambridge, MA: Harvard University Press, 1967).
—*Roman Social Relations, 50 BC to AD 284* (New Haven: Yale University Press, 1974).
—*Paganism in the Roman Empire* (New Haven: Yale University Press, 1981).
McDonald, W.A., 'Archaeology and Saint Paul; Journey in Greek Lands. Part III: Corinth', *BA* 4 (1942), pp. 36-48.
Magie, D., *Roman Rule in Asia Minor to the End of the Third Century after Christ* (2 vols.; New York: Arno, 1975).
Malherbe, A.J., 'The Corinthian Collection', *RestQ* 3 (1959), pp. 221-33.
—'The Inhospitality of Diotrephes', in *God's Christ and his People: Studies in Honor of Nils Alstrup Dahl* (ed. J. Jervell and W.A. Meeks; Oslo: Universitetsforlaget, 1977).
—*Social Aspects of Early Christianity* (Philadelphia: Fortress Press, 1983).
—'Exhortation in First Thessalonians', *NovT* 25 (1983), pp. 238-56.
—*Moral Exhortation: A Greco-Roman Sourcebook* (Philadelphia: Fortress Press, 1986).
—*Paul and the Thessalonians* (Philadelphia: Fortress Press, 1987).
Malina, B., 'Does *Porneia* mean "Fornication"?', *NovT* 14 (1972), pp. 10-17.
—*The New Testament World: Insights from Cultural Anthropology* (Atlanta: John Knox, 1981).
—'The Social Sciences and Biblical Interpretation', *Int* 37 (1982), pp. 229-42.
Manson, T.W., 'St Paul in Ephesus: (3) The Corinthian Correspondence', *BJRL* 26 (1941–42), pp. 101-20.
Marrou, H.I., *A History of Education in Antiquity* (London: Sheed & Ward, 1956).
Marshall, A.J., 'Roman Women and the Provinces', *Ancient Society* 6 (1975), pp. 109-27.
Marshall, P., *Enmity in Corinth: Social Conventions in Paul's Relations with the Corinthians* (Tübingen: Mohr, 1987).
Martin, L.H., *Hellenistic Religions: An Introduction* (Oxford: Oxford University Press, 1987).
Martin, R.P., *2 Corinthians* (Waco, TX: Word Books, 1986).
Martin, T.R., 'Inscriptions at Corinth', *Hesp* 46 (1977), pp. 178-98.
Marx, K., and F. Engels, *On Religion* (Moscow: Progress, 1975).
Massie, J., *I and II Corinthians* (New York: Frowde, 1902).
Mathews, J.B., 'Hospitality and the New Testament Church: A Historical and Exegetical Study' (PhD dissertation, Princeton University, 1965).
Mathews, S., 'The Social Origins of Theology', *AJS* 18 (1912), pp. 289-317.
Mauss, M., *The Gift: Forms and Functions of Exchange in Archaic Societies* (Glencoe: Free Press, 1954).
Mayer, A.C., 'System and Network: An Approach to the Study of Political Process in Dewas', in *Indian Anthropology: Essays in Memory of D.N. Majundar* (ed. T.N. Madan and G. Sarana; Bombay: Asian Publishing House, 1962).
—'The Significance of Quasi-Groups in the Study of Complex Societies', in *The Social Anthropology of Complex Societies* (ed. M. Banton; London: Tavistock, 1966).

Bibliography 209

Meeks, W.A., *The Writings of St Paul* (New York: Norton, 1972).
—'The Social Context of Pauline Theology', *Int* 37 (1982), pp. 266-77.
—*The First Urban Christians: The Social World of the Apostle Paul* (New Haven: Yale University Press, 1983).
—'A Hermeneutics of Social Embodiment', *HTR* 79 (1986), pp. 176-86.
—*The Moral World of the First Christians* (London: SPCK, 1987).
Meinardus, O.F.A., *St Paul in Greece* (New York: Caratzas Brothers, 1979).
Merklein, H., 'Die Einheitlichkeit des ersten Korintherbriefes', *ZNW* 75 (1984), pp. 153-83.
Meritt, B.D., 'Greek Inscriptions', *Hesp* 11 (1942), pp. 275-303.
Metzger, B.M., 'Considerations of Method in the Study of Mystery Religions', *HTR* 48 (1955), pp. 1-20.
Meyer, H.A.W., *A Critical and Exegetical Handbook to the Epistles to the Corinthians* (2 vols.; Edinburgh: T. & T. Clark, 1883, 1884).
Meyer, L.H., and G.F. Snyder, 'Sexuality: Its Social Reality and Theological Understanding in I Corinthians 7', in *SBL 1980 Seminar Papers* (ed. P.J. Achtemeier; Chico, CA: Scholars Press, 1980).
Millar, F.G.B., 'Some Evidence on the Meaning of Tacitus *Annals XII*.60', *Historia* 13 (1964), pp. 180-87.
—'The Development of Jurisdiction by Imperial Procurators: Further Evidence', *Historia* 14 (1965), pp. 362-67.
—'Epictetus and the Imperial Court', *JRS* 55 (1965), pp. 141-48.
—'The Emperor, the Senate and the Provinces', *JRS* 56 (1966), pp. 156-66.
—*The Roman Empire and its Neighbours* (London: Duckworth, 1967).
—'The World of the Golden Ass', *JRS* 71 (1981), pp. 65-75.
—'Empire and City, Augustus to Julian: Obligations, Excuses and Status', *JRS* 83 (1983), pp. 76-96.
Miller, G., 'ΑΡΧΟΝΤΩΝ ΤΟΥ ΑΙΩΝΟΥ ΤΟΥΤΟΥ—A New Look at I Corinthians 2.6-8', *JBL* 91 (1972), pp. 522-28.
Minear, P.S., 'Christ and the Congregation: I Corinthians 5–6', *RevExp* 80 (1983), pp. 341-50.
Mitchell, J.C., 'Theoretical Orientations in African Urban Studies', in *The Social Anthropology of Complex Societies* (ed. M. Banton; London: Tavistock, 1966).
—(ed.) *Social Networks in Urban Situations: Analyses of Personal Relationships in Central African Towns* (Manchester: Manchester University Press, 1969).
Moffatt, J., *The First Epistle of Paul to the Corinthians* (London: Hodder & Stoughton, 1938).
—'The First and Second Epistles of Paul the Apostle to the Thessalonians', in *The Expositor's Greek Testament*, IV (Grand Rapids: Eerdmans, 1988).
Momigliano, A., 'Herod of Judaea', in *Cambridge Ancient History*, X (ed. S.A. Cook, F.E. Adcock and M.P. Charlesworth; Cambridge: Cambridge University Press, 1934).
—*On Pagans, Jews and Christians* (Middletown: Wesleyan, 1987).
Mommsen, T., *The History of Rome* (London: Dent & Dutton, 1930).
Morris, L., *The First Epistle of Paul to the Corinthians* (London: Tyndale Press, 1958).
Mott, S.C., 'The Greek Benefactor and Deliverance from Moral Distress' (PhD dissertation, Harvard University, 1971).

—'The Power of Giving and Receiving: Reciprocity in Hellenistic Benevolence', in *Current Issues in Biblical and Patristic Interpretation* (ed. G. Hawthorne; Grand Rapids: Eerdmans, 1975).

Moule, C.F.D., 'Obligation in the Ethic of Paul', in *Christian History and Interpretation* (ed. W.R. Farmer, C.F.D. Moule and R.R. Niebuhr; Cambridge: Cambridge University Press, 1967).

Munck, J., *Paul and the Salvation of Mankind* (London: SCM Press, 1959).

—*The Acts of the Apostles* (Garden City, NY: Doubleday, 1967).

Murphy, D.J., 'The Dead in Christ: Paul's Understanding of God's Fidelity: A Study of I Corinthians 15' (PhD dissertation, Union Seminary, 1977).

Murphy-O'Connor, J., 'I Corinthians V, 3–5', *RB* 84 (1977), pp. 239-45.

—'Corinthian Slogans in I Cor. 6.12-20', *CBQ* 40 (1978), pp. 391-96.

—'I Cor., VIII, 6: Cosmology or Soteriology?', *RB* 85 (1978), pp. 253-67.

—'Freedom or the Ghetto (I Cor., VIII, 1–13; X, 23–XI, 1)', *RB* 85 (1978), pp. 543-74.

—*I Corinthians* (Dublin: Veritas, 1979).

—'Food and Spiritual Gifts in I Cor. 8.8', *CBQ* 41 (1979), pp. 292-98.

—' "Baptized for the Dead" (I Cor., XV, 29). A Corinthian Slogan?', *RB* 88 (1981), pp. 532-43.

—*St Paul's Corinth: Texts and Archaeology* (Wilmington, DE: Michael Glazier, 1983).

—'The Corinth St Paul Saw', *BA* 47 (1984), pp. 147-59.

—'Philo and 2 Cor. 6.14–7.1', *RB* 95 (1988), pp. 55-69.

—'The First Letter to the Corinthians', in *New Jerome Biblical Commentary* (Englewood Cliffs, NJ: Prentice-Hall, 1990).

Nickle, K.F., *The Collection: A Study in Paul's Strategy* (London: SCM Press, 1966).

Nilsson, M.P., *The Dionysiac Mysteries of the Hellenistic and Roman Age* (Lund: Gleerup, 1957).

Nock, A.D., 'The Historical Importance of Cult-Associations', *CR* 38 (1924), pp. 105-109.

—*Conversion: The Old and the New in Religion from Alexander the Great to Augustine of Hippo* (Oxford: Clarendon Press, 1933).

—'Religious Developments from the Close of the Republic to the Death of Nero', in *Cambridge Ancient History*, X (ed. S.A. Cook, F.E. Adcock and M.P. Charlesworth; Cambridge: Cambridge University Press, 1934).

—'The Gild of Zeus Hypsistos', *HTR* 29 (1936), pp. 39-88.

—'The Cult of Heroes', *HTR* 37 (1944), pp. 141-74.

—*St Paul* (London: Oxford University Press, 1946).

—'Early Gentile Christianity and its Hellenistic Background', in *Essays on Religion and the Ancient World*, I (Oxford: Clarendon Press, 1972).

—*Essays on Religion and the Ancient World* (ed. Z. Stewart; 2 vols.; Oxford: Clarendon Press, 1972).

Nutton, V., 'The Beneficial Ideology', in *Imperialism in the Ancient World* (ed. C.R. Whittaker and P. Garnsey; Cambridge: Cambridge University Press, 1978).

Ogilvie, R.M., *The Romans and their Gods* (London: Hogarth Press, 1969).

Oliver, J.H., 'Lollia Paulina, Memmius Regulus and Caligula', *Hesp* 35 (1966), pp. 150-53.

—'The Epistle of Claudius which Mentions the Proconsul Junius Gallio', *Hesp* 40 (1971), p. 239.

—'Panachaeans and Panhellenes', *Hesp* 47 (1978), pp. 185-95.
Ollrog, W.-H., *Paulus und seine Mitarbeiter: Untersuchungen zu Theorie und Praxis der paulinischen Mission* (Neukirchen: Erziehungsverein, 1979).
O'Neill, J.C., 'I Corinthians 15.29', *ExpTim* 91 (1980), pp. 310-11.
Orr, D.G., 'Roman Domestic Religion: The Evidence of the Household Shrines', *ANRW* II.16.2 (1978), pp. 1557-91.
Orr, W.F., and J.A. Walther, *I Corinthians* (Garden City, NY: Doubleday, 1976).
Osborn, E., *Ethical Patterns in Early Christian Thought* (Cambridge: Cambridge University Press, 1976).
Oster, R.E., 'When Men Wore Veils to Worship: The Historical Context of I Corinthians 11.4', *NTS* 34 (1988), pp. 481-505.
Pagels, E., *The Gnostic Paul* (Philadelphia: Fortress Press, 1975).
Paine, R., 'What is Gossip about? An Alternative Hypothesis', *Man* ns 2 (1967), pp. 278-85.
Parry, R., *The First Epistle of Paul the Apostle to the Corinthians* (Cambridge: Cambridge University Press, 1926).
Patte, D., *Paul's Faith and the Power of the Gospel: A Structural Introduction to the Pauline Letters* (Philadelphia: Fortress Press, 1983).
Pearce, T., 'The Role of the Wife as *custos*', *Eranos* 72 (1974), pp. 16-33.
Pearson, B.A., *The Pneumatikos–Psychikos Terminology: A Study in the Theology of the Corinthian Opponents of Paul and its Relation to Gnosticism* (Missoula, MT: Scholars Press, 1973).
Peristiany, J.G., (ed.), *Honour and Shame: The Values of Mediterranean Society* (London: Weidenfeld & Nicolson, 1965).
Petersen, N., *Rediscovering Paul: Philemon and the Sociology of Paul's Narrative World* (Philadelphia: Fortress Press, 1985).
Pfitzner, V., *Paul and the Agon Motif* (Leiden: Brill, 1967).
Pherigo, L.P., 'Paul and the Corinthian Church', *JBL* 68 (1949), pp. 341-50.
Phipps, W.E., 'Is Paul's Attitude toward Sexual Relations Contained in 1 Cor. 7.1?', *NTS* 28 (1982), pp. 125-31.
Pierce, C.A., *Conscience in the New Testament* (London: SCM Press, 1955).
Pitt-Rivers, J.A., *The People of the Sierra* (New York: Criterion, 1954).
—'Honour and Social Status', in *Honour and Shame: The Values of Mediterranean Society* (ed. J.G. Peristiany; London: Weidenfeld & Nicolson, 1965).
Poland, F., *Geschichte des griechischen Vereinswesens* (Leipzig: Teubner, 1909).
Pomeroy, S.B., 'Selected Bibliography on Women in Antiquity', *Arethusa* 6 (1973), pp. 125-57.
—*Goddesses, Whores, Wives and Slaves: Women in Classical Antiquity* (New York: Schocken Books, 1975).
Pomtow, H., 'Delphische Neufunde V: Zusätze und Nachträge', *Klio* 17 (1921), pp. 153-203.
Pope, R.M., 'Studies in Pauline Vocabulary of Indwelling Power', *ExpTim* 22 (1911), pp. 312-33.
Powell, B., 'Greek Inscriptions from Corinth', *AJA* 7 (1903), pp. 26-71.
Powell, J.D., 'Peasant Society and Clientelist Politics', *American Political Science Review* 64 (1970), pp. 411-26.

Price, F.V., 'Only Connect? Issues in Charting Social Networks', *SR* 29 (1981), pp. 283-312.
Price, S.R.F., *Rituals and Power: The Roman Imperial Cult in Asia Minor* (Cambridge: Cambridge University Press, 1984).
—'Gods and Emperors: The Greek Language of the Roman Imperial Cult', *JHS* 104 (1984), pp. 79-95.
Radcliffe-Brown, A.R., 'On Social Structure', in *Social Networks* (ed. S. Leinhardt; New York: Academic, 1977).
Raditsa, L.F., 'Augustus' Legislation concerning Marriage, Procreation, Love Affairs and Adultery', *ANRW* II.13 (1980), pp. 278-339.
Raeder, M., 'Vikariatstaufe in I Cor. 15.29?', *ZNW* 46 (1955), pp. 258-60.
Ramsay, W.M., 'Historical Commentary on the Epistles to the Corinthians', *Exp* 6.1 (1900), pp. 19-31, 91-111, 203-17, 273-89, 380-87.
—*St Paul the Traveller and the Roman Citizen* (London: Hodder & Stoughton, 1920).
Rawson, B.M., 'Roman Concubinage and Other *de facto* Marriage', *TAPA* 104 (1974), pp. 279-305.
—(ed.), *The Family in Ancient Rome: New Perspectives* (London: Croom Helm, 1986).
Reisser, H., 'πορνεύω', *NIDNTT*, I, pp. 497-501.
Reitzenstein, R., *Hellenistic Mystery-Religions: Their Basic Ideas and Significance* (trans. J.E. Steely; Pittsburgh: Pickwick Press, 1978).
Reumann, J., ' "Stewards of God"—Pre-Christian Religious Application of OIKONOMOS in Greek', *JBL* 77 (1958), pp. 339-49.
Rhodes, P.J., *The Athenian Boule* (Oxford: Clarendon Press, 1972).
Richards, J.R., 'Romans and I Corinthians: Their Chronological Relationship and Comparative Dates', *NTS* 13 (1966), pp. 14-30.
Richardson, P., 'Judgment, Immortality, and Sexual Ethics in I Corinthians 6', in *SBL 1980 Seminar Papers* (ed. P.J. Achtemeier; Chico, CA: Scholars Press, 1980).
—'Pauline Inconsistency: I Corinthians 9.19-23 and Galatians 2.11-14', *NTS* 26 (1980), pp. 347-62.
—'On the Absence of "Anti-Judaism" in I Corinthians', in *Anti-Judaism in Early Christianity* (ed. P. Richardson *et al*.; Waterloo: Wilfrid Laurier University Press, 1986).
Ridgway, B.S., 'Sculpture from Corinth', *Hesp* 50 (1981), pp. 422-48.
Rissi, M., *Die Taufe für die Toten* (Zurich: Zwingli Verlag, 1962).
Robertson, A., *Word Pictures in the New Testament*, III and IV (Grand Rapids: Baker Book House, 1930).
Robertson, A., and A. Plummer, *A Critical and Exegetical Commentary on the First Epistle of St Paul to the Corinthians* (New York: Charles Scribner's Sons, 1911).
Robinson, H.S., *Corinth: A Brief History of the City and a Guide to the Excavations* (Athens: American School of Classical Studies, 1964).
Robinson, J.A.T., *The Body: A Study in Pauline Theology* (London: SCM Press, 1952).
Rodd, C.S., 'On Applying a Sociological Theory to Biblical Studies', *JSOT* 19 (1981), pp. 95-106.
Roetzel, C.J., *Judgment in the Community: A Study in the Relationship between Eschatology and Ecclesiology in Paul* (Leiden: Brill, 1972).
Rohrbaugh, R.L., 'Methodological Considerations in the Debate over Social Class Status of Early Christians', *JAAR* 52 (1984), pp. 519-46.

Roniger, L., 'Modern Patron–Client Relations and Historical Clientelism: Some Clues from Ancient Republican Rome', *AES* 24 (1983), pp. 63-95.
Rordorff, W., 'Was wissen sir über die christlichen Gottesdiensträume?', *ZNW* 55 (1964), pp. 110-28.
Rostovtzeff, M., *The Social and Economic History of the Roman Empire* (Oxford: Clarendon Press, 2nd edn, 1957).
Rowland, C., *Christian Origins: An Account of the Setting and Character of the Most Important Messianic Sect of Judaism* (London: SPCK, 1985).
Rudd, N., *Themes in Roman Satire* (London: Duckworth, 1986).
Ruef, J.S., *Paul's First Letter to Corinth* (Harmondsworth: Penguin Books, 1971).
Ryberg, I.S., *Rites of the State Religion in Roman Arts* (Memoirs of the American Academy in Rome, 22; Rome: American Academy in Rome, 1955).
Sänger, D., 'Die Δυνατοί in 1 Kor. 1.26', *ZNW* 76 (1985), pp. 285-91.
Saller, R.P., 'Promotion and Patronage in Equestrian Careers', *JRS* 70 (1980), pp. 44-63.
—*Personal Patronage under the Early Empire* (Cambridge: Cambridge University Press, 1982).
—'Martial on Patronage and Literature', *CQ* 33 (1983), pp. 246-57.
—'*Familia, Domus*, and the Roman Conception of the Family', *Phoenix* 38 (1984), pp. 336-55.
—'Roman Dowry and the Devolution of Property in the Principate', *CQ* 34 (1984), pp. 195-205.
—'Patria Potestas and the Stereotype of the Roman Family', *Continuity and Change* 1 (1986), pp. 7-22.
Sampley, J.P., 'Societas Christi: Roman Law and Paul's Conception of the Christian Community', in *God's Christ and his People: Studies in Honor of Nils Alstrup Dahl* (ed. J. Jervell and W.A. Meeks; Oslo: Universitetsforlaget, 1977).
—*Pauline Partnership in Christ: Christian Community and Commitment in Light of Roman Law* (Philadelphia: Fortress Press, 1980).
Sandelin, K.-G., *Die Auseinandersetzung mit der Weisheit in 1. Korinther 15* (Abo: Abo Akademi, 1976).
Sanders, B., 'Imitating Paul: 1 Cor. 4.16', *HTR* 74 (1981), pp. 353-63.
Sanders, E.P., *Paul, the Law and the Jewish People* (London: SCM Press, 1983).
Sanders, J.T., *Ethics in the New Testament* (London: SCM Press, 1975).
Sandys, J.E. (ed.), *A Companion to Latin Studies* (Cambridge: Cambridge University Press, 3rd edn, 1921).
Schaps, D., *Economic Rights of Women in Ancient Greece* (Edinburgh: Edinburgh University Press, 1959).
Schlatter, D., *Die korinthische Theologie* (Gütersloh: Bertelsmann, 1914).
—*The Church in the New Testament Period* (London: SPCK, 1955).
—*Paulus der Bote Jesu* (Stuttgart: Calwer Verlag, 1956).
—*Die Korintherbriefe* (Stuttgart: Calwer Verlag, 1962).
Schlier, H., 'βέβαιος, κτλ.', *TDNT*, I, pp. 600-603.
Schmidt, S.W., *et al.* (eds.), *Friends, Followers and Factions: A Reader in Political Clientelism* (Berkeley: University of California Press, 1977).
Schmithals, W., *Gnosticism in Corinth: An Investigation of the Letters to the Corinthians* (Nashville: Abingdon Press, 1971).
—'Die Korintherbriefe als Briefsammlung', *ZNW* 64 (1973), pp. 263-88.

Schnackenburg, R., *Baptism in the Thought of St Paul* (trans. G.R. Beasley-Murray; Oxford: Basil Blackwell, 1964).

Schöllgen, G., 'Was wissen wir über die Sozialstruktur der paulinischen Gemeinden?', *NTS* 34 (1988), pp. 71-82.

Schrage, W., *The Ethics of the New Testament* (trans. D.E. Green; Philadelphia: Fortress Press, 1988).

Schreiber, A., *Die Gemeinde in Korinth: Versuch einer gruppen-dynamischen Betrachung der Entwicklung der Gemeinde von Korinth auf der Basis des ersten Korintherbriefs* (Münster: Aschendorff, 1977).

Schütz, J.H., *Paul and the Anatomy of Apostolic Authority* (Cambridge: Cambridge University Press, 1975).

Schumacher, R., *Die soziale Lage der Christen im apostolischen Zeitalter* (Paderborn: Ferdinand Schöningh, 1924).

Schweitzer, A., *The Mysticism of Paul the Apostle* (London: A. & C. Black, 1931).

Schweizer, E., 'Die Bekehrung des Apollos, Apg. 18.24-26', *EvT* 15 (1955), pp. 247-54.

Scott, J.C., 'Patron-Client Politics and Political Change in Southeast Asia', *American Political Science Review* 65 (1972), pp. 91-114. Reprinted in *Friends, Followers and Factions* (ed. S.W. Schmidt, L. Guasti, C.H. Landé and J.C. Scott; Berkeley: University of California Press, 1977).

—'Patronage or Exploitation?', in *Patrons and Clients in Mediterranean Societies* (ed. E. Gellner and J. Waterbury; London: Duckworth, 1977).

Scott, K., 'Honorific Months', *YCS* 2 (1931), pp. 201-78.

—'The Significance of Statues in Precious Metals in Emperor Worship', *TAPA* 62 (1931), pp. 101-23.

—'Humor at the Expense of the Ruler Cult', *CP* 27 (1932), pp. 317-28.

Scranton, R.L., *Monuments in the Lower Agora and North of the Archaic Temple. Corinth: Results*, I.3 (Princeton: American School of Classical Studies at Athens, 1951).

Scroggs, R., *The Last Adam: A Study in Pauline Anthropology* (Philadelphia: Fortress Press, 1966).

—'Paul: ΣΟΦΟΣ and ΠΝΕΥΜΑΤΙΚΟΣ', *NTS* 14 (1967), pp. 33-55.

—'Paul and the Eschatological Woman', *JAAR* 40 (1972), pp. 283-303.

—'The Sociological Interpretation of the New Testament: The Present State of Research', *NTS* 26 (1980), pp. 164-79.

—*The New Testament and Homosexuality: Contextual Background for Contemporary Debate* (Philadelphia: Fortress Press, 1983).

Scullard, H.H., *Festivals and Ceremonies of the Roman Republic* (London: Thames & Hudson, 1981).

Sellin, G. von, *Der Streit um die Auferstehung der Toten: Eine religionsgeschichtliche und exegetische Untersuchung von 1 Korinther 15* (Göttingen: Vandenhoeck & Ruprecht, 1986).

—'Hauptprobleme des ersten Korintherbriefes', *ANRW* II.25.4 (1987), pp. 2940-3044.

—'I Kor. 5–6 und der "Vorbrief" nach Korinth' (SNTS Seminar Paper, 1989).

Selter, F., 'πλεονεξία', *NIDNTT*, I, pp. 137-39.

Sevenster, J.N., *Paul and Seneca* (Leiden: Brill, 1961).

Shanor, J., 'Paul as Master Builder: Construction Terms in First Corinthians', *NTS* 34 (1988), pp. 461-71.

Shaw, B.D., 'The Divine Economy: Stoicism as Ideology', *Latomus* 44 (1985), pp. 16-54.

Bibliography 215

Shaw, G., *The Cost of Authority: Manipulation and Freedom in the New Testament* (Philadelphia: Fortress Press, 1982).

Sherwin-White, A.N., *Roman Society and Roman Law in the New Testament* (Oxford: Clarendon Press, 1963).

—*The Letters of Pliny: A Historical and Social Commentary* (Oxford: Clarendon Press, 1966).

—*The Roman Citizenship* (Oxford: Clarendon Press, 2nd edn, 1973).

Sider, R.J., 'The Pauline Conception of the Resurrection of the Body in 1 Corinthians XV.35-54', *NTS* 21 (1975), pp. 428-39.

Smith, D.E., 'The Egyptian Cults at Corinth', *HTR* 70 (1977), pp. 201-31.

—'Social Obligation in the Context of Communal Meals: A Study of the Christian Meal in I Corinthians in Comparison with Greco-Roman Communal Meals' (unpublished ThD dissertation, Harvard University, 1980).

Smith, J., 'The Social Description of Early Christianity', *Religious Studies Review* 2 (1975), pp. 19-25.

Smith, K.K., 'Greek Inscriptions from Corinth, II', *AJA* 23 (1919), pp. 331-93.

Smith, W.S., 'Husband vs. Wife in Juvenal's Sixth Satire', *CW* 73 (1980), pp. 323-32.

Snow, D.A., L.A. Zurcher, Jr, and S. Ekland-Olson, 'Further Thoughts on Social Networks and Movement Recruitment', *Sociology* 17 (1983), pp. 112-20.

Snyder, W.F., 'Public Anniversaries in the Roman Empire: The Epigraphical Evidence for their Observance during the First Three Centuries', *YCS* 7 (1940), pp. 223-317.

Soden, H.F. von, 'Sacrament and Ethics in Paul', in *The Writings of St Paul* (ed. W.A. Meeks; New York: Norton, 1972).

Spörlein, B., *Die Leugnung der Auferstehung: Eine historisch-kritische Untersuchung zu 1 Kor 15* (Regensburg: Friedrich Pustet, 1971).

Srinivas, M.N., and A. Beteille, 'Networks in Indian Social Structure', *Man* 64 (1964), pp. 165-68.

Stambaugh, J.E., and D.L. Balch, *The New Testament in its Social Environment* (Philadelphia: Westminster Press, 1986).

Ste. Croix, G.E.M. de, 'Suffragium: From Vote to Patronage', *BJS* 5 (1954), pp. 33-48.

—*The Class Struggle in the Ancient Greek World* (London: Gerald Duckworth, 1981).

Stein, A., 'Wo trugen die korinthischen Christen ihre Rechtshändel aus?', *ZNW* 59 (1968), pp. 86-90.

Stevenson, G.H., *Roman Provincial Administration* (Oxford: Basil Blackwell, 1939).

Stevenson, G.H., and A. Momigliano, 'Rebellion within the Empire', in *Cambridge Ancient History*, X (ed. S.A. Cook, F.E. Adcock and M.P. Charlesworth; Cambridge: Cambridge University Press, 1934).

Stillwell, R., *The Theatre. Corinth · Results*, II (Princeton: American School of Classical Studies at Athens, 1952).

Stillwell, R., R.L. Scranton and S.E. Freeman, *Architecture. Corinth: Results*, I.2 (Cambridge, MA: Harvard University Press, 1941).

Stowers, S.K., 'Social Status, Public Speaking and Private Teaching: The Circumstances of Paul's Preaching Activity', *NovT* 26 (1984), pp. 59-82.

—*Letter-Writing in Greco-Roman Antiquity* (Philadelphia: Westminster Press, 1986).

Strobel, A., 'Der Begriff des "Hauses" im griechischen und römischen Privatrecht', *ZNW* 56 (1965), pp. 91-100.

Sturgeon, M.C., *Sculpture: The Reliefs from the Theatre. Corinth: Results*, IX.2 (Princeton: American School of Classical Studies at Athens, 1977).

Styler, G.M., 'The Basis of Obligation in Paul's Christology and Ethics', in *Christ and Spirit in the New Testament: Studies in Honour of C.F.D. Moule* (ed. B. Lindars and S.S. Smalley; Cambridge: Cambridge University Press, 1973).

Sundberg, A.C., 'Sadducees', in *Interpreter's Dictionary of the Bible*, IV (Nashville: Abingdon Press, 1962).

Swift, E.H., 'A Group of Roman Imperial Portraits at Corinth', *AJA* 25 (1921), pp. 142-59, 248-65, 337-63.

—'A Group of Roman Imperial Portraits at Corinth', *AJA* 26 (1922), pp. 131-47.

Syme, R., *The Roman Revolution* (Oxford: Oxford University Press, 1939).

—*Some Arval Brethren* (Oxford: Clarendon Press, 1980).

Talbert, C., *Reading Corinthians: A Literary and Theological Commentary on 1 and 2 Corinthians* (New York: Crossroad, 1987).

Tarn, W.W., 'The Hellenistic Ruler Cult and the Daemon', *JHS* 48 (1928), pp. 206-19.

Taylor, L.R., '*Augustales*, *Seviri Augustales*, and *Seviri*: A Chronological Study', *TAPA* 45 (1914), pp. 231-53.

—*The Divinity of the Roman Emperor* (Middletown: American Philological Association, 1931).

—*Party Politics in the Age of Caesar* (Berkeley: University of California Press, 1949).

—'Freedmen and Freeborn in the Epitaphs of Imperial Rome', *AJP* 82 (1961), pp. 113-32.

Taylor, L.R., and A.B. West, 'The Euryclids in Latin Inscriptions from Corinth', *AJA* 30 (1926), pp. 389-400.

Theissen, G., *The Social Setting of Pauline Christianity: Essays on Corinth* (Philadelphia: Fortress Press, 1982).

Thiselton, A.C., 'Realized Eschatology at Corinth', *NTS* 24 (1977–78), pp. 510-26.

Thompson, K.C., 'I Cor. 15.29 and Baptism for the Dead', in *Studia Evangelica*, II (ed. F.L. Cross; Berlin: Akademie Verlag, 1964).

Thrall, M.E., *The First and Second Letter of Paul to the Corinthians* (Cambridge: Cambridge University Press, 1965).

—'The Pauline Use of Συνείδησις', *NTS* 14 (1967), pp. 118-25.

—'The Meaning of οἰκοδομέω in relation to the Concept of συνείδησις (I Cor. 8.10)', in *Studia Evangelica*, IV (ed. F.L. Cross; Berlin: Akademie-Verlag, 1968).

—'The Problem of II Cor. VI. 14–VII.1 in Some Recent Discussion', *NTS* 24 (1977), pp. 132-48.

Tod, M.N., *Sidelights on Greek History: Three Lectures on the Light Thrown by Greek Inscriptions on the Life and Thought of the Ancient World* (Oxford: Basil Blackwell, 1932).

Tomlinson, R.A., *Epidauros* (Austin, TX: University of Texas Press, 1983).

Toynbee, J.M.C., 'Dictators and Philosophers in the First Century AD', *GR* 13 (1944), pp. 43-58.

—*Death and Burial in the Roman World* (London: Thames & Hudson, 1971).

Treggiari, S., *Roman Freedom during the Late Republic* (Oxford: Clarendon Press, 1969).

—'Jobs in the Household of Livia', *PBSR* 43 (1975), pp. 48-77.

—'Family Life among the Staff of the Volusii', *TAPA* 105 (1975), pp. 393-401.

—'Intellectuals, Poets and their Patrons in the First Century BC', *Classical News and Views* 21 (1977), pp. 24-29.

Bibliography 217

—'Consent to Roman Marriage: Some Aspects of Law and Reality', *Classical Views* 26 (1982), pp. 34-44.

Troeltsch, E., *The Social Teaching of the Christian Churches* (London: George Allen & Unwin, 1931).

Tuckett, C.M., 'I Corinthians and Q', *JBL* 102 (1983), pp. 607-19.

Turner, V.W., *The Ritual Process: Structure and Anti-Structure* (Chicago: Aldine, 1969).

Verhey, A., *The Great Reversal: Ethics and the New Testament* (Grand Rapids: Eerdmans, 1984).

Verner, D.C., *The Household of God: The Social World of the Pastoral Epistles* (Chico, CA: Scholars Press, 1983).

Veyne, P. (ed.), *A History of Private Life*, I (Cambridge: Belknap, 1987).

Vielhauer, P., 'Paulus und die Kephaspartei in Korinth', *NTS* 21 (1975), pp. 341-52.

Vischer, L., *Die Auslegungsgeschichte von 1. Kor. 6.1-11* (Tübingen: Mohr, 1955).

Vögtle, A., *Die Tugend- und Lasterkataloge im Neuen Testament* (Münster: Aschendorff, 1936).

Vogliano, A., 'La grande iscrizione Bacchica del Metropolitan Museum: I', *AJA* 37 (1933), pp. 215-31.

Vollgraff, W., 'Inscriptions d'Argos', *BCH* 28 (1904), pp. 420-29.

Währisch, H., 'λοιδορέω', *NIDNTT*, III, pp. 346-47.

Waele, F.J. de, 'A Roman Market at Corinth', *AJA* 34 (1930), pp. 432-54.

Wagner, G., *Pauline Baptism and the Pagan Mysteries: The Problem of the Pauline Doctrine of Baptism in Romans VI.1-11, in the Light of its Religio-Historical 'Parallels'* (trans. J.P. Smith; Edinburgh: Oliver & Boyd, 1967).

Wallace-Hadrill, A., 'Family and Inheritance in the Augustan Marriage Laws', *PCPhS* 27 (1981), pp. 58-80.

Wallis, R., and S. Bruce, 'Network and Clockwork', *Sociology* 16 (1982), pp. 102-107.

Waltzing, J., *Étude historique sur les corporations professionelles chez les Romains* (4 vols.; Louvain: Peeters, 1895–1900).

Waterbury, J., 'An Attempt to put Patrons and Clients in their Places', in *Patrons and Clients in Mediterranean Societies* (ed. E. Gellner and J. Waterbury; London: Duckworth, 1977).

Watson, A., *The Laws of Succession in the Later Roman Republic* (Oxford: Clarendon Press, 1971).

Watson, F., '2 Cor. 10–13 and Paul's Painful Letter to the Corinthians', *JTS* 35 (1984), pp. 324-46.

—*Paul, Judaism and the Gentiles: A Sociological Approach* (Cambridge: Cambridge University Press, 1986).

Weaver, P.R.C., 'Social Mobility in the Early Roman Empire: The Evidence of Imperial Freedmen and Slaves', *PP* 37 (1967), pp. 3-20.

—*Familia Caesaris: A Social Study of the Emperor's Freedmen and Slaves* (Cambridge: Cambridge University Press, 1972).

Wedderburn, A.J.M., 'The Body of Christ and Related Concepts in I Corinthians', *SJT* 24 (1971), pp. 74-96.

—'The Problem of the Denial of the Resurrection in I Corinthians XV', *NovT* 23 (1981), pp. 229-41.

—*Baptism and Resurrection: Studies in Pauline Theology against its Graeco-Roman Background* (Tübingen: Mohr, 1987).

Weingrod, A., 'Patrons, Patronage and Political Parties', *CSSH* 10 (1968), pp. 377-400. Reprinted in *Friends, Followers and Factions* (ed. F.W. Schmidt, L. Guasti, C.H. Landé and J.C. Scott; Berkeley: University of California Press, 1977).

—'Patronage and Power', in *Patrons and Clients in Mediterranean Societies* (ed. E. Gellner and J. Waterbury; London: Duckworth, 1977).

Weinstock, S., *Divus Julius* (Oxford: Clarendon Press, 1971).

Weiss, B., *A Commentary on the New Testament*. III. *Romans to Colossians* (New York: Funk & Wagnalls, 1906).

Weiss, J., *Der erste Korintherbrief* (Göttingen: Vandenhoeck & Ruprecht, 9th edn, 1910).

—*The History of Primitive Christianity*, I (London: Macmillan, 1937).

Welborn, L.L., 'On the Discord in Corinth: I Corinthians 1-4 and Ancient Politics', *JBL* 106 (1987), pp. 85-111.

—'A Conciliatory Principle in 1 Cor. 4.6', *NovT* 29 (1987), pp. 320-46.

Wellmann, B., 'Network Analysis: Some Basic Principles', in *Sociological Theory* (ed. R. Collins; San Francisco: Jossey-Bass, 1983).

Wendland, H.-D., *Die Briefe an die Korinther* (Göttingen: Vandenhoeck & Ruprecht, 11th edn, 1965).

Westermann, W.L., 'Between Slavery and Freedom', *AHR* 50 (1945), pp. 213-27.

Wheeldon, P.D., 'The Operation of Voluntary Association and Personal Networks on the Political Processes of an Inter-Ethnic Community', in *Social Networks in Urban Situations* (ed. J.C. Mitchell; Manchester: Manchester University Press, 1969).

White, L.M., '*Domus Ecclesiae—Domus Dei*: Adaptation and Development in the Setting for Early Christian Assembly' (PhD dissertation, Yale University, 1983).

White, P., 'The Friends of Martial, Statius and Pliny, and the Dispersal of Patronage', *HSCP* 79 (1975), pp. 265-300.

—'*Amicitia* and the Profession of Poetry in Early Imperial Rome', *JRS* 68 (1978), pp. 74-92.

Whiteley, D.E.H., *The Theology of St Paul* (Oxford: Basil Blackwell, 1974).

Whitten, N.E., Jr, and A.W. Wolfe, 'Network Analysis', in *The Handbook of Social and Cultural Anthropology* (ed. J.I. Honigmann; Chicago: Rand–McNally, 1974).

Wibbing, S., *Die Tugend- und Lasterkataloge in Neuen Testament* (Berlin: Töpelmann, 1959).

Wieser, T., 'Community: Its Unity, Diversity and Universality', *Semeia* 33 (1985), pp. 83-95.

Wilckens, U., *Weisheit und Torheit: Eine exegetisch-religionsgeschichtliche Untersuchung zu 1 Kor. 1 und 2* (Tübingen: Mohr, 1959).

Wilken, R.L., 'Collegia, Philosophical Schools, and Theology', in *The Catacombs and the Colosseum* (ed. S. Benko and J.J. O'Rourke; Valley Forge: Judson, 1971).

—*The Christians as the Romans Saw Them* (New Haven: Yale University Press, 1984).

Williams, C.K., 'The Refounding of Corinth: Some Roman Religious Attitudes', in *Roman Architecture in the Greek World* (ed. S. Macready and F.H. Thompson; London: Society of Antiquaries, 1987).

Williams, C.K., and O.H. Zervos, 'Corinth, 1981: East of the Theater', *Hesp* 51 (1982), pp. 115-63.

—'Corinth, 1986: Temple E and East of Theater', *Hesp* 56 (1987), pp. 1-46.

Williams, G.W., 'Some Aspects of Roman Marriage Ceremonies and Ideals', *JRS* 48 (1958), pp. 16-29.

—'Poetry in the Moral Climate of Augustan Rome', *JRS* 52 (1962), pp. 28-46.
Willis, W., *Idol Meat in Corinth: The Pauline Argument in I Corinthians 8 and 10* (Chico, CA: Scholars Press, 1985).
—'An Apostolic Apologia: The Form and Function of I Corinthians 9', *JSNT* 24 (1985), pp. 33-48.
Wills, L., 'The Form of the Sermon in Hellenistic Judaism and Early Christianity', *HTR* 77 (1984), pp. 277-99.
Wilson, J.H., 'The Corinthians Who Say There is No Resurrection of the Dead', *ZNW* 59 (1968), pp. 90-107.
Wilson, R.McL., *Gnosis and the New Testament* (Philadelphia: Fortress Press, 1968).
—'How Gnostic were the Corinthians?', *NTS* 19 (1972), pp. 65-74.
Winter, B., 'The Public Honouring of Christian Benefactors: Romans 13.3-4 and 1 Peter 2.14-15', *JSNT* 34 (1988), pp. 87-103.
Wirszubski, Ch., *Libertas as a Political Idea at Rome during the Late Republic and Early Principate* (Cambridge: Cambridge University Press, 1950).
Wiseman, J., 'The Gymnasium Area at Corinth, 1969–1970', *Hesp* 41 (1972), pp. 1-42.
—'Corinth and Rome I: 228 BC–AD 267', *ANRW* II.7.1 (1979), pp. 438-58.
Wiseman, T., *Roman Political Life 90 BC–AD 69* (Exeter: Exeter University Press, 1985).
Wistrand, E., *The So-Called Laudatio Turiae: Introduction, Text, Translation and Commentary* (Lund: Acta Universitatis Gothoburgensis, 1976).
Witherington, B., *Women in the Earliest Churches* (Cambridge: Cambridge University Press, 1988).
Wolf, E., 'Kinship, Friendship and Patron–Client Relations', in *The Social Anthropology of Complex Societies* (ed. M. Banton; London: Tavistock, 1966). Reprinted in *Friends, Followers and Factions* (ed. S.W. Schmidt, L. Guasti, C.H. Landé and J.C. Scott: Berkeley: University of California Press, 1977).
Wolff, C., *Der erste Brief des Paulus an die Korinther. II. Auslegung der Kapitel 8-16* (Berlin: Evangelische Verlagsanstalt, 1982).
Wuellner, W.H., 'Haggadic Homily Genre in 1 Corinthians 1–3', *JBL* 89 (1970), pp. 199-204.
—'The Sociological Implications of I Corinthians 1.26-28 Reconsidered', in *Studia Evangelica*, VI (ed. E.A. Livingstone; Berlin: Akademie-Verlag, 1973).
—'Tradition and Interpretation of the "Wise–Powerful–Noble" Triad in I Cor. 1.26', in *Studia Evangelica*, VII (ed. E.A. Livingstone; Berlin: Akademie-Verlag, 1982).
—'Where is Rhetorical Criticism Taking Us?', *CBQ* 49 (1987), pp. 448-63.
Yarbrough, O.L., *Not Like the Gentiles: Marriage Rules in the Letters of Paul* (Atlanta: Scholars Press, 1985).
Young, F.M., 'Notes on the Corinthian Correspondence', in *Studia Evangelica*, VII (ed. E.A. Livingstone: Berlin: Akademie-Verlag, 1982).
Young, F., and D.F. Ford, *Meaning and Truth in 2 Corinthians* (London: SPCK, 1987).
Young, N.H., '*PAIDAGOGOS*: The Social Setting of a Pauline Metaphor', *NovT* 29 (1987), pp. 150-76.
Youtie, H.C., 'The *Kline* of Seraphis', *HTR* 41 (1948), pp. 9-20.
Zaas, P., 'I Corinthians 6.9ff.; Was Homosexuality Condoned in the Corinthian Church?', in *SBL 1979 Seminar Papers* (ed. P. Achtemeier; Missoula, MT: Scholars Press, 1979).

—'As I Teach Everywhere, in Every Church: A Study of the Communication of Morals in Paul' (PhD dissertation, Chicago University, 1982).
—' "Cast Out the Evil Man from Your Midst" (I Cor. 5.13b)', *JBL* 103 (1984), pp. 259-61.
—'Catalogues and Context: I Corinthians 5 and 6', *NTS* 34 (1988), pp. 622-29.

Ziesler, J., *Pauline Christianity* (Oxford: Oxford University Press, 1983).

INDEXES

INDEX OF REFERENCES

OLD TESTAMENT

Leviticus		27.20	132	Ezekiel	
18.8	130, 132			22.27	139
		Jeremiah			
Deuteronomy		22.17	139		
22.30	132				

NEW TESTAMENT

Luke		24.27	78	1.12	87, 94
1.4	172	25.3	79	1.13-17	131
10.3-8	108	25.9	79	1.13	176
		25.25-27	78	1.14-16	85
Acts		26.30-32	78	1.14	89, 90
13.8	72			1.16	88
16.16-24	80	Romans		1.17	104
16.20	80	4.4	106	1.26-31	13
17.5-9	102	12.4-5	176	1.26-27	128
18.1-17	86	13.1-6	97	1.26	11, 93, 97, 145, 163, 181
18.5	84	16.1-2	85, 101, 102		
18.7	90	16.21	85	1.27	178
18.8	89	16.22	85	1.29	131
18.12-17	79	16.23	85, 90, 92, 102, 155, 172, 173	2.1-5	104
18.17	85, 89			2.1	178
18.18	84			2.6–3.3	104
18.24				2.7	178
–19.1	85, 103	1 Corinthians		2.15-16	131
18.24-28	103	1–4	11, 12, 139	3.3	176
18.24	105	1.1	100, 169	3.5-9	85, 103
19.1	106	1.5	131	3.5	85
23.29	78	1.10–4.21	12, 101	3.6	106
23.35	78	1.10	94, 176	3.8	98, 106, 107
24.1-2	78	1.11	85, 91, 94, 170	3.9	103
24.26	78			3.10	100

3.13-15	106	5.11	139, 140, 180	8.5	146
3.14	103	5.13	130, 171, 180	8.7-13	182
3.18-19	128	6	133	8.7	145
3.18	131	6.1-11	119, 123, 124, 125, 139, 163	8.8-12	141
3.21	131, 170			8.8-9	124
4.1-5	106, 172, 173			8.8	143, 156
4.1	172, 178	6.1-6	181	8.9	145, 155, 182
4.3	172	6.1	85, 86, 114, 123, 126, 127, 135, 138, 163, 181, 182	8.10-11	154
4.6	103, 131, 139			8.10	114, 141-43, 155, 157, 171, 178
4.7	131				
4.8	131, 170				
4.10	171, 178			8.11-12	182
4.11	97	6.2-6	123	8.11	182
4.12	98	6.2-3	180	8.12	182
4.14-21	98, 99	6.2	181	8.13	107, 182
4.14-16	99	6.4	181	9	87, 107, 108, 155
4.14-15	100	6.5	128, 129, 181		
4.15	175	6.6	114	9.1-23	172, 173
4.17	84, 85, 99	6.7-8	123, 126, 127	9.1-18	107, 108
4.18-21	99	6.7	126	9.1-6	98
4.18	99, 100, 131, 139, 154	6.8	126	9.1-3	100, 107
		6.9-10	126, 127	9.1-2	174
4.19-21	100	6.9	126	9.3-14	174
4.19-20	104	6.10	126, 127	9.3-6	155
5–7	133, 138	6.12-20	135	9.3	173
5.1–6.11	116, 124	6.12	124, 130, 131, 166, 170	9.4-6	155
				9.6	107
5	22, 23, 133, 139, 179, 180	6.13	124, 131	9.12	107, 108, 173, 174
		6.18	131		
5.1-13	130, 179	6.20		9.15-18	174
5.1-5	180	–7.40	125	9.15	174
5.1	85, 114, 124, 125, 130, 133, 138, 139, 163, 170	6.20	170, 172	9.16-17	174
		7	133	9.17-18	106
		7.1	85, 135	9.22	178
		7.2ff.	22	9.23	174
5.2-5	140	7.2	132	9.24-27	149
5.2	130, 131, 139, 154, 170, 180	7.23	170	10.1-22	114, 141, 143, 144, 163
		7.25	85		
		8.1		10.7-8	142
5.3-5	130, 171, 180	–11.1	107	10.14-22	142, 146, 172
5.4-5	180	8–10	139, 141, 143, 152	10.14	142, 171
5.6-7	181			10.16-22	141, 143
5.6	130, 131, 170	8.1		10.16-17	176
5.7	130, 170, 180	–10.22	142	10.22	97, 171
5.8	171	8.1-3	131, 154	10.23	
5.9	85, 95, 113, 133	8.1	85, 139, 143, 163	–11.1	141, 142
				10.23-24	182
5.10	113	8.4	118, 143, 163		

Index of References

10.23	124, 130, 145, 166	14.26	184	10.10	104
		14.28	178	11.7-15	108
10.29	145	14.29	184	11.23-27	98
10.31	172	14.34-35	184	12.11-13	108
11.2-16	184	15.9	100		
11.3-16	22	15.10	98	*Galatians*	
11.3	183	15.12	162, 163	3.18	126
11.17-34	87, 94, 110, 183	15.19	163, 165	4.30	126
		15.29	119, 144, 157-59	5.21	126
11.18-19	176				
11.18	85	15.30-32	158	*Philippians*	
11.21-22	183	15.32	165	2.19-24	98
11.21	111	15.34	163		
11.22	111, 183	15.50	126	*Ephesians*	
11.29	183	16.1-4	185	1.22	177
11.33	183	16.1	85	4.15	177
12–14	97	16.2	185	5.23	177
12.1	85	16.3	186		
12.12-27	177	16.4	186	*Colossians*	
12.12-13	95	16.5	98	1.18	177
12.12	176	16.5-9	84	2.19	177
12.13	177	16.6-7	98		
12.18-20	176	16.6	98	*1 Thessalonians*	
12.18	177	16.7	98	2.7	100
12.19-20	177	16.10-11	84, 85	2.17–3.13	98, 99
12.21	177	16.10	99	2.17-18	98
12.22-26	178	16.11	99	3.6	100
12.22	178	16.12	85, 103, 106	4.3-6	95
12.23	178	16.15-18	88	4.9-10	95
12.24	178	16.15-16	96, 97	5.12-13	97
12.25-26	178	16.15	88		
12.27	176	16.17-18	95, 96	*1 Timothy*	
13.2	178	16.17	85, 90	4.12	99
13.4	139	16.18	90		
14.1-33	183	16.19	84	*2 Timothy*	
14.1-5	184	16.22	84	2.18	117
14.1	184				
14.2	178	*2 Corinthians*		*Titus*	
14.3	184	1.19	84	3.1	97
14.12-13	184	6.14–7.1	133	3.13	106
14.17-19	184	10–13	171		

APOCRYPHA AND PSEUDEPIGRAPHA

Jubilees		*2 Maccabees*		*4 Maccabees*	
33.10-13	132	4.50	139	5.1-38	145
		5.27	145		

Wisdom of Solomon
14.27	143	15.2-3	143

ANCIENT AUTHORS

Andocides		44.2-4	63	5.12-15	73
4.13	138	45.2-3	56	5.15-18	74
		45.7-8	64	5.15-23	74
Appian		45.12-13	149	5.24-25	74
Roman History		46.8	80	6	135
8.20.136	40	50.3	64	6.135-41	138
		77/78.		9.59	73
Aristotle		34-35	72		
The Athenian Constitution				Livy	
45.3	173	Gaius		2.32	176, 177
55.2	173	1.63	132		
55.2-4	173	2.286	137	Lysias	
				32.10	126
Demosthenes		Horace		32.17	126
21.80	126	*Epistles*		32.22	126
21.157	126	1.7	72		
47.35	172	1.18	74	Martial	
		1.19.35	72	*Epigrams*	
Digest				1.20	72
2.4.4	70	*Satires*		3.60	72-74
37.15.9	70	1.9.56-58	75	4.49	73
47.22.1	64	2.6	73	6.48	73
		2.6.40-41	72, 73	6.11	74
Dio Cassius		2.7.32-34	73, 74	10	73
43.40.3-5	40			10.4	73
54.16.1	137	Isaeus		10.26	75
55.23	76	6.4	126	10.28	75
58.25	53	6.12-13	173	10.75	73
59.9	50	8.3	126	10.82	74
59.12	54, 136				
60.13	70	Josephus		Polybius	
		Antiquities of the Jews		4.6	48
Dio Chrysostom		19.8-10	55		
Or.				Ovid	
7.21-63	76	Juvenal		*Fasti*	
10	80	*Satires*		5.419-44	160
17	139	1.52	73		
31.121	149	1.52.5	73	Pausanias	
40.10-11	149	1.95-138	74	2.1.2	40
41.2	63	1.100-101	75	2.2.2	60
43.1	149	1.128	73, 74	7.17.4	46
43.6	80	3.189	75		
43.11	78	5	72		

Index of References

Persius		3.12	73	Ps-Socratic Epistles	
Prologue	73	3.12.2	74	8.9	72
		3.19	137	9	73
Satires		3.21	72		
1	72	3.21.3	73	*Res gestae divi Augusti*	
1.50-56	73	4.9	57	4.2	42
1.54	73	5.4	78	9	42
1.108-109	72	5.19	72	19-21	42
		6.23.2	105		
Petronius		6.33.6	127	Seneca	
Satyricon		7.22.2	105	*De Ben.*	
14	72	8.12	73	6.34.2	75
29	69	10.13	162		
34-35	73	10.14	162	*De Brev. Vit.*	
41	73	10.27	56	2.4	81
46	69	10.34	64	11.4	75
48	69, 73, 105	10.35	162	14.3	75
52	69	10.79.3	59	14.4	74
55	73	10.94	56	20.1	75
57	69	10.96.10	151		
71	69	10.100	162	*De Clementia*	
77	69	13	78	1.3.5	176
		87	56	1.4.3	176
Philostratus				1.5.1	176
Lives of the Sophists		Pliny the Elder			
600	73	*Natural History*		*De Const.*	
		9.117-18	136	10.2	75
Plato					
Orphica Fragment		Plutarch		*De Ira*	
232	159, 165	*Ages*		3.8.6	74
		4.2	126	3.35	74
Republic					
326 B-C	122	*Antony*		Stobaeus	
364E		67	48	*Anthologium*	
-365A	159, 165			3.40.9	51
371C	97	*Caesar*			
		57	40	Strabo	
Pliny				8.5.5	49
Epistles		*Cato the Elder*		8.6.23	40
1.4	137	24.4	134	17.3.15	40
1.14.9	136				
1.19.2	136	*Comparison of*		Suetonius	
2.6	74	*Aristides and Cato*		*Augustus*	
2.9.4	105	6.1	134	56	77
2.11	78				
2.13.6-7	105	*Moralia*		*Caligula*	
3.2.3	105	207F	49	25	136
3.9	78	814D	75		

Claudius		Tiberius		6.18	49
18	62	33	77	12.1	136
25	70			12.22	136
		Vespasian		12.45	62
Gaius		8.4	46	14.17	65
25	54			14.47	53
		Tacitus		16.32	72
Nero		Annals			
23-24	45	3.25	135, 137	History	
		5.11	54	4.10	72
		6.4	54		

INDEX OF AUTHORS

Abbott, F.F. 58, 72
Alexander, C. 69
Altman, M. 153
Angus, S. 161
Arnold, W.T. 58
Aune, D. 127

Badian, E. 39
Bagdikian, A. 40, 53, 58, 59, 62, 80
Balch, D. 104
Balsdon, J.P.V.D. 74
Banks, R. 21
Barnes, J.A. 34
Barrett, C.K. 86-89, 91, 94, 98, 99, 103, 104, 107, 108, 111-15, 125, 131, 132, 135, 138, 141, 145, 146, 155, 158, 159, 161, 163, 170-72, 174, 180-86
Baur, F.C. 88
Beasley-Murray, G.R. 158, 159, 161, 165
Beker, J.C. 175, 176
Bernard, J.H. 124, 125
Best, E. 176
Biers, W.R. 57
Bloch, M. 31
Boissevain, J. 31-34, 121
Bonner, C. 178
Bornkamm, G. 86, 116
Bouchier, E.S. 58
Bowersock, G. 39, 48-50, 105, 153
Braund, D.C. 38, 42, 43, 45, 46, 49, 52-56, 63, 137, 147-50, 152, 155, 156, 161, 173
Broneer, O. 40, 149
Bruce, F.F. 72, 90, 104, 105, 126, 147

Brunt, P.A. 52, 56, 136
Buckland, W.W. 71
Bünker, M. 101
Bultmann, R. 15, 16, 144, 163, 165
Burton, G.P. 78

Cadbury, H.J. 92
Cartledge, P. 48-51, 56
Charlesworth, M.P. 50, 54, 55
Clarke, E.G. 143
Conzelmann, H. 79, 86, 87, 91, 96, 97, 106, 115, 119, 126, 127, 132, 133, 141, 145-47, 155, 158, 159, 163, 171, 174, 176, 180, 183, 185, 186
Corbett, P.E. 132, 138
Cornford, F.M. 122
Countryman, L.W. 96
Cranfield, C.E.B. 101
Crook, J.A. 39, 70, 71, 76, 132, 134, 137, 138
Csillag, P. 136
Cumont, F. 69

Dahl, N.A. 11, 16, 87, 88, 91, 94-96, 100, 103, 117, 139, 167
Daube, D. 132, 133
Davis, J.A. 118
Dean, L.R. 53, 62
Deissmann, A. 13, 21, 146
Delcor, M. 123, 181
Delling, F. 139
Dill, S. 65-68
Dobschütz, E. von 13-15, 18, 22, 23, 91, 111, 127, 133
Duff, A.M. 40, 59, 66, 70, 71
Dunn, J.D.G. 101, 115, 145, 176, 180

Edlund, E.M.I. 39
Edwards, K.N. 44, 60, 61
Ehrenberg, V. 42, 43, 46, 49, 52, 53, 55, 63, 137, 147-52, 155, 156, 161
Eisenstadt, S.N. 30, 31, 169
Ellis, E.E. 114, 117
Engels, F. 13
Ewald, G.H. 127

Fee, G.D. 87-92, 97-100, 103, 104, 106, 107, 109, 113, 115, 124-26, 132, 142, 144, 159, 161, 174, 180, 184-86
Ferguson, J. 161
Filson, F.V. 15
Findlay, G.G. 85, 88, 89, 97, 99, 100, 103, 106, 186
Finley, M.I. 15, 28, 29
Fiorenza, E.S. 83, 84, 91, 93, 96, 101, 108, 112, 123, 125, 127, 132, 133, 135, 139, 142, 167, 184
Fitzgerald, J.T. 103
Foerster, W. 146
Ford, D.F. 103
Forkman, G. 139, 171, 180
Foschini, B.M. 158-60, 165
Frank, R.I. 135
Freeman, S.E. 44, 45
Fuller, R.H. 16, 125, 127, 181
Funk, R.W. 98
Furnish, V. 45, 79, 93

Gager, J. 13, 15, 17, 29
Gardner, J.F. 132, 137
Garnsey, P. 24, 39, 53, 56, 58, 62, 67, 70, 76, 105, 125, 128, 129, 132, 134, 138, 170
Geagan, D.J. 57
Gelzer, M. 39, 66, 75, 105
Georgi, D. 114, 115, 129
Gill, D.W.J. 44, 45, 151
Godet, F. 158
Graindor, P. 55
Grant, R.M. 104
Guggenheim, S. 31

Haenchen, E. 79, 80
Hallett, J.P. 135

Headlam, A.C. 101
Hengel, M. 87
Hock, R.F. 25, 27, 73, 98, 105-109, 173
Hollmann, G. 161
Hopkins, M.K. 47, 65
Horsley, R.A. 104, 115, 117-19, 123, 124, 129, 131, 141, 143, 144, 155, 182
Hurd, J.C. 16, 85-88, 95, 103, 113, 123, 141-143, 158, 159, 163, 165, 166, 176

Johnson, A.C. 58
Johnson, F.P. 44, 72, 164
Jolowicz, H.F. 52, 80
Jones, A.H.M. 42, 43, 46, 49, 52, 53, 55, 63, 76, 137, 147, 148-52, 155, 156, 161
Jones, C.P. 58, 78, 80
Judge, E.A. 16-21, 23, 24, 26, 27, 78, 88, 90, 91, 101, 109, 110, 168, 173

Käsemann, E. 16, 107, 115-17, 123, 144, 170, 174, 176, 177, 180
Kautsky, K. 13, 17
Keck, L.E. 13, 131, 141, 178
Kelly, J.M. 39, 72
Kenny, M. 31
Kent, J.H. 40, 43-45, 47, 48, 51, 52, 54, 56, 57, 59, 60-63, 65, 91, 136, 148, 151, 153
Kim, C.H. 96
Koester, H. 116, 124, 143, 163

Lacey, W.K. 138
Landé, C.H. 30
Lattimore, O. 39
Lemarchand, R. 30
Levick, B. 54
Lewis, N. 55, 58, 66, 69, 71, 72, 76, 161
Leitzmann, H. 99
Lightfoot, J.B. 91, 181
Lisle, R. 146
Lutz, C.E. 51, 134

MacDowell, D.M. 173

Index of Authors

MacMullen, R. 66, 67, 154
MacRae, G.W. 115
Malherbe, A.J. 17, 21, 89, 101, 106, 110, 129
Malina, B. 27, 29, 30
Marshall, I.H. 72
Marshall, P. 17, 23-27, 88, 90, 91, 96, 105, 107, 109, 110, 170, 174
Mauss, M. 23
Martin, T.R. 57
Mayer, A. 34
Meeks, W.A. 14, 25, 26, 34, 68, 85, 87, 89-93, 96, 97, 101, 103, 104, 106, 110, 111, 116, 123, 125, 127, 141, 158, 176, 180, 181, 184, 185
Meritt, B.D. 43, 47, 50, 153
Meyer, H.W.A. 133
Millar, F. 52, 53, 56, 59, 78
Minear, P.S. 123
Mitchell, J.C. 33, 34, 84
Moffatt, J. 15, 16, 89, 91, 127, 131, 134, 140, 142, 145, 146, 159, 174, 180
Momigliano, A. 45
Munck, J. 16, 87, 104, 105
Murphy-O'Connor, J. 103, 111, 116, 131, 134, 142, 143, 146, 157-59, 171, 172, 180, 181, 183, 184

Nickle, K. 186
Nock, A.D. 47, 148, 151, 153, 161, 163

Oepke, A. 159
Ogilvie, R.M. 70, 144, 150, 160, 161
Oliver, J.H. 54, 57, 136
O'Neill, J.C. 158
Orr, W.F. 85, 96, 114, 135, 145, 159

Parry, R. 159, 170, 173
Pearson, B.A. 116
Pitt-Rivers, J.A. 31
Plummer, A. 90, 91, 106, 114, 123, 125, 132, 144, 145, 155, 181, 185
Price, F.V. 34
Price, S.R.F. 47, 147-49, 151-54, 161

Radcliffe-Brown, A.R. 34

Raeder, M. 158, 159
Rawson, B. 134
Reinhold, M. 55, 58, 66, 69, 71, 72, 76, 161
Reitzenstein, R. 159, 161
Rhodes, P.J. 173, 186
Richardson, P. 124
Ridgway, B.S. 44, 153
Rissi, M. 158, 159
Robertson, A.T. 90, 91, 96, 103, 106, 114, 123, 125, 132, 144, 145, 155, 181, 185
Robinson, J.A.T. 176
Rohrbaugh, R.L. 26
Roniger, L. 30, 31, 169
Rowland, C. 177
Rudd, N. 40, 74
Ryberg, I.S. 47, 65, 150

Saller, R.P. 24, 30, 39, 40, 52, 53, 55, 56, 58, 67, 78, 105, 132, 134, 136-38, 170
Sandars, T.C. 70, 132, 137
Sampley, J.P. 182
Sanday, W. 101
Sandys, J.E. 74
Schmithals, W. 16, 86, 114-16, 124, 131, 141-43, 155, 159, 160, 163
Schnackenburg, R. 159
Schütz, J. 21
Schulz, F. 125
Schweitzer, A. 159
Scott, K. 153
Scranton, R.L. 40, 60
Scroggs, R. 17
Scullard, H.H. 160
Selter, F. 139
Shaw, G. 126, 167, 168, 176, 182
Sherk, R.K. 38, 54, 55, 64-66, 68, 71, 161, 164
Smallwood, E.M. 42, 45, 46, 49, 52-56, 63, 147, 148, 173
Smith, D.E. 25
Snyder, W.F. 46
Soden, H. von 141, 144
Spawforth, A. 48-51, 56
Stambaugh, J. 104

Ste. Croix, G.E.M. de 17, 39, 41, 77, 125
Stevenson, G.H. 58, 68
Stowers, S.K. 96
Sullivan, J.P. 69, 74
Sundberg, A.C. 163
Swift, E.H. 44, 164
Syme, R. 39, 50, 54

Talbert, C.H. 108, 124, 129-31, 135, 141, 144, 158
Taylor, L.R. 47, 54, 65, 90, 150, 152, 153
Taylor, N. 39
Theissen, G. 17, 21, 22, 26, 27, 85, 87, 89-91, 93-95, 97, 105, 108, 111, 115, 120, 125, 127-29, 141, 145, 146, 151, 152, 154, 156, 158, 168, 183
Thiselton, A.C. 115, 117, 123, 131, 135, 141, 158, 163
Thompson, K.C. 158
Tod, M.N. 65
Treggiari, S. 40

Verner, D.C. 21
Veyne, P. 129
Vielhauer, P. 103
Vogliano, A. 69

Wagner, G. 144
Wallace-Hadrill, A. 137
Walther, J.A. 85, 96, 114, 135, 145, 159
Weaver, P.R.C. 93
Wedderburn, A.J.M. 117, 158, 160, 161, 163, 165
Weingrod, A. 33, 39
Weiss, J. 159, 163
Wellman, B. 34, 122
West, A.B. 38, 43, 44, 46, 47, 49-51, 53-57, 59, 61-63, 136, 148, 149, 152
White, L.M. 21, 85, 100, 101
Wilckens, U. 115
Wilken, R.L. 67
Williams, C.K. 40, 45
Willis, W. 25, 27, 108, 141, 142, 145, 146, 155, 171
Wilson, R.McL. 115
Winter, B. 173
Wiseman, J. 40, 44, 45, 51, 60
Wolf, E.R. 31

Yarbrough, O.L. 184
Young, F. 103

Zaas, P. 127
Zervos, O.H. 40

WITHDRAWN